Prentice Hall LITERATURE

PENGUIN EDITION

D1560569

Unit One
Resources

Grade Six

PEARSON

Upper Saddle River, New Jersey
Boston, Massachusetts
Chandler, Arizona
Glenview, Illinois

BQ Tunes Credits
Keith London, Defined Mind, Inc., Executive Producer
Mike Pandolfo, Wonderful, Producer
All songs mixed and mastered by Mike Pandolfo, Wonderful
Vlad Gutkovich, Wonderful, Assistant Engineer
Recorded November 2007 – February 2008 in SoHo, New York City, at
Wonderful, 594 Broadway

ISBN–13: 978-0-13-366429-4
ISBN–10:   0-13-366429-5

3 4 5 6 7 8 9 10   12 11 10 09

PEARSON

CONTENTS

"Why Monkeys Live in Trees" by Julius Lester

"The Case of the Monkeys That Fell from the Trees" by Susan E. Quinlan

Writing Workshop: Description—Descriptive Essay

Writing Workshop: Revising for Errors with Possessive Pronouns

Benchmark Test 1

Skills Concept Map 2

"My Papa, Mark Twain" by Susy Clemens

"Stage Fright" by Mark Twain

Name _____ Date _____

About the Unit Resources

The *Prentice Hall Literature Unit Resources* provide manageable, comprehensive, and easy-to-use teaching materials to support each Student Edition unit. You can use these resources to address your students' different ability levels and learning styles, customize instruction to suit your teaching needs, and diagnose and assess student progress. All of these materials are also available at *PHLitOnline*, a rich, online source of personalized instruction and activities.

Here is a brief description of each element of the *Unit Resources*:

UNIT-LEVEL FEATURES

Big Questions (grades 6–10)

Support for the Big Questions includes complete lyrics to BQ Tunes (engaging songs that incorporate Big Question Vocabulary; available on CD); unit-opener worksheets that practice Big Question Vocabulary, an Applying the Big Question chart, re-rendered from the Student Edition.

Essential Questions (The American Experience; The British Tradition)

Support for the Essential Questions includes unit-opener worksheets that focus on each Essential Question individually and a worksheet to support the end-of-unit Essential Question Workshop.

Skills Concept Maps

Each map presents a graphic look at the relationship between the literature and the skills taught in the unit, with space provided for students' notes.

Vocabulary Workshop, Writing Workshop, and Communications Workshop support

End-of-unit worksheets provide opportunities for students to practice vocabulary, and gather and organize information for their Student Edition assignments.

SELECTION-LEVEL SUPPORT

Vocabulary and Reading Warmups

These exercises and easy reading passages provide selection vocabulary practice for students reading at one or two levels below grade level.

Writing About the Big Question (grades 6–10)

These worksheets tie the Big Question to individual selections, while giving students additional practice using the Big Question Vocabulary.

Literary Analysis, Reading, and Vocabulary Builder

A series of worksheets that provide extra practice on each of the main skill strands in the Student Edition. You can find more support for the Literary Analysis and Reading strands in the separate Graphic Organizers Transparencies component.

Integrated Language Skills

The Student Edition Integrated Language Skills features are supported by grammar worksheets and additional pages containing graphic organizers and questions to help students gather and organize information to complete their Student Edition Writing and Listening and Speaking or Research and Technology assignments.

Enrichment

These activities give opportunities for advanced students to focus more closely on topics related to the content or theme of the literature selection.

Name _____   Date _____

ASSESSMENT

Diagnostic Tests

The beginning of each Unit 1 Resources book features a Diagnostic Test. Thereafter, each even-numbered Benchmark Test ends with a 20-question diagnostic component called Vocabulary in Context. Teachers desiring a larger sample for measuring students' reading ability can find an additional 20 questions at *PHLitOnline*.

Benchmark Tests

Twelve Benchmark Tests, spaced evenly throughout the year, assess students' mastery of literary, reading, vocabulary, grammar, and writing skills. A diagnostic Vocabulary in Context, described above, ends each even-numbered Benchmark Test.

Open-Book Tests

For every selection or grouping of selections, there is an Open-Book Test featuring short-answer and extended-response questions and opportunities for oral response. Most Open-Book-Tests also contain a question requiring students to represent information in a graphic organizer. These tests are available as a computer test bank on CD-ROM and at *PHLitOnline*.

Selection Tests

For every selection or grouping of selections, there are two closed-book Selection Tests (A and B) featuring multiple-choice and essay questions. Both tests assess essentially the same material; however Test A is designed for lower-level students, and Test B is designed for students average and above.

ADDITIONAL SUPPORT IN *UNIT ONE RESOURCES*

Pronunciation Guide

A two-page student guide to understanding diacritical marks given in standard dictionary pronunciations; includes practice

Form for Analyzing Primary Source Documents

In support of Primary Sources features in *The American Experience* and *The British Tradition*, a form for analyzing various types of primary sources.

Teaching Guides

To support fluency monitoring, Guide for Assessing Fluency; to support vocabulary instruction through music, a Guide for Teaching with BQ Tunes.

Name _____   Date _____

Guide for Assessing Fluency

The students' *All-in-One Workbooks* feature a series of twelve expository and narrative reading passages to be used to assess reading fluency. The passages have lexiles of increasing difficulty within the grade level range. They are designed to test students' reading accuracy and pace. An optional question is provided to assess comprehension.

The following oral reading rates are recommended goals:

ORAL READING RATES	
Grade	Words per Minute
6	115–145 with 90% accuracy
7	147–167 with 90% accuracy
8	156–171 with 90% accuracy
9–10	180–200 with 90% accuracy

Instructional Routine

- Hold reading practice sessions. Choose an appropriate practice passage of about 250 words from the literature students are studying or from another source. You will find a lexile score for each literature selection in your *Teacher's Edition* Time and Resource Managers. You may also use as practice passages the Warm-ups in the *Unit Resources* books and, for grade 6–8, articles in the *Discoveries* series and *Real-Life Readings*.

- Students should read the passage once silently, noting any unfamiliar words. Have them define or explain those words before reading the passage aloud. (Students may add these words to a *Word Wall* later.)

- Then, have students work in pairs to rehearse their oral fluency. (Alternatively, you may lead the class in a choral reading of a single passage.)

- After students have read the passage(s) with understanding, they may time themselves or each other for practice before the formal timed readings are conducted.

Formal Fluency Assessment

- From the students' All-in-One Workbook, select a passage at the appropriate lexile level.

- Using an audio recorder, instruct the student to read the passage aloud at a normal pace. Alternatively, you may ask the student to read as you follow along, marking the text. Time the student for one minute.

- Note these types of errors: mispronunciations, omissions, reversals, substitutions, and words with which you have to help the student, after waiting two or three seconds.

- Mark the point in the passage that the student reaches after one minute.

- Use the formula below for determining accuracy and rate.

- Determine the rate by calculating the total number of WCPM (words correct per minute) and comparing the student's results against the goals indicated in the chart above.

- Analyze the results and create a plan for continued student improvement.

Name _____ Date _____

Guide for Assessing Fluency

Calculating Fluency

Use this formula to calculate reading fluency:

> Total words read correctly (both correctly read and self-corrected) in one minute *divided by* total words read (words read correctly + errors) × 100 = % accuracy

$$\frac{\text{number of words read correctly}}{\text{number of words read}} \times 100 = \text{WCPM}$$

Example: $\frac{137}{145} \times 100 = 94\%$

Post-reading Comprehension Activity

A short test item allows you quickly to assess student's comprehension. The items include these formats:

- matching
- fill-in-the-blank
- true/false
- short answer

If the student demonstrates difficulty in understanding the passage, you may remediate using selected leveled resources in the *Prentice Hall Literature* program. These components include the Vocabulary and Reading Warm-ups in the *Unit Resources*; the *Reading Kit* Practice and Assess pages, which are aligned with specific skills; and the scaffolded support for comprehension and other ELA skills in the *Reader's Notebooks: Adapted* and *English Learner's Versions*.

Pronunciation Key Practice—1

Throughout your textbook, you will find vocabulary features that include pronunciation for each new word. In order to pronounce the words correctly, you need to understand the symbols used to indicate different sounds.

Short Vowel Sounds

These sounds are shown with no markings at all:

a   as in <u>a</u>t, c<u>a</u>p   e   as in <u>e</u>nd, f<u>ea</u>ther, v<u>e</u>ry
i   as in <u>i</u>t, g<u>y</u>m, <u>ea</u>r   u   as in m<u>u</u>d, t<u>o</u>n, tr<u>ou</u>ble

Long Vowel Sounds

These sounds are shown with a line over the vowel:

ā   as in <u>a</u>te, r<u>ai</u>n, br<u>ea</u>k   ē   as in s<u>ee</u>, st<u>ea</u>m, p<u>ie</u>ce
ī   as in n<u>i</u>ce, l<u>ie</u>, sk<u>y</u>   ō   as in n<u>o</u>, <u>oa</u>t, l<u>ow</u>

A. DIRECTIONS: *Read aloud the sounds indicated by the symbols in each item. Then write the word the symbols stand for.*

1. kap _____   6. ker _____
2. kāp _____   7. wird _____
3. tīp _____   8. swet _____
4. klōz _____   9. swēt _____
5. tuf _____   10. nīt _____

Other Vowel Sounds

Notice the special markings used to show the following vowel sounds:

ä   as in father, far, heart   ô   as in all, law, taught
oo   as in look, would, pull   ōō   as in boot, drew, tune
yōō   as in cute, few, use   oi   as in oil, toy, royal
ou   as in out, now   ʉ   as in her, sir, word

B. DIRECTIONS: *Read aloud the sounds indicated by the symbols in each item. Then write the word the symbols stand for.*

1. boi _____   6. wʉrk _____
2. kär _____   7. lʉr _____
3. kood _____   8. kôt _____
4. lōōz _____   9. myōō _____
5. kroun _____   10. rä _____

Pronunciation Key Practice—2

Some Special Consonant Sounds

These consonant sounds are shown by special two-letter combinations:

hw as in which, white   zh as in vision, treasure
sh as in shell, mission, fiction   th as in threw, nothing
ŋ   as in ring, anger, pink   *th* as in then, mother
ch as in chew, nature

Syllables and Accent Marks

Your textbook will show you how to break a word into syllables, or parts, so that you can pronounce each part correctly. An accent mark (´) shows you which syllable to stress when you pronounce a word. Notice the differences in the way you say the following words:

bā´ bē   ō bā´   den´ im   dē nĭ´

Sounds in Unaccented Syllables

You will often see the following special symbols used in unaccented syllables. The most common is the schwa (ə), which shows an unaccented "uh" sound:

ə   as in ago, conceited, category, invisible
'l as in cattle, paddle
'n as in sudden, hidden

Light and Heavy Accents

Some long words have two stressed syllables: a heavy stress on one syllable and a second, lighter stress on another syllable. The lighter stress is shown by an accent mark in lighter type, like this: (´)

C. DIRECTIONS: *With a partner, read aloud the sounds indicated by the symbols in each item. Say the words that the symbols stand for.*

1. kôr´əs   5. mezh´ ər   9. fər bid´'n
2. kəm pash´ən   6. des´ pər ā´ shən   10. hwim´ pər
3. brē´ *thi*ŋ   7. im´ə cho͝or´   11. fun´ də ment´ 'l
4. ig nôrd´   8. plunj´ iŋ   12. rek´ əg nīz´

D. DIRECTIONS: *With a partner, read aloud the sounds indicated by the symbols in the following lines. Each group of lines represent the words of a small poem.*

1. ī ēt mī pēz wi*th* hun´ ē.   2. dōnt wᵤr´ ē if yo͝or jäb iz smôl
    ĭv dun it ôl mī līf.   and yo͝or ri wôrdz´ är fyo͞o.
    it māks *th*ə pēz tāst fun´ ē.   ri mem´ bər *that th*ə mīt´ ē ōk
    but it kēps *th*em än *th*ə nīf.   wuz wuns ə nut līk yo͞o.

BQ Tunes Activities

Use **BQ Tunes** to engage students in learning each unit's Big Question vocabulary and introduce the issue that the Big Question raises. You can access **BQ Tunes** recordings and lyrics at *PHLitOnline* or in *Hear It*, the Prentice Hall Audio Program. The lyrics are also provided in your **Unit Resources** books and in the students' **All-in-One Workbooks**. Below are suggested activities for using the songs with your class. Each activity takes 20–25 minutes. Students should have copies of the lyrics available.

Listening Exercise

OBJECTIVE: *To familiarize students with the song vocabulary and initiate discussion of definitions*

1. Instruct students to listen to the selected song, listing words that they do not know.
2. Play the selected song.
3. Afterward, ask students to raise their hands if they know the definitions of words they listed, and call on individuals to share their definitions. Write the words on the board as they are called out.
4. Then, ask students to share words for which they did *not* know the definitions, and call on them individually. Write the words on the board as they are called out.
5. Direct students to turn to the selected lyrics and instruct students to infer definitions for the remaining words in the lyrics. If they experience difficulty, encourage them to work in pairs or direct them to a dictionary.
6. Play the song again, and instruct students to read the lyrics to reinforce the exercise.

Vocabulary Game Exercise

OBJECTIVE: *To reinforce students' knowledge of Big Question vocabulary in the songs, and to initiate class discussion of definitions.*

1. Divide the students into two teams, each on one side of the room.
2. Play the selected song to the class. Then, play it again as students follow along reading the lyrics.
3. Afterward, read the song's lyrics aloud and, alternating sides, ask each team to define key words as you come upon them. Award a point for each correct definition.
4. Write the words on the board as they are defined, and keep score as the teams win points.
5. Declare the team with the most points the winners.
6. Review vocabulary missed by both teams, and field any questions the students may have.

BQ Tunes Activities

Writing Exercise, Stage 1

OBJECTIVE: *To build students' writing skills, leveraging newly acquired vocabulary*

1. Instruct students to write three contextual sentences, each using a single vocabulary word present in the selected song. The sentences *do not* have to be related to one another.
2. Allow 5 to 7 minutes for students to complete the task.
3. Afterward, ask random students to read what they have composed.
4. Then, ask the class if the sentences satisfied the "contextual" criteria, and discuss the responses.
5. Repeat with as many students as time permits.
6. Field any questions the students may have.

Writing Exercise, Stage 2

OBJECTIVE: *To build students' composition skills, leveraging newly acquired vocabulary*

1. Instruct students to write three contextual sentences, each using a single vocabulary word present in the selected song. The sentences *must* be related to one another, as in a paragraph.
2. Allow 5 to 7 minutes for students to complete the task.
3. Afterward, ask random students to read what they've composed.
4. Then, ask the class if the sentences satisfied the "contextual" criteria and the "relationship" criteria, and discuss the responses.
5. Repeat with as many students as time permits.
6. Field any questions the students may have.

BQ Tunes

Get My Point Across, performed by Hydra

If I win that means that's your loss /
I guess that makes me the new boss /
and I don't even have to go and use brute force / Nah,
I just have to get my point across

Have to get my point across
I just have to get my point across
Have to get my point across

This is not an act this is **fact** / a true non fiction description /
no need to interact you can sit back and listen /
too many rappers rap but that's all contradiction /
they act one way in their rap but that's not how they're living /
if all that were true they would all be in prison / instead we fall victim to
the **fiction** they've written / they made it up, yup, imaginary ideas / is it a **fantasy** or
should we believe what we hear? /
So we're here to question them yea, **investigate** them /
see if they can **prove** or give **evidence** of what they're saying / just a verbal
discussion with words in a song / I think they're lying let's see if they can prove me
wrong /
Let's get it on . . .

If I win that means that's your loss /
I guess that makes me the new boss /
and I don't even have to go and use brute force / Nah,
I just have to get my point across
Have to get my point across
I just have to get my point across
Have to get my point across

Now it's my **opinion,** my personal view / you shouldn't even want to do
The things they say they do / I mean most of it is criminal (criminal), and if your song
was a police interview well that would be the end of you / come on now who you
kidding? You? /
you, never do that stuff you say you do, it's all too **unbelievable** /
It's not conceivable to put into my mind /

Continued

that anything you say is true so why don't you stop lying /

why don't you stop trying to be a gangster just end it /

write about your actual life man keep it **realistic** /

it's one thing to create a character to be artistic /

but they act like that's really them so the point, they missed it /

so that's why I dissed it, after putting it to the **test** /

I tried to see if it was genuine but found out it was less /

So I'm not going to rest until I can decide who's real /

And **determine** who's just acting for the money and the deal but either way...

If I win that means that's your loss /

I guess that makes me the new boss /

and I don't even have to go and use brute force / Nah,

I just have to get my point across

Have to get my point across

I just have to get my point across

Have to get my point across

See I studied you dudes' moves I research your ways /
you only say what you say cuz you think that it pays /

sometimes it does but at least show what's next /

and doing negative eventually has negative effects /

Use better judgment making **decisions** on what you say in songs /

Or I will pull your card if what you're saying is wrong /

And I will never lose, I've got the title I earned it /

You know what I'm saying's **true** listen the hook **confirms** it.

If I win that means that's your loss /

I guess that makes me the new boss /

and I don't even have to go and use brute force / Nah,

I just have to get my point across

Have to get my point across

I just have to get my point across

Have to get my point across

Song Title: **Get My Point Across**
Artist: Performed by Hydra
Vocals: Rodney "Blitz" Willie
Lyrics by Rodney "Blitz" Willie
Music composed by Keith "Wild Child" Middleton
Produced by Keith "Wild Child" Middleton
Technical Production: Mike Pandolfo, Wonderful
Executive Producer: Keith London, Defined Mind

Unit 1: Fiction and Nonfiction
Big Question Vocabulary—1

The Big Question: How do we decide what is true?

In your textbook, you learned words that will help you talk about what is true and what may not be true. These words can be useful in classroom discussions and when talking to friends in everyday conversation.

fantasy: an idea or a belief that is not based on facts

fiction: a story or book that is about imaginary people and events

realistic: based on what is actually possible rather than on how a person might like things to be

true: based on facts

unbelievable: hard to believe because it does not seem probable

---

Lacy told the following story to Bill, Stuart, and Kim: "I was at home, minding my own business, when the doorbell rang. My mom opened the door to a woman that I never saw before. She was wearing lots of shiny jewelry and a long silver gown. She had a magic wand. She said, 'Lacy, there you are! Come here my child, and I will grant you three wishes!' I wished for three things. The next thing I knew all three wishes came true!"

Each of Lacy's friends had a different reaction to the story.

DIRECTIONS: *Use the word(s) given in parentheses to write what each friend said to Lacy.*

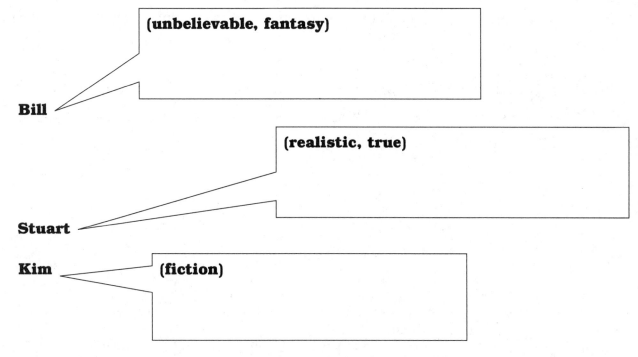

Bill **(unbelievable, fantasy)**

Stuart **(realistic, true)**

Kim **(fiction)**

Name _____ Date _____

Unit 1: Fiction and Nonfiction
Big Question Vocabulary—2

The Big Question: How do we decide what is true?

People must learn facts in order to make decisions. The following words can help you talk about how to separate facts from opinions.

decision: a choice or judgment that a person makes after discussion or thought

determine: to find out the facts about something

fact: a piece of information known to be true

opinion: a person's belief about something

prove: to show that something is true by using facts and information

DIRECTIONS: *Fill in the dialogue using the word(s) in parentheses.*

"I think that you should study hard and get good grades so you can go to a good college," Mario's father told him.

1. Mario did not believe that he needed better grades to go to a good college. He said to his father: **(opinion)** "_____

   _____"

2. His father wanted to do some research to see if he was correct. He said: **(determine, fact)** "_____

   _____"

3. They looked at some college Web sites and Mario discovered that he would need A's and B's to be considered. His sister asked what they were doing. Mario responded: **(prove)** _____

   _____"

4. Based on what he saw, Mario spent the afternoon studying instead of going to the park. He told his friends: **(decision)** "_____

   _____"

Unit 1: Fiction and Nonfiction
Big Question Vocabulary—3

The Big Question: How do we decide what is true?

Sometimes it takes work to find out the truth. The following words will help you talk about how people work to get at the truth.

confirm: show that something is definitely true by getting more proof

evidence: a fact, an object, or a sign that makes you believe something is true

investigate: to try to find out the truth about something

study: to find out more about a subject

test: to examine something in order to get information

DIRECTIONS: *Read the passage. Then, fill in the dialogue using the words in parentheses.*

"Aha! said Dr. Trooper. "My experiment will prove that I am correct. Carrots improve eyesight!"

"How do you know that?" asked Mia.

"My dear, it has been my life's work," said Dr. Trooper. "Come to my laboratory. Let me show you."

Mia followed Dr. Trooper into his laboratory. In the laboratory, they found Doug, Dr. Trooper's assistant. He was eating carrots and reading very fine print on a sheet of paper.

Mia asked, "What are you doing?"

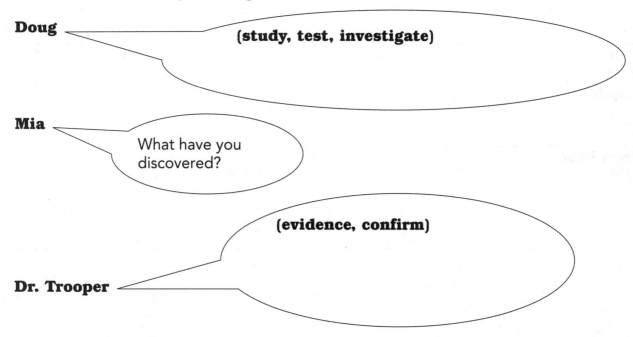

Doug (study, test, investigate)

Mia What have you discovered?

(evidence, confirm)

Dr. Trooper

Name _____ Date _____

Unit 1: Fiction and Nonfiction
Applying the Big Question

 How do we decide what is true?

DIRECTIONS: *Complete the chart below to apply what you have learned about how to decide what is true. One row has been completed for you.*

Example	Information, situation, or event	True/untrue	How I decided	What I learned
From Literature	In "Greyling," a seal becomes a child.	Untrue	I know that an animal cannot change into a human.	I can sometimes use my own knowledge to decide what is true.
From Literature				
From Science				
From Social Studies				
From Real Life				

Diagnostic Test

Identify the answer choice that best completes the statement.

1. The cat jumped into my lap, and I_____ its back.
   A. stroked
   B. spine
   C. shrugged
   D. snorted

2. When she asked her children to do chores, they complained and_____ about it.
   A. insisted
   B. stalling
   C. ignored
   D. grumbled

3. Kneeling in the grass, I looked for a four-leaf_____ .
   A. clover
   B. beneath
   C. fruit
   D. examine

4. When our cat was 3 weeks old, it weighed very little and was very_____ .
   A. raggedy
   B. related
   C. skinny
   D. picky

5. We brought our dog home when he was just a_____ .
   A. kin
   B. pup
   C. lad
   D. human

6. When you buy a dozen eggs, you have a total of_____ eggs.
   A. eleven
   B. twelve
   C. fifteen
   D. forty

7. The lawyer listened carefully while the_____ spoke about the case.
   A. clues
   B. expert
   C. advising
   D. evidence

8. I was not paying attention because I was_____ by the loud noises.
   - A. hushed
   - B. distracted
   - C. observed
   - D. suspicious

9. You should go to lunch now;_____ , you will have to wait for an hour.
   - A. plus
   - B. otherwise
   - C. seldom
   - D. wherever

10. After he fell and hit his head, he looked_____ .
   - A. jabbed
   - B. bulged
   - C. dazed
   - D. obliged

11. Because the tea was so hot, I just_____ it.
   - A. sipped
   - B. delicious
   - C. plucked
   - D. cautious

12. She is so young, yet she skates_____ well for her age.
   - A. rarely
   - B. actual
   - C. remarkably
   - D. vaguely

13. Mom stores our cans and boxes of food in the_____ .
   - A. pantry
   - B. warehouses
   - C. basin
   - D. arches

14. If you ever see that type of snake, beware of its_____ .
   - A. coiled
   - B. deadly
   - C. fangs
   - D. poisonous

15. When iron nails are left out in the rain, they become_____ .
   A. absorbed
   B. chemicals
   C. silvery
   D. rusty

16. As I was riding my bike, those annoying_____ kept flying into my face.
   A. brows
   B. storks
   C. gnats
   D. kennels

17. Your new black car looks very shiny and_____ .
   A. features
   B. sleek
   C. particularly
   D. apparent

18. The police officer was able to_____ the bank robber from a photo.
   A. fascinate
   B. involve
   C. endure
   D. identify

19. The letters *a*, *e*, *i*, *o*, and *u* are known as_____ .
   A. vowels
   B. phrases
   C. constants
   D. observations

20. After I came inside from the storm, my socks were so wet that I_____ them out.
   A. clasped
   B. suspended
   C. inhabited
   D. wrung

21. We did not find the cat outside, so we looked_____ the house again.
   A. basement
   B. upside
   C. within
   D. opposite

Name _____ Date _____

22. The king wanted to hear the important news only from the_____ himself.
   A. royal
   B. messenger
   C. folk
   D. dignity

23. We stayed overnight right on the beach in a small_____ .
   A. acre
   B. overhead
   C. hearth
   D. cottage

24. Monday started out like any other day—just another_____ day.
   A. ordinary
   B. alert
   C. intensity
   D. daily

25. This is an unusual name, and I do not know how to_____ it.
   A. hesitate
   B. exchange
   C. introducing
   D. pronounce

26. Every July, we have a family picnic with all of my_____ .
   A. boyfriends
   B. generations
   C. relatives
   D. various

27. That small hole in my favorite shirt needs to be_____ .
   A. mended
   B. laced
   C. embroidered
   D. sturdy

28. Thank you for your help—I will always remember your actions with_____ .
   A. envy
   B. behavior
   C. valuable
   D. gratitude

29. Eat right and exercise, and you will be a_____ person.
   A. vain
   B. healthy
   C. solemn
   D. exhausted

30. At times, you may have to pay extra for something that is top_____ .
   A. appealing
   B. collecting
   C. quality
   D. produced

31. Turtles have become well known for their_____ in movement.
   A. flex
   B. memory
   C. slowness
   D. balancing

32. My favorite chair is so soft and_____ to sit in.
   A. raw
   B. cozy
   C. nimble
   D. coarse

33. When the rough game ended, several of our players were_____ .
   A. tending
   B. plastered
   C. appreciation
   D. bruised

34. The movie was enjoyed by the reporter whose job it was to_____ it.
   A. review
   B. note
   C. record
   D. produce

35. The vegetables that I planted in my garden have_____ .
   A. devoured
   B. sprouted
   C. powdered
   D. mowed

36. She twisted her ankle and has been_____ all day.
   A. enabling
   B. glinting
   C. hobbling
   D. favored

37. What was the_____ of the water when it began to boil?
   A. meter
   B. recipe
   C. temperature
   D. calendar

Name _____ Date _____

38. The badly hurt animal was crying in _____ .
    A. shame
    B. distress
    C. stricken
    D. painful

39. Nothing tastes better to me than a delicious red, ripe _____ .
    A. strawberry
    B. banana
    C. mushroom
    D. biscuit

40. I ate my dinner so fast that I developed _____ .
    A. hiccups
    B. toleration
    C. homesick
    D. complicated

Name _____

Unit 1: Fiction and Nonfiction Skills Concept Map—1

How do we decide what is true?

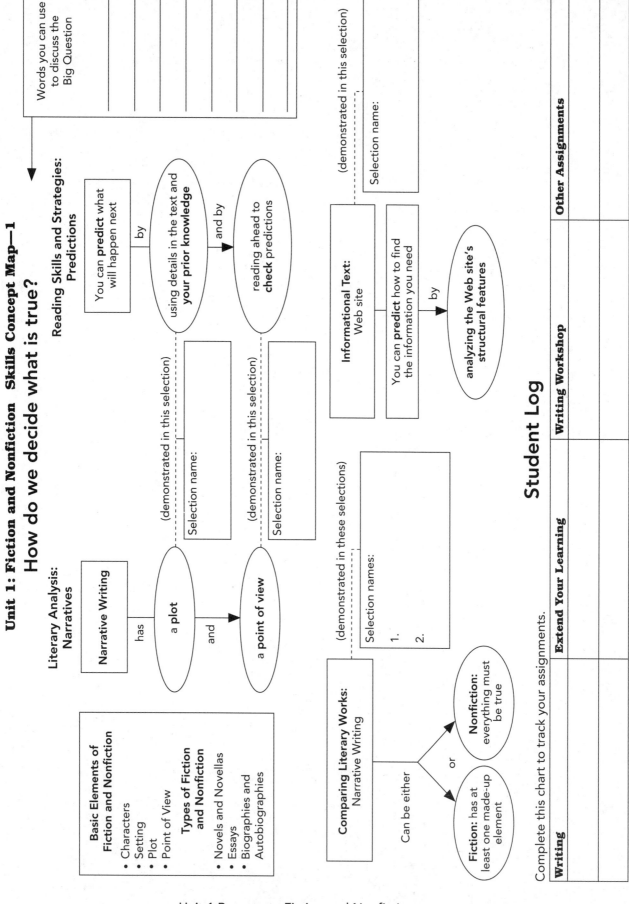

Literary Analysis:
Narratives

Narrative Writing — has → a plot — and → a point of view

(demonstrated in this selection)
Selection name: _____

(demonstrated in this selection)
Selection name: _____

Reading Skills and Strategies:
Predictions

You can **predict** what will happen next — by → using details in the text and **your prior knowledge** — and by → reading ahead to **check** predictions

(demonstrated in this selection)
Selection name: _____

Informational Text:
Web site

You can **predict** how to find the information you need — by → analyzing the Web site's structural features

Words you can use to discuss the Big Question

Basic Elements of Fiction and Nonfiction
• Characters
• Setting
• Plot
• Point of View

Types of Fiction and Nonfiction
• Novels and Novellas
• Essays
• Biographies and Autobiographies

Comparing Literary Works:
Narrative Writing

Can be either — or

Nonfiction: everything must be true

Fiction: has at least one made-up element

(demonstrated in these selections)
Selection names:
1.
2.

Student Log

Complete this chart to track your assignments.

Writing	Extend Your Learning	Writing Workshop	Other Assignments

Unit 1 Resources: Fiction and Nonfiction

Vocabulary Warm-up Word Lists

Study these words from "Greyling" and "My Heart Is in the Highlands." Then, complete the activities.

Word List A

childhood [CHYLD hood] *n.* the time when a person is a child
   Anna looked back on her youth, remembering <u>childhood</u> as a happy time.

delicious [di LISH us] *adj.* great tasting or great smelling
   I can't stop eating those <u>delicious</u> oatmeal raisin cookies.

foam [FOHM] *n.* mass of tiny bubbles
   When Sheila opened the can of soda, <u>foam</u> sprayed out.

mansions [MAN shuhnz] *n.* houses that are very big and grand
   The rich woman owned two <u>mansions</u> with many elegant rooms.

mended [MEND id] *v.* fixed; repaired
   A balloon cannot be <u>mended</u>; if it pops, just throw it out.

memories [MEM uh reez] *n.* things that you remember from the past
   Jack has great <u>memories</u> of the party; he recalls that it was fun.

relatives [REL uh tivs] *n.* family members
   Uncle Jack, my cousin Steve, and Grandma Lil are my favorite <u>relatives</u>.

stunned [STUHND] *v.* extremely shocked or surprised
   I was so sure my team was going to win that when we lost I was <u>stunned</u>.

Word List B

driftwood [DRIFT wood] *n.* pieces of wood that float up on a beach
   We found enough <u>driftwood</u> on the beach to make a big bonfire.

dwell [DWEL] *v.* to think about for a long time
   When Leslie and Will <u>dwell</u> on their problems, they always feel sad.

endure [en DOOR] *v.* put up with something
   The noise was so loud that Tammy found it hard to <u>endure</u>.

fiction [FIK shuhn] *n.* stories about characters and events that are not real
   I like reading <u>fiction</u> more than I like reading about real life.

grieving [GREE ving] *v.* feeling terribly sad
   Charlotte was <u>grieving</u> for weeks when her best friend moved far away.

rebuilding [ree BIL ding] *v.* completely fixing, putting something back together
   Workers spent weeks <u>rebuilding</u> a home that was damaged by the storm.

sleek [SLEEK] *adj.* shiny and smooth
   Trevor washed and waxed his car; it had never looked so <u>sleek</u> before.

technique [tek NEEK] *n.* a way of doing something that requires skill
   I practiced the new batting <u>technique</u> that my coach had shown me.

Name _____ Date _____

"Greyling" and "My Heart Is in the Highlands" by Jane Yolen
Vocabulary Warm-up Exercises

Exercise A *Fill in each blank in the paragraph below with an appropriate word from Word List A. Use each word only once.*

Jon was keeping a family journal. He asked some [1] _____ to recall

their earliest [2] _____. Jon's grandfather was the first to talk about his

[3] _____.

"When I was small, everything seemed bigger," he said. "Small houses seemed like

enormous [4] _____. The little trees in our backyard towered into the

sky. One day I fell out of one. I sat on the ground feeling [5] _____.

My leg was broken. The bones [6] _____ fine, but I was stuck in bed

for weeks. Mom brought me ice cream sodas to cheer me up. I thought they tasted

[7] _____. I'd scrape up the last bit of [8] _____ from the

bottom of the cup, using my straw."

Exercise B *Decide whether each statement below is true or false. Then, circle T or F, and explain your answer.*

1. A cat is one animal that has a *sleek* appearance.
   T / F _____

2. Reading a lot is a good *technique* for improving your vocabulary.
   T / F _____

3. You will often find *driftwood* under trees at the top of a mountain.
   T / F _____

4. *Rebuilding* a town destroyed by an earthquake is a job that can be done in a day.
   T / F _____

5. Most people find that vacations are hard to *endure*.
   T / F _____

6. Movies about people who don't really exist are works of *fiction*.
   T / F _____

7. You will probably find many *grieving* people at a funeral.
   T / F _____

8. You *dwell* on a problem when you spend just one second thinking about it.
   T / F _____

Name _____ Date _____

"Greyling" and "My Heart Is in the Highlands" by Jane Yolen
Reading Warm-up A

Read the following passage. Pay special attention to the underlined words. Then, read it again, and complete the activities. Use a separate sheet of paper for your written answers.

"Time to see Auntie Jane and Uncle Reggie again," said Mollie's mother. "It's been so long since we have gone to Scotland. You've grown so much that they will not recognize you."

At first, Mollie was <u>stunned</u> by her mother's announcement. The news was completely unexpected. Just the week before, her mother was helping her pick out a summer camp. Now she wouldn't be going to camp; she was going to be traveling to Scotland. She tried to picture her <u>relatives</u> in her mind. The <u>memories</u> of her aunts and uncles were foggy and indistinct. It had been almost eight years since the last trip. She could barely remember the visit to Scotland the family had taken earlier in her <u>childhood</u>. At the time, she had been just six years old.

Mollie remembered the countryside and the buildings better than the people. As a six-year-old, Scotland had seemed like a fairyland. <u>Mansions</u> sat atop rolling green hills. These were extremely big houses; they looked almost like castles. In fact, some of them were castles, inhabited long ago by princes and kings.

Sitting on the couch, she let her mind wander back in time. Now she remembered a picnic on a cliff overlooking the water. The images in her mind grew clearer. She could see waves gently breaking, leaving traces of <u>foam</u> on the rocks below. Now she remembered the food, so different from what she was used to eating. Instead of sandwiches there had been pastries filled with meat, and so absolutely <u>delicious</u> that she had asked for seconds. For dessert there was a type of fruitcake, filled with tiny bits of nuts and lemon peel. Afterwards, playing with her cousins, Mollie had fallen and torn her shirtsleeve.

"Don't worry," said Uncle Reggie. "As soon as we get back to the house we'll have that <u>mended</u>."

1. Underline the phrase that explains why Mollie is <u>stunned</u>. What might leave you *stunned*?

2. Underline two <u>relatives</u> of Mollie and her mother who are named in this story. Then, explain what *relatives* are.

3. What is the likely reason that Mollie's <u>memories</u> are so foggy? Define *memories*.

4. Underline the words that name an age that is part of <u>childhood</u>. List the age when you think *childhood* ends.

5. Underline the words that tell the meaning of <u>mansions</u>. What kind of people might live in *mansions*?

6. Circle the words that tell what leaves traces of <u>foam</u>. Name somewhere else *foam* might be found.

7. Write a sentence describing what Mollie thought was <u>delicious</u>. What is something you find *delicious*?

8. Write a sentence explaining what Mollie needs to have <u>mended</u> and why.

Name _____   Date _____

"Greyling" and "My Heart Is in the Highlands" by Jane Yolen
Reading Warm-up B

Read the following passage. Pay special attention to the underlined words. Then, read it again, and complete the activities. Use a separate sheet of paper for your written answers.

Fishermen know that their jobs are dangerous. They cannot <u>dwell</u> too much upon these dangers. If they thought about them, fishermen would not be capable of doing their jobs. Still, they realize that danger is not <u>fiction</u> but an everyday fact of life.

Fishermen in smaller boats face the greatest risks, but all fishermen are aware of possible hazards at sea. In dense dark fog, a sea craft can lose its course, run aground, or collide with another ship. Equipment failure is something fishermen must also be prepared to handle. Engines sometimes fail. Radios, so important when the need for assistance arises, may malfunction. When something serious happens, <u>rebuilding</u> equipment at sea is not always an option. That's why fishermen carry backup equipment such as flares or signal flags.

The biggest danger, however, is getting caught in an unexpected storm. Even a <u>sleek</u> fishing vessel that cuts easily through the water cannot always outrace a storm. Each year, many fishing boats are destroyed by the elements. Constant pounding by the waves is more than some boats can <u>endure</u>. Boats crack apart and the pieces wash up on an ocean beach as <u>driftwood</u>.

Although these hazards at sea seem pretty scary, expert fishermen are knowledgeable in every <u>technique</u> of safe sailing. They know what to do when rough weather arises. Safety equipment and lifeboats and life preservers are kept in good repair and replaced when necessary. It is always "safety first" when working at sea, because no fisherman wants to be the one who doesn't return, leaving a <u>grieving</u> family behind!

1. Underline the nearby phrase that has the same meaning as <u>dwell</u>.

2. Circle the nearby word that means the opposite of <u>fiction</u>.

3. Explain why you think <u>rebuilding</u> at sea might be hard.

4. Write a sentence describing two things you think have a <u>sleek</u> look.

5. What is it that some boats cannot <u>endure</u>? Tell what happens to these boats.

6. Write a sentence telling where the passage says you can find <u>driftwood</u>.

7. Underline the word that explains what type of fisherman knows every <u>technique</u> of the sea.

8. Explain what it means for a fisherman's family to be <u>grieving</u>.

Jane Yolen
Listening and Viewing

Segment 1: Meet Jane Yolen
- According to Jane Yolen, writers have a love-hate relationship with movies. Why does she think that it is important to read a book even if there is a movie version of it? Which do you usually prefer, the book or the movie? Why?

_____

_____

_____

_____

Segment 2: Fiction and Nonfiction
- Jane Yolen says writers often take something old and make it new again. How does she accomplish this with the story of the selchie? How is this story a combination of fiction and nonfiction?

_____

_____

_____

_____

Segment 3: The Writing Process
- How does Jane Yolen gather ideas for stories? Where do you get your ideas for stories?

_____

_____

_____

_____

Segment 4: The Rewards of Writing
- According to Jane Yolen, what is the real reward of writing?

_____

_____

_____

_____

Learning About Fiction and Nonfiction

Literature may be either **fiction** or **nonfiction.** The following chart compares and contrasts these two types of literature.

Characteristics	Fiction	Nonfiction
Features	Fiction tells about *imaginary* people or animals called **characters**. They experience a series of made-up events called the **plot**. The plot contains a problem, or **conflict**, that the characters must solve.	Nonfiction tells about *real* people, animals, places, things, experiences, and ideas. Nonfiction contains only facts and ideas.
Sample Forms	short stories, novels	articles, essays, biographies, authobiographies
Author's Purpose	to entertain	to explain, inform, persuade, to entertain

A. DIRECTIONS: *Read each item. Decide whether it is an element of fiction or nonfiction, and then write* fiction *or* nonfiction *on the line provided.*

_____ 1. a story about a talking horse

_____ 2. a newspaper article that describes farming in France

_____ 3. a magazine article that explains how to make a kite

_____ 4. a novel in which a boy turns into a bird

B. DIRECTIONS: *This paragraph begins a piece of literature. Read it carefully. Then, decide whether it is fiction or nonfiction. Circle your choice. Then, on the lines below, explain what information led you to make your choice.*

Jerry was eager to perform with Harry in the school talent show. He had practiced with Harry for three days. Jerry was sure that Harry would be able to solve the math problem. After all, Harry was a hard worker. He was also a very smart dog.

Circle your choice: FICTION   NONFICTION

Explain your choice:

_____

_____

_____

Name _____ Date _____

Model Selection: Fiction

Fiction is writing that tells about imaginary people or animals called **characters.** They experience a series of made-up events called the **plot.** The plot contains a problem, or **conflict,** that characters solve. The action takes place at a certain time and location, called the **setting**.

The plot is told by a speaker called the **narrator.** If the narrator is a character, he or she tells the story in **first-person point of view.** If the narrator stands outside the story, he or she tells it in **third-person point of view.**

DIRECTIONS: *"Greyling" is a piece of fiction. Use this chart to provide details about its characters, plot, setting, and narrator.*

Element of Fiction	Details
Characters	_____ _____ _____
Plot	What conflict, or problem, do the characters face? _____ _____
Narrator	Is the narrator inside or outside the story? _____ Does the narrator use the first-person or the third-person point of view? _____ What hints in the story led to your answers? _____ _____ _____ _____
Setting	_____ _____

"My Heart Is in the Highlands" by Jane Yolen
Learning About Nonfiction

Nonfiction is writing that tells about real people, animals, places, things, experiences, and ideas. Examples include biographies, autobiographies, letters, articles, essays, journals, speeches, and diaries.

Unlike fiction, which contains made-up details and characters, nonfiction presents facts and discusses ideas. Nonfiction is told from the **author's perspective,** or point of view. The author has a definite **purpose for writing.** That purpose might be:

- to explain ("How To Make a Mask")
- to entertain ("My Funny Experience")
- to share thoughts and experiences ("My Trip to Spain")
- to persuade ("Support Our Soccer Team!")
- to inform ("The Products of India")

A. DIRECTIONS: *Answer the following questions about "My Heart Is in the Highlands."*

1. What real people does it mention? _____

2. In what real location does it take place? _____

3. Summarize the real experience that the author shares. _____

_____

_____

4. List three facts that the author presents. _____

_____

_____

5. Summarize the author's point of view about her fiction writing. _____

_____

_____

B. DIRECTIONS: *Authors often have more than one purpose in mind when they write a piece of nonfiction. Jane Yolen had two purposes in mind when she wrote "My Heart Is in the Highlands." Look at the list of purposes at the top of this page. Tell which two purposes she had for writing. Support your answer with examples.*

_____

_____

_____

_____

_____

_____

Name _____ Date _____

"Greyling" and "My Heart Is in the Highlands" by Jane Yolen
Open-Book Test

Short Answer *Write your responses to the questions in this section on the lines provided.*

1. An author lived in Africa in the 1990s. She writes about her own experiences there from a first-person point of view. Is her writing fiction or nonfiction? Explain.

   _____

   _____

2. An author writes a book set during the Revolutionary War. George Washington appears in the book, but the main character is made up by the author. Is the book fiction or nonfiction? Explain.

   _____

   _____

   _____

3. You are reading an exciting book of fiction about a journey into outer space. It describes the adventures of several characters on dangerous missions. Briefly describe what an exciting nonfiction book on the same subject might tell about.

   _____

   _____

   _____

4. Where does "Greyling" take place, and why is that setting important to the story?

   _____

   _____

   _____

5. How do the fisherman and his wife feel about keeping Greyling from the sea? Support your answer with details from the story.

   _____

   _____

   _____

6. When he found Greyling, the fisherman "looked to the town on the great grey cliffs that sheared off into the sea." What word in the quote helps you determine the meaning of *sheared*? Explain.

   _____

   _____

   _____

Unit 1 Resources: Fiction and Nonfiction

7. If she had been able, would the fisherman's wife have stopped Greyling from diving into the sea to save her husband? Support your answer with details from the story.

_____

_____

_____

_____

8. In "My Heart Is in the Highlands," Yolen says that all fiction uses memory. Then she more precisely calls it "re-memory." Explain why *re-memory* is a more accurate word for what the fiction writer uses.

_____

_____

_____

_____

9. "My Heart Is in the Highlands" is a work of nonfiction. In the left column of the chart, write details that show the speech is nonfiction. In the right column, explain the importance of each detail to the speech.

Details of Nonfiction	Importance to Speech

10. Using information from "My Heart Is in the Highlands," explain how an author creates a character for a work of fiction.

_____

_____

_____

Essay

Write an extended response to the question of your choice or to the question or questions your teacher assigns you.

11. Why do Greyling's parents think "this way is best" when he finally returns to the sea? Explain your answer in a brief essay. Support your ideas with examples from the story.

12. The fisherman and his wife keep Greyling's true identity secret from him and keep him away from the sea. Write a brief essay to tell if you think his parents are being loving or selfish. Use examples from the story to support your response.

13. In "My Heart Is in the Highlands," Yolen describes "little building blocks" she uses to write fiction. In a brief essay, discuss two building blocks from Yolen's own history that she might have used to create "Greyling." Use details from both Yolen's introduction to "Greyling" and the story itself in your response.

14. **Thinking About the Big Question: How do we decide what is true?** Greyling does not know the truth of his identity, although there are signs in the novel that might help him figure it out. In an essay, tell what signs Greyling chooses to ignore and why he might do so. Consider how he feels when he discovers the truth at the end of the story. Use examples from the story to support your response.

Oral Response

15. Go back to question 4, 5, 8, or 9 or to the question your teacher assigns to you. Take a few minutes to expand your answer and prepare an oral response. Find additional details in "Greyling" or "My Heart Is in the Highlands" that support your points. If necessary, make notes to guide your response.

"Greyling" and "My Heart Is in the Highlands" by Jane Yolen
Selection Test A

Learning About Fiction and Nonfiction *Identify the letter of the choice that best answers the question.*

_____ 1. Which statement is true about fiction?
   A. It can contain imaginary people and animals.
   B. It can contain only facts and ideas.
   C. It can contain only real people and animals.
   D. It can take place only in the present time.

_____ 2. Which statement is true about nonfiction?
   A. It contains a series of made-up events.
   B. It contains characters who face a problem.
   C. It can contain only imaginary people.
   D. It can contain only facts and ideas.

_____ 3. Which term names the problem that characters in a story must face and solve?
   A. the setting
   B. the novel
   C. the conflict
   D. the essay

_____ 4. Which of the following is an example of fiction?
   A. article
   B. story
   C. essay
   D. biography

_____ 5. Which of the following is an example of nonfiction?
   A. a story about a dog that talks
   B. a tale about a man who barks
   C. an article about a doghouse
   D. a letter a dog wrote

Critical Reading

_____ 6. Who is the narrator of "Greyling"?
   A. the fisherman
   B. the fisherman's wife
   C. Greyling
   D. a storyteller who is not a character

_____ 7. What is the setting of "Greyling"?
    A. a village by the sea
    B. a magic village under the sea
    C. a ship at the bottom of the sea
    D. a seal colony in the Arctic Sea

_____ 8. Why is the fisherman's wife sad at the beginning of "Greyling"?
    A. She misses a friend who has moved away.
    B. Her husband is in danger on his boat.
    C. She wishes that she had a child.
    D. Her child has left her and gone off to sea.

_____ 9. In "Greyling," why do the fisherman and his wife avoid letting Greyling go into the sea?
    A. They are afraid that he will drown.
    B. They don't want him to become a fisherman.
    C. They are afraid that a shark might attack him.
    D. They are afraid that he might become a seal.

_____ 10. In "Greyling," why does Greyling come back once a year?
    A. He loves the fisherman and his wife and wants to visit them.
    B. He likes to be around people instead of seals.
    C. He wants to make sure that the fisherman is safe.
    D. He hopes to attend the yearly fisherman's festival.

_____ 11. What is the setting of "My Heart Is in the Highlands"?
    A. a village by the sea
    B. Scotland
    C. an imaginary highway
    D. Denver

_____ 12. Which statement from "My Heart is in the Highlands" is true about the cottages?
    A. They are made with wood from very old forests.
    B. They are made with steel from old factories.
    C. They are made with stones from older buildings.
    D. They are made with sand from the sea.

____ 13. According to Yolen in "My Heart Is in the Highlands," what "stones from the past" does she use to build her stories?

    A. her memories

    B. her future

    C. her conflicts

    D. her hopes

____ 14. According to "My Heart Is in the Highlands," from whom does Yolen take, or "thieve," real-life details that she uses in her stories?

    A. the fisherman and his wife

    B. Greyling

    C. people who build stone cottages

    D. her friends and family

____ 15. What two things does Yolen compare in "My Heart Is in the Highlands"?

    A. her husband's thoughts and her thoughts

    B. science fiction and computer science

    C. stone cottages and her stories

    D. toads and selchies

Essay

16. At the end of "Greyling," the fisherman says that Greyling has "gone where his heart calls." What does he mean?

17. Name two people or events you know about that you might use in a piece of fiction. Describe each as it exists in real life, without getting too personal. Then, explain how you'd "reshape" each one, changing it and adding details from your imagination.

18. **Thinking About the Big Question: How do we decide what is true?** Greyling does not know the truth about who he is, although there are signs in the story that might help him figure it out. In an essay, tell one sign Greyling chooses to ignore and why he might do so. Use details from the story to support your response.

"Greyling" and "My Heart Is in the Highlands" by Jane Yolen
Selection Test B

Learning About Fiction and Nonfiction *Identify the letter of the choice that best completes the statement or answers the question.*

____ 1. Which statement is true about <u>nonfiction</u>?
   A. It can contain imaginary characters.
   B. It presents only made-up details and facts.
   C. It presents only conflict and resolution.
   D. It presents only facts and ideas.

____ 2. Which statement is true about <u>fiction</u>?
   A. It can contain only real people.
   B. It can contain imaginary people.
   C. It cannot contain any facts.
   D. It cannot contain any details.

____ 3. Which of the following is the best description of the <u>plot</u> of a piece of fiction?
   A. the main character
   B. the location of the story
   C. the series of made-up events
   D. the point of view

____ 4. Which statement is true about a work of fiction in which the narrator is a character in the story?
   A. It is told in the first-person point of view.
   B. The narrator knows what the other characters think.
   C. It is told in the third-person point of view.
   D. The narrator knows what the other characters want.

____ 5. Which of the following groups contains only examples of <u>nonfiction</u>?
   A. biography, novel
   B. short story, diary
   C. autobiography, letter
   D. essay, story

____ 6. Which of the following is an example of <u>fiction</u>?
   A. a letter from a spider
   B. a report that compares types of spiders
   C. an essay about spiders
   D. an article on how spiders spin webs

Critical Reading

____ 7. Which statement is true about "Greyling"?
   A. Its narrator is the fisherman.
   B. Its narrator is the fisherman's wife.
   C. Its narrator is Greyling.
   D. Its narrator is not a character.

_____ 8. At the beginning of "Greyling," what conflict do the main characters face?
A. They are very poor, and they do not have enough food.
B. Their fishing boat is destroyed in a bad storm.
C. They are sad because they have no children.
D. They are sad because seals do not live along the shore.

_____ 9. Which statement best explains why the fisherman in "Greyling" wrapped the seal in his shirt and hurried home?
A. He was afraid that someone else would claim the seal.
B. He thought his wife would want the seal in place of a child.
C. He knew that it was against the law to adopt a wild seal.
D. He had always wanted to have a selchie.

_____ 10. Greyling often looks out to sea as he grows up. Why is he "longing and grieving in his heart"?
A. He worries that the fisherman might drown in a storm at sea.
B. He longs to return to the sea but doesn't understand why.
C. He is lonely because people are not friendly toward him.
D. He is sad because he cannot take the place of a real child.

_____ 11. Why does Greyling pull free from his mother's arms and dive off the cliff into the sea?
A. He wants to save his father.
B. He wants to show that he is brave.
C. He has begun to change into a seal.
D. He doesn't want to obey any rules.

_____ 12. When is the fisherman's wife's conflict about Greyling returning to the sea resolved?
A. when Greyling returns from the sea and promises never to leave her again
B. when Greyling promises to protect the fisherman during bad storms
C. when she learns that the fisherman has found another seal for her to raise
D. when she realizes that Greyling will be happier living in the sea

_____ 13. Which statement best summarizes what the fisherman and his wife learn at the end of "Greyling"?
A. Parents need to keep a close watch on their children.
B. Sometimes you need to let go of someone you love.
C. Selchies cannot be trusted to do what they are told.
D. Neighbors need to learn to help their neighbors.

_____ 14. Which is the best definition of the word *Highlands*, as Yolen uses it in "My Heart Is in the Highlands"?
A. long road trips that she took with her family
B. castles and mansions in the city of Edinburgh
C. the high, small country towns of Scotland
D. camping vacations that she took with children

_____ 15. Which statement is true about the buildings that Yolen writes about in "My Heart Is in the Highlands"?
   A. They are made from the wood of ancient trees.
   B. They are made from stones from older buildings.
   C. They are huts that were built by local fishermen.
   D. They remind her of the home she lived in as a child.

_____ 16. What does Yolen mean when she says that "All fiction uses memory"?
   A. Fiction writers often use memories from their own lives when they create their stories.
   B. Writers often place clues in a story to help readers make predictions.
   C. Fiction writers often make up details to make their stories more memorable.
   D. Both authors and readers must try to remember the main events in a piece of fiction.

_____ 17. What warning does Yolen give to her readers in "My Heart Is in the Highlands"?
   A. If you get to know her, details about you might show up in her stories.
   B. If you get to know her, you may want to learn more about buildings.
   C. If you visit Scotland, you may never want to return home again.
   D. If you visit Scotland, you may find a selchie or a toad by the sea.

_____ 18. According to "My Heart Is in the Highlands," Yolen's friends and family members may have difficulty identifying themselves in her stories. Why?
   A. She always makes up different names for them.
   B. She usually puts them in unfamiliar or unrealistic settings.
   C. She often changes them into different characters, such as animals.
   D. She often changes the colors of their eyes to match stormy skies.

Essay

19. In "Greyling," Greyling longs for the sea but loves the couple who raised him. Explain how he resolves this conflict. Do you think his solution will make him happier than he was as a young man? Explain why or why not.

20. Yolen may have "reshaped" real-life events and details to create the events and characters in "Greyling." Think about the character of Greyling. What type of real person might Yolen have based him on? What conflict might that real person have faced? How might he have solved the conflict? How might his parents have felt about his solution? Use examples from the story in your response.

21. **Thinking About the Big Question: How do we decide what is true?** Greyling does not know the truth of his identity, although there are signs in the novel that might help him figure it out. In an essay, tell what signs Greyling chooses to ignore and why he might do so. Consider how he feels when he discovers the truth at the end of the story. Use examples from the story to support your response.

Vocabulary Warm-up Word Lists

Study these words from "Stray." Then, complete the activities.

Word List A

abandoned [uh BAN duhnd] *v.* tossed aside; left behind
   The ghost town was filled with <u>abandoned</u> houses.

automobiles [AW tuh moh beelz] *n.* passenger vehicles with four wheels and an engine
   <u>Automobiles</u> are expensive; it costs a lot of money to buy a car.

cough [KAWF] *v.* make a rough, harsh noise while forcing out air
   When the nurse heard me <u>cough</u>, he gave me some medicine.

exhausted [eg ZAWST id] *adj.* very tired and worn out
   Tracy felt <u>exhausted</u> after running seven miles.

ignore [ig NAWR] *v.* pay no attention to something
   From now on I will <u>ignore</u> you when you say such foolish things.

mildly [MYLD lee] *adv.* gently, with little force
   The wind blew so <u>mildly</u> that I couldn't get my kite into the air.

sipped [SIPT] *v.* drank slowly
   Sherry gulped her milk shake down, but I <u>sipped</u> mine to make it last.

warehouse [WAIR hows] *n.* a building where things are stored
   We don't have that bicycle in the store, but we'll get you one from the <u>warehouse</u>.

Word List B

biscuit [BIS kit] *n.* small, round type of bread
   I'd rather have a <u>biscuit</u> than toast with my eggs.

distress [dis TRES] *n.* difficulty, pain, or sadness
   Sharon was filled with <u>distress</u> when she saw the impossible job she had to do.

grudgingly [GRUHJ ing lee] *adv.* not happily, in a resentful or reluctant way
   She didn't want to share and gave me a taste <u>grudgingly</u>.

icicles [EYE si kuhls] *n.* long thin pieces of ice that hang down
   The spring sun started to melt the <u>icicles</u> hanging from our roof.

scraps [SKRAPS] *n.* small pieces (of food, paper, wood, fabric, etc.)
   After building the bookcase, we swept up the <u>scraps</u> of wood that were left over.

starvation [star VAY shun] *n.* the act of suffering from not enough food
   Ancient peoples faced <u>starvation</u> if they couldn't find food.

timidly [TIM id lee] *adv.* shyly, in a frightened way
   Dave spoke <u>timidly</u> since he wasn't sure that his answer was correct.

trudged [TRUHJD] *v.* plodded; walked slowly and with effort
   The rancher <u>trudged</u> through the snow in search of his lost cattle.

"Stray" by Cynthia Rylant
Vocabulary Warm-up Exercises

Exercise A *Fill in each blank in the paragraph below with an appropriate word from Word List A. Use each word only once.*

Shaun's mom heard him [1] _____. She made him some tea. After he [2] _____ the tea, Shaun felt better and decided to go to work. Shaun worked in a [3] _____ filled with [4] _____. These cars had been [5] _____ by their owners. Shaun liked his work even though it was tiring and left him feeling [6] _____. One thing about the job that bothered him [7] _____ was the noise from the trucks unloading the cars. At first he tried to [8] _____ the noise. Then he started wearing earplugs.

Exercise B *Write a complete sentence to answer each question. For each item, use a word from Word List B to replace the underlined word or phrase without changing its meaning.*

1. What is one kind of <u>bread</u> people like to eat in the morning?
   _____

2. What is something you would only do <u>reluctantly</u>?
   _____

3. Describe a situation in which you might speak <u>shyly</u>.
   _____

4. What could cause people to experience <u>a suffering from the lack of food</u>?
   _____

5. Why did the emergency workers <u>plod</u> through the wreckage?
   _____

6. When you cut out paper dolls, <u>small pieces</u> of paper are left over. Name another activity in which <u>small pieces</u> are left over.
   _____

7. In which season would you find <u>pieces of ice</u> hanging from trees?
   _____

8. What is something that would cause you to feel <u>pain or sadness</u>?
   _____

"Stray" by Cynthia Rylant
Reading Warm-up A

Read the following passage. Pay special attention to the underlined words. Then, read it again, and complete the activities. Use a separate sheet of paper for your written answers.

Most of us look forward to wintertime. Winter is the season of holidays, parties, and a nice vacation from school. Winter can also be a time to be careful, and not just because you are more likely to cough and give someone your cold. If you live in a northern climate, winter means cold weather and snow. Snow is great for skiing and sledding, but it can also produce dangerous conditions.

Snowstorms can appear suddenly. They may begin mildly with just a few flakes, but then they take a turn for the worse. Roads can become slippery and ice-covered. That makes driving hazardous. Automobiles are harder to control on snow and ice. Sharp turns can lead to spins and skids. Your braking distance, or the distance it takes to stop your vehicle, grows longer.

Local governments understand this. That is why there is usually a fleet of snowplows ready to clear the roads when severe weather strikes. There is also a warehouse for storing salt. Salt is used to melt snow and ice on the roads.

Still, people should take responsibility for their own safety. Drivers need to be careful and pay attention to weather forecasts. Even with salt and snowplows, it can be unwise to ignore weather warnings. After a big storm, you will encounter abandoned cars along the sides of roadways. People have left them behind after swerving and getting stuck in the snow. These people may have wished that they had stayed at home and sipped hot chocolate instead of driving.

Another wintertime danger is overexertion. Sidewalks get slippery and dangerous, too. So after snow accumulates, people pick up their shovels to clear them off. Shoveling snow is hard work, however. It is easy to become exhausted. People must be careful not to tire themselves out doing it.

All in all, winter *is* a great time of year. Still, it pays to be a little careful when the snowflakes start to fall.

1. Underline the word that helps you understand what cough means. Then, write a sentence describing when you might *cough*.

2. Circle the words that describe a snowstorm that begins mildly. Define *mildly*.

3. Underline the verb that helps you to understand what automobiles are for. Describe your favorite kinds of *automobiles*.

4. Circle the words that tell you what a warehouse is used for. List some other things that might be kept in one.

5. Underline the nearby words that mean the opposite of ignore. Then, write a sentence using the word *ignore*.

6. Underline the words that tell where abandoned cars are found. Describe what probably happens to these cars.

7. Explain why hot chocolate is sipped rather than gulped.

8. Underline a phrase that tells why you can become exhausted shoveling snow. List three other activities that can leave you *exhausted*.

"Stray" by Cynthia Rylant
Reading Warm-up B

Read the following passage. Pay special attention to the underlined words. Then, read it again, and complete the activities. Use a separate sheet of paper for your written answers.

Most people love their pets. Sometimes, however, people fail to realize how much care and attention animals need. Sadly, these pet owners may abandon their pets. The poor animals end up living on the street.

Former house pets can have an especially hard time living on their own. They may have difficulty finding food. In fact, many are at risk of <u>starvation</u>. Stray dogs and cats hang around outside dumps, looking for <u>scraps</u> to chew on. Indeed, an old <u>biscuit</u>, stale bread, or cold spaghetti is delicious to a homeless animal.

Sometimes, restaurant owners will <u>grudgingly</u> feed strays leftover food. If they do it too often, though, the strays might hang around and bother customers. Handouts and scraps are hardly enough to survive on.

Luckily, there are groups that work to help stray animals. You have probably seen them as they have <u>trudged</u> through empty houses and garbage dumps. These rescue groups collect stray animals. Then, they take them to shelters. At shelters, the former strays get food; they also get medical care if they are sick.

One such group is Stray Rescue of St. Louis. For several years, it has been helping to save stray animals from hunger, illness, and other conditions that cause <u>distress</u>. It finds animals that have been left in empty houses or public parks. Then, it does everything it can to find the pets new homes. The group points out that former strays make great pets. These animals may act <u>timidly</u> at first. Soon, however, they get over their fear and show their new owners love, affection, and loyalty.

The next time you see a stray dog begging for food, or a shivering cat trying to keep warm in a cardboard box covered with <u>icicles</u>, contact a local animal rescue group.

1. Underline the phrase that tells you why animals are at risk of <u>starvation</u>. Write a sentence telling what these animals need.

2. Write a sentence explaining why <u>scraps</u> wouldn't help these strays very much.

3. Write a sentence describing what an old <u>biscuit</u> might look, taste, or feel like.

4. In your own words, tell why restaurant owners might act <u>grudgingly</u> when feeding strays.

5. Circle the words that tell where rescue workers have <u>trudged</u>. Explain what *trudged* means.

6. Underline two words that help you understand the meaning of <u>distress</u>. Then, write a sentence using the word.

7. Underline the nearby word that tells what animals overcome when they stop acting <u>timidly</u>.

8. Describe what the weather might be like when <u>icicles</u> cover a cardboard box.

Name _____ Date _____

"**Stray**" by Cynthia Rylant
Writing About the Big Question

How do we decide what is true?

Big Question Vocabulary

confirm	decision	determine	evidence	fact
fantasy	fiction	investigate	opinion	prove
realistic	study	test	true	unbelievable

A. *Use one or more words from the list above to complete each sentence.*

1. Some scientists decided to _____ the effects on people of having pets.

2. They found scientific _____ that people with pets are happier.

3. The _____ also showed that people with pets live longer.

4. The results _____ that having a pet can be good for you.

B. *Respond to each item with a complete sentence.*

1. Describe a pet that you have had or would like to have.

_____

_____

2. Explain how the pet you described helped or would help you. Use at least two Big Question vocabulary words.

_____

_____

C. *In "Stray," Doris is upset because her parents tell her they cannot afford to keep the stray dog she found. Is it true that keeping a dog as a pet can be expensive? Complete the sentence below. Then, write a short paragraph connecting this situation to the Big Question.*

Dog owners spend money on _____

_____

_____

_____

_____

_____

Unit 1 Resources: Fiction and Nonfiction

Name _____ Date _____

Reading: Use Prior Knowledge to Make Predictions

A **prediction** is a logical guess about what will happen next in a story. You can **use your prior knowledge** to help you make predictions. To do this, relate what you already know to the details in a story. For example, you have prior knowledge about stray animals. If you haven't seen one, you have read about them. You know how they look. You know how they make you feel. Then, as you read details about the abandoned puppy in "Stray," you are ready to make a **prediction,** a logical guess, about what might happen next.

What if your prediction turns out to be wrong? No problem. Part of the fun of reading is adjusting your predictions as you get more details. As you read, use story clues and your own knowledge to make predictions along the way.

DIRECTIONS: *You have prior knowledge about dogs. You know a lot about how children relate to adults in a family. You have prior knowledge about families that have little money. Start with your prior knowledge. Combine it with a detail from the story. Then, make a prediction on the chart that follows. One entry has been modeled for you.*

Prior Knowledge About Strays		Detail From Story		Prediction
They're hungry.	+	This one shivers with cold.	=	Doris will bring it in and feed it.
1. About dogs	+		=	
2. About children and adults in a family	+		=	
3. About families with little money	+		=	

Name _____   Date _____

"**Stray**" by Cynthia Rylant
Literary Analysis: Plot

The **plot** of "Stray" is the arrangement of events in the story. The elements of plot include:

- **Exposition:** introduction of the setting, characters, and basic situation
- **Conflict:** the story's central problem
- **Rising action:** events that increase the tension
- **Climax:** high point of the story when the story's outcome becomes clear
- **Falling action:** events that follow the climax
- **Resolution:** the final outcome

All the events in a plot follow one after another in a logical way. Like most stories, "Stray" centers on a conflict or struggle. You keep reading because you want to find out who will win the conflict or how the problem will be solved. At the climax of the story, you know who wins. The problem is solved. The story ends.

A. DIRECTIONS: *The following questions focus on the exposition, the rising action, and the falling action in "Stray." Answer each question in the space provided.*

1. The exposition introduces the setting, characters, and basic situation. Here is one exposition detail:

   Exposition detail: Snow has fallen.

   What is another exposition detail?

   Exposition detail: _____

   _____

2. The events in the rising action come before the climax. There are many events in the rising action of "Stray." Here is one event in the rising action:

   Rising action event: Doris meets the dog.

   On the following lines, write two additional events that happen in the rising action.

   Rising action events:

   a. _____

   _____

   b. _____

   _____

3. In "Stray," the story winds up quickly after the climax. Here is one event in the falling action:

   Falling action event: Mr. Lacey tells Doris he took the dog to the pound.

   What is another event that happens in the falling action?

   Falling action event: _____

   _____

Name _____   Date _____

"Stray" by Cynthia Rylant
Vocabulary Builder

Word List

exhausted   grudgingly   ignore   starvation   timidly   trudged

A. DIRECTIONS: *In each question below, think about the meaning of the underlined word from the Word List. Then, answer the questions.*

1. If a puppy enters a room <u>timidly</u>, is he running or moving cautiously? Why?

   Answer: _____

   Explanation: _____

2. If you admire someone, will you help that person <u>grudgingly</u> or willingly? Explain.

   Answer: _____

   Explanation: _____

3. If a team chooses to <u>ignore</u> its coach, might the coach be pleased or angry? Why?

   Answer: _____

   Explanation: _____

4. If someone <u>trudged</u> through the woods, would she move quickly? Why or why not?

   Answer: _____

   Explanation: _____

5. If you are <u>exhausted</u>, what might you do? Why?

   Answer: _____

   Explanation: _____

6. If a bear eats too much, would it face <u>starvation</u>? Why?

   Answer: _____

   Explanation: _____

B. Word Study. *The Latin suffix -ation changes a verb to a noun. It means the condition of being ___ed (past tense verb). Change each underlined verb into a noun by adding -ation. Answer the question using the new word.*

1. How might a mother and her child feel if they were to <u>separate</u> in a crowd?

   _____

2. What do you like to <u>converse</u> about?

   _____

3. What things do you <u>admire</u> in a person?

   _____

"Stray" by Cynthia Rylant
Enrichment: Make a Poster; Write an Article

Every day people drop off unwanted animals at animal shelters. Pet overpopulation has caused many shelters, like the one Mr. Lacey visited, to become very crowded. You may be able to help some of these animals find good homes. You can make a poster or write an article for your school newspaper.

A. DIRECTIONS: *In the space below, design a poster that calls attention to the animals waiting in animal shelters. Decide what kind of animal you will draw. Then sketch it in the rectangle. Leave space for two or three words in big letters at the top. That will be your eye-catching title. On the lines following the heading* **Information,** *give the address and phone number of the nearest animal shelter.*

Title: _____

Information:

_____

_____

_____

B. DIRECTIONS: *If you already have a pet, you can write an article for your school paper. Give students the information they need about owning a pet. Here are questions you might want to answer in your article. (You may have to do some research before answering some of the questions.) Jot down your notes on the lines below.*

1. How much time does your pet need from you every day? _____

2. What is the cost of caring for your pet? Tell how often someone might pay these costs. You don't need to give exact figures. Just tell about how much each item costs.

   - food _____   - license (if it's a dog) _____
   - shots _____   - checkups and medical care _____
   - toys _____   - purchase price of pet (if any) _____

3. What is the biggest advantage of having a pet like yours? _____

   _____

4. What is the biggest disadvantage of having a pet like yours? _____

   _____

Name _____ Date _____

"Stray" by Cynthia Rylant
Open-Book Test

Short Answer *Write your responses to the questions in this section on the lines provided.*

1. In "Stray," the puppy wags its tail *timidly*. How does Doris behave *timidly* when her father sees the dog?

   _____

   _____

   _____

2. The author of "Stray" writes, "Mrs. Lacey grudgingly let Doris feed it table scraps." Explain how the word *grudgingly* reveals Mrs. Lacey's feelings about the dog.

   _____

   _____

   _____

   _____

3. Use your prior knowledge about how children feel about their pets. Explain how this knowledge helps you predict how Doris will feel about the stray.

   _____

   _____

   _____

   _____

4. In "Stray," why do Doris's parents ignore her when she points out how good the dog is?

   _____

   _____

   _____

   _____

5. Mrs. Lacey tells Doris to act more grown-up when the puppy has to leave. What does Mrs. Lacey want Doris to do?

   _____

   _____

   _____

6. In the plot diagram, write two events that are part of the rising action of "Stray." Then, on the lines below, explain how each event helps to increase tension in the story.

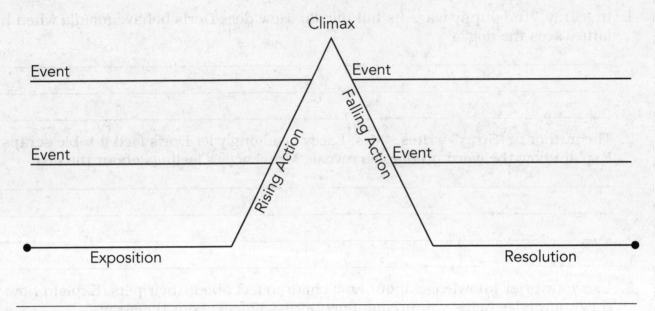

_____

_____

_____

_____

_____

7. When Doris cries herself to sleep in "Stray," what prediction do Doris and the reader make about the dog's fate? Give two examples from the story that support this prediction.

_____

_____

_____

_____

8. The falling action of "Stray" shows a different side of Doris's father. How is he different? Why does the author wait for the falling action to show this side of him? Explain your answer.

_____

_____

_____

_____

9. Near the end of "Stray," Mrs. Lacey smiles at her husband and shakes her head "as if she would never, ever, understand him." Explain her reaction.

_____

_____

_____

10. Think about what the story suggests will happen to the stray. Then consider what really happens. Why does the resolution come as a surprise? Use details from the story to support your answer.

_____

_____

_____

_____

Essay

Write an extended response to the question of your choice or to the question or questions your teacher assigns you.

11. Think about Doris's relationship with her parents in "Stray." How do they treat her? How does she get along with them? Also consider how the story ends. In a brief essay, describe Doris's relationship with her parents. Use examples from the story to support your answer.

12. At the beginning of "Stray," Doris's parents want her to learn to make sensible choices in life. What do they wind up learning themselves by the end of the story? Use examples from the story to support your answer.

13. Near the end of "Stray," Doris walks into the kitchen to fix herself some dinner. Why do her parents choose not to tell her right away that they kept the dog? Use details from the story to support your response.

14. **Thinking About the Big Question: How do we decide what is true?** At the beginning of "Stray," Doris decides that her parents will not let her keep the dog. Write an essay in which you discuss how Doris comes to this conclusion and why it turns out not to be true. Support your ideas with examples from the story.

Oral Response

15. Go back to question 4, 6, 8, or 10 or to the question your teacher assigns to you. Take a few minutes to expand your answer and prepare an oral response. Find additional details in "Stray" that support your points. If necessary, make notes to guide your response.

Name _____ Date _____

"**Stray**" by Cynthia Rylant
Selection Test A

Critical Reading *Identify the letter of the choice that best answers the question.*

____ 1. How can you make a good guess about what will happen in a story?

    A. You connect what you know to what you don't know.

    B. You relate your prior knowledge to clues in the story.

    C. You read the same kind of story.

    D. You combine your prior knowledge with what your friends tell you.

____ 2. Use your prior knowledge about strays to help you answer this question: If Doris does not take in the puppy, what is least likely to happen to it?

    A. It might become mean and attack someone.

    B. A mother dog who had recently lost her puppy might take care of it.

    C. Another animal might attack it.

    D. Another family might take it in.

____ 3. Why doesn't Doris give the dog a name?

    A. She hasn't yet thought of the perfect name for it.

    B. She has been too sad and worried to think about a name.

    C. She thinks the dog's next owners should name it.

    D. She does not want to become too attached to the dog.

____ 4. Using your prior knowledge about families and pets, what leads you to think that Doris's parents will not let her keep the puppy?

    A. Parents want to know all about a puppy's background. Her parents don't know anything about this puppy's background.

    B. Many parents think that a small dog might be less trouble and would eat less than a big one. This puppy looks as if it will grow up to be a big dog.

    C. Families that have never had a dog before are not likely to take in a dog off the streets.

    D. Families need to talk before making important decisions. Doris's parents won't talk with her about the dog.

____ 5. At what point in the plot of "Stray" does Mr. Lacey make the following statement?

    "I don't know where it came from," he said mildly, "but I know for sure where it's going."

    A. exposition

    B. rising action

    C. climax

    D. falling action

Unit 1 Resources: Fiction and Nonfiction

___ 6. Which of the following words best describes Mrs. Lacey?
   A. sensible
   B. selfish
   C. stubborn
   D. generous

___ 7. How does Doris know that the puppy is a good dog?
   A. It cries for its mother in the night.
   B. It always tries to go into the kitchen.
   C. It doesn't tear up things in the basement.
   D. It is completely housebroken.

___ 8. After her father takes the puppy away, what does Doris do?
   A. She cries herself to sleep.
   B. She runs down the road after the car.
   C. She talks to her mother about how upset she is.
   D. She goes to school.

___ 9. Which of these events happens in the falling action, after the climax of "Stray"?
   A. Mr. Lacey agrees to let the dog sleep in the basement.
   B. Mrs. Lacey tells Doris she should try to act more grown up.
   C. Mr. Lacey drives away with the dog.
   D. Mr. Laccy tells Doris he brought the dog back.

___ 10. What does Mrs. Lacey mean when she tells Doris to act more grown-up?
   A. She wants Doris to do her chores without being asked.
   B. She wants Doris to stop crying about the puppy.
   C. She wants Doris to stop sleeping all afternoon.
   D. She wants Doris to be able to argue with her parents without getting so upset.

Vocabulary and Grammar

___ 11. Why does Doris speak timidly to her mother?
   A. Her mother has told her that speaking loudly is rude.
   B. She fears what her mother will say.
   C. She does not want to wake up her father.
   D. She is a calm child who prefers to speak quietly.

____ **12.** How can you tell whether a noun is a *proper noun*?

    A. It names something important, such as *president* or *mother.*

    B. It is capitalized even if it is a noun that does not begin a sentence.

    C. It will be a general name for a group of people, places, or things.

    D. It will end with an apostrophe.

____ **13.** How many nouns (common and proper) are in the following sentence?

    On Saturday, nine days after the dog had arrived, the sun was shining.

    A. one

    B. two

    C. three

    D. four

____ **14.** Why does Mrs. Lacey grudgingly let Doris feed the dog table scraps?

    A. She feels sorry that table scraps are all that is left.

    B. She is happy that there is something left to give.

    C. She fears that the dog will eat some of Doris's food.

    D. She resents having to give food to the dog.

Essay

15. In five or six sentences, sum up the plot of "Stray." Include the words that name three of the elements of plot: conflict, rising action, and resolution. Remember to tell only the important events that happen in the story.

16. In this story, Doris's parents hoped by their actions to teach Doris a lesson about life. Tell what lesson Doris's parents wanted her to learn. Explain whether you think she did or did not learn that lesson. Then write what you think Doris did learn from her experience.

17. **Thinking About the Big Question: How do we decide what is true?** At the beginning of "Stray," Doris decides that her parents will not let her keep the dog because they cannot afford a pet. In an essay, discuss why Doris's conclusion turns out not to be true. Support your ideas with examples from the story.

"**Stray**" by Cynthia Rylant
Selection Test B

Critical Reading *Identify the letter of the choice that best answers the question.*

____ 1. To make a logical guess about what will happen in a story you combine
   A. prior knowledge with what you already know.
   B. prior knowledge with a detail from the story.
   C. a prediction with a logical guess about the story.
   D. what the story says with clues from other stories.

____ 2. In the exposition of "Stray," the weather is important because
   A. Mr. Lacey can take the dog to the pound.
   B. the Laceys cannot use their phone to find out who abandoned the dog.
   C. the puppy needs help to survive in the snow.
   D. the puppy has lost its way in the snow.

____ 3. The following statement from Mr. Lacey indicates the beginning of which plot element in "Stray"?

   "I don't know where it came from," he said mildly, "but I know for sure where it's going."

   A. exposition
   B. conflict
   C. climax
   D. resolution

____ 4. If Doris does not take in the puppy, what is least likely to happen to it? Base your answer on your prior knowledge of strays and your common sense.
   A. It might become mean and attack someone.
   B. A wild dog who had recently lost her puppy might adopt it.
   C. Another animal might attack it.
   D. Another family might take it in.

____ 5. Doris does not give the dog a name because
   A. she hasn't found the perfect name yet.
   B. she has been too upset to think about a name.
   C. she thinks the dog's next owners should name it.
   D. she does not want to grow too attached to the dog.

____ 6. Doris's most important reason for wanting to keep the puppy is that
   A. she knows it will grow up to be a big dog.
   B. she thinks playing with the puppy will be fun.
   C. she wants the love and companionship of a pet.
   D. she is looking forward to training the puppy.

____ 7. What makes you think Doris's parents will not let her keep the puppy?
   A. The puppy has been abandoned.
   B. The puppy is on its way to being a big dog.
   C. Mrs. Lacey doesn't like to waste food.
   D. Doris's parents refuse to talk to her about the dog.

____ 8. Which choice best describes Mrs. Lacey?
    A. mean and selfish
    B. practical and sensible
    C. unreasonable and stubborn
    D. generous and warm

____ 9. Doris doesn't argue about the puppy with her parents because
    I. she is afraid of her parents.
    II. she knows it is useless.
    III. she is, by nature, a quiet child.
    IV. she thinks that if she keeps quiet, they will change their minds.
    A. I and II
    B. I and IV
    C. II and III
    D. III and IV

____ 10. Doris tries not to cry when her father prepares to take away the puppy because
    A. she does not want to look like a baby.
    B. she realizes that her parents are being sensible.
    C. she does not want to make her father angry.
    D. she still hopes that he will change his mind.

____ 11. Doris's parents do not wish to keep the puppy because
    A. the puppy looks sick.
    B. the puppy does not have a name.
    C. the puppy will grow to be a large dog.
    D. of the expense.

____ 12. Based on the way the story ends, which phrase best describes Mr. Lacey?
    A. more softhearted than he wants his family to think he is
    B. mean and insensitive toward his daughter
    C. sensitive and understanding toward his daughter
    D. less softhearted than his wife

____ 13. When Mrs. Lacey smiles at her husband near the end of the story, her smile shows that
    A. she finds Mr. Lacey's actions funny.
    B. she thinks he has behaved foolishly.
    C. she knew all along that he would keep the puppy.
    D. she is surprised at his unusual behavior.

Vocabulary and Grammar

____ 14. A puppy abandoned on a snowy road is most likely to wag its tail timidly when it is
    A. cold.
    B. frightened.
    C. excited.
    D. happy.

_____ **15.** Mrs. Lacey grudgingly let Doris feed the puppy table scraps because Mrs. Lacey
   A. does not like dogs.
   B. resents the fact that Mr. Lacey and Doris leave food on their plates.
   C. wants to cook more food.
   D. is reluctant to give it any food at all.

_____ **16.** In which sentence does the word *ignore* make the most sense?
   A. The hungry puppy chose to ignore its food.
   B. We ignore the forecasts of rain when we remember to put on slickers and boots.
   C. My sister tells me I should ignore anyone who teases me in a mean way.
   D. Knowing he needed help, Tom continued to ignore every offer of assistance.

_____ **17.** Which choice best defines a proper noun?
   A. a name for something with only one correct meaning
   B. a special name for one person, such as a nickname
   C. a category or type of a person, place, or thing
   D. a specific person, place, or thing

_____ **18.** How many nouns are in the following sentence?
      In January, a puppy wandered close to the Laceys' small house.

   A. one
   B. two
   C. three
   D. four

_____ **19.** Which of the following sentences includes the incorrect possessive form of a noun?
   A. The puppies' paws were covered with mud.
   B. After five minute's time, the children's mother called them in.
   C. The animals' cages needed to be cleaned.
   D. Doris was the Laceys' daughter.

Essay

20. Early in the story, both of Doris's parents feel it is important for Doris to learn that the family can afford only the essential things in life. They also want her to learn that she cannot have everything she wants. In the end, Doris learns quite a different lesson. In an essay, write what you think Doris learns from her experience. Explain how she might use what she learns later in life.

21. When Mr. Lacey brings the dog back from the pound, Doris is asleep. However, Mr. Lacey does not awaken her. Why do you think the author chose to have him wait and tell Doris later? Write an essay about the way the story ends. Include your opinion of the resolution, and back up your opinion with reasons.

22. **Thinking About the Big Question: How do we decide what is true?** At the beginning of "Stray," Doris decides that her parents will not let her keep the dog. Write an essay in which you discuss how Doris comes to this conclusion and why it turns out not to be true. Support your ideas with examples from the story.

Vocabulary Warm-up Word Lists

Study these words from "The Homecoming." Then, complete the activities.

Word List A

aroma [uh ROH muh] *n.* pleasant smell
  The aroma of the cooking hamburgers made everyone feel hungry.

advising [ad VY zing] *v.* telling someone how to do something
  My math teacher was advising me to spend more time studying.

bulged [BUHLJD] *v.* stuck out, appeared swollen
  My stomach bulged after I ate double desserts.

distracted [dis TRAK tid] *adj.* with weakened concentration, without focus
  Because of all the noise, I felt distracted and I couldn't concentrate.

interesting [IN tuh res ting] *adj.* attracting your interest or curiosity
  Trevor found the program so interesting that he didn't want to turn it off.

jabbed [JABD] *v.* made a poking or punching movement
  He jabbed his hand into the freezing water to feel how cold it was.

odd [AHD] *adj.* strange, weird, hard to explain
  Selena made an odd choice in picking a horror film; she hates scary movies.

recipe [RES i pee] *n.* instructions for how to cook something
  I'm a terrible cook, but I followed the recipe and the dish came out great!

Word List B

chess [CHES] *n.* a two-person game played on a checkered board
  In chess, players take turns moving their pieces across the board.

energy [EN er jee] *n.* strength to do an activity
  Climbing up the hill took away all our energy.

firewood [FYR wood] *v.* logs or twigs that are used for burning in a fire
  We gathered old branches to use as firewood in our campfire.

hatchet [HACH it] *n.* a small axe used as a tool to cut wood
  The lumberjack used the hatchet to cut branches and the axe to cut logs.

homecoming [HOHM kuhm ing] *n.* going back home after a trip
  The homecoming felt great; we had been gone for so long.

involved [in VAHLVD] *v.* took part or was active in something
  Chazz was very involved in sports until he broke his leg.

shooing [SHOO ing] *v.* motioning or yelling to drive someone or something away
  She tried shooing away the dog, but it jumped up and licked her.

wooded [WooD id] *adj.* covered with trees
  Before they cut down all the trees, this area was completely wooded.

"**The Homecoming**" by Laurence Yep
Vocabulary Warm-up Exercises

Exercise A *Fill in each blank in the paragraph below with an appropriate word from Word List A. Use each word only once.*

It felt [1] _____ to be in the new house. All of our belongings were still in huge boxes that [2] _____ at the sides. Our cat seemed unhappy; she [3] _____ her paw at the door over and over, begging to go out. My dad was busy talking to the movers, [4] _____ them about where to put furniture. We showed a movie to my little sister to keep her [5] _____ and out of the way. She seemed to find it very [6] _____. In the kitchen, my brother cooked from a favorite dinner [7] _____. Soon I smelled the familiar [8] _____ of my brother's yummy chicken stew. Luckily, some things were still the same.

Exercise B *Revise each sentence so that the underlined vocabulary word is used in a logical way. Be sure to keep the vocabulary word in your revision.*

Example: When the temperature grew colder, everyone <u>removed</u> their jackets.
When the temperature grew warmer, everyone <u>removed</u> their jackets.

1. I want to go to sleep since I have so much <u>energy</u>.

   _____

2. It is easy to find <u>firewood</u> in places where there aren't any trees.

   _____

3. A <u>hatchet</u> is a useful tool for cutting bread.

   _____

4. I was so <u>involved</u> in my book that I really wanted to stop reading.

   _____

5. Harold was a big fan of games so he hated playing <u>chess</u>.

   _____

6. In fall, the ground is covered with leaves because the area is not <u>wooded</u>.

   _____

7. Denise really wanted Jackson to join us so she began <u>shooing</u> him away.

   _____

8. We had been gone for almost five minutes, so people were excited about our <u>homecoming</u>.

   _____

"The Homecoming" by Laurence Yep
Reading Warm-up A

Read the following passage. Pay special attention to the underlined words. Then, read it again, and complete the activities. Use a separate sheet of paper for your written answers.

Sherry didn't realize what she was getting into when she invited Howard to help make chocolate-chip cookies for the party.

From the minute Howard walked in the door, his behavior was extremely <u>odd</u>. Everything he did seemed strange. Before even saying hello, he grabbed a bunch of chocolate chips. He stuffed so many in his mouth that his cheeks <u>bulged</u> like balloons. Soon, however, Sherry wished that his mouth had stayed full. As soon as he started talking, everything became worse.

"Where did you get this <u>recipe</u>, Sherry?" Howard asked. "This recipe looks awful. I have a good one, but I think you need a better brand of chocolate chips. I don't like the way these chips smell. They have a weird <u>aroma</u>."

The aroma couldn't have been *that* weird. Howard <u>jabbed</u> his hand into the container of chips a second time.

"I don't think you set the temperature right, Sherry," said Howard, glancing at the oven. "In my opinion, I think if you really want to make delicious cookies, we should use margarine instead of butter."

Sherry was not easily <u>distracted</u>, but Howard's chatter made her lose her concentration. She knocked over the mixing bowl, sending a mess of milk, eggs, and flour onto the floor. Howard looked at the mess. He was about to say something, but before he could, Sherry was pushing him toward the door.

"Howard, I thought having you here would make cooking more <u>interesting</u>. Now I'm looking forward to a boring afternoon. I'm tired of you <u>advising</u> me. I don't need someone telling me how to do everything. So, if you don't mind, I'll see you at the party."

1. Underline the nearby word that has the same meaning as <u>odd</u>. Describe a behavior that you would find *odd*.

2. Underline the words that explain why Howard's cheeks <u>bulged</u>. Tell what *bulged* means.

3. What does this <u>recipe</u> probably describe how to prepare? Name a favorite *recipe* of yours.

4. Circle the nearby word that has the same meaning as <u>aroma</u>. Name something you think has an unusual *aroma*.

5. Describe the action Howard made when he <u>jabbed</u> his hand into the container.

6. Underline the words that tell why Sherry is <u>distracted</u> now. Describe something that might leave you feeling *distracted*.

7. Circle the nearby word that has the opposite meaning of <u>interesting</u>. Define *interesting*.

8. Give one example of how Howard has been <u>advising</u> Sherry.

"The Homecoming" by Laurence Yep
Reading Warm-up B

Read the following passage. Pay special attention to the underlined words. Then, read it again, and complete the activities. Use a separate sheet of paper for your written answers.

Are you tired of sitting at home, watching television, playing games like chess, and reading books? Maybe it's time you got active and took a trip into the woods. Hiking and backpacking take energy, but they are great activities. They'll help you get physically fit, and allow you to experience the feeling of being close to nature.

There's nothing like walking into a wooded area after months of being trapped in the city. It just feels great to be surrounded by trees. Trees aren't just beautiful; they're useful, too. When you are camping in the woods, it's not hard to find firewood. You'll appreciate this at the end of a hard day's hike when you're ready to cook dinner over a fire. There is nothing like the feeling of chopping wood with a hatchet, then making a fire and cooking a meal outdoors.

Of course, there are some downsides to dining in the wilderness. Mosquitoes, spiders, and ticks call the woods home. Bring the insect repellent, and don't be upset if you have to spend some time shooing the flies away from your food. Overcoming difficulties like bugs and bad weather are just part of the fun. It's also what makes a homecoming such fun as well. After a few days in the wilderness, it's nice to get back home to hot showers and fly-free food.

Does all this sound interesting? If so, it's not hard to get started. Find out if your school has a camping or hiking club. Or talk to your parents and see if you can get them involved in outdoor activities. Once they start participating in these types of activities, it might be hard to get them to stop!

1. Underline the word that tells the category of chess. Describe one quality you need to play **chess**.

2. According to the passage, what activities take energy? List two other activities that take lots of **energy**.

3. Underline the phrase that tells you what it's like to be in a wooded area. Name two living things you might see there.

4. Explain why it's not hard to find firewood in these surroundings.

5. Underline the phrase that tells you what a hatchet is used for. Name another tool that can be used for this purpose.

6. Write a sentence explaining what you want flies to do when you are shooing them.

7. In your own words, explain what homecoming means.

8. Circle the nearby word with a similar meaning to involved. Then, list two activities you would like to get **involved** in.

Name _____ Date _____

"The Homecoming" by Laurence Yep
Writing About the Big Question

How do we decide what is true?

Big Question Vocabulary

confirm	decision	determine	evidence	fact
fantasy	fiction	investigate	opinion	prove
realistic	study	test	true	unbelievable

A. *Use one or more words from the list above to complete each sentence.*

1. Some _____ stories describe events that could really happen.

2. Their characters and settings are _____, just like life.

3. Other stories, like folk tales and fairy tales, are set in a _____ world.

4. Things happen that are strange and _____.

B. *Respond to each item with a complete sentence.*

1. Describe a realistic story you have read. Tell how it is like real life.

   _____

   _____

2. Describe a fantasy story you have read. Explain how it is different from real life.

   _____

   _____

C. *In "The Homecoming," the main character, a woodcutter, is a busybody. He is so distracted with everybody else's business that he has no time to cut wood. Is he really a woodcutter? Complete the sentence below. Then, write a short paragraph connecting this situation to the Big Question.*

   If a woodcutter never cuts wood, he is _____

   _____

   _____

   _____

   _____

   _____

   _____

   _____

Unit 1 Resources: Fiction and Nonfiction

"The Homecoming" by Laurence Yep

Reading: Use Prior Knowledge to Make Predictions

A **prediction** is a logical guess about what will happen next in a story. You can **use your prior knowledge** to help you make predictions. To do this, relate what you already know to details in a story. For example, you have prior knowledge about board games like chess. If you haven't played chess, you have read about it. You may have played a similar game like checkers or Monopoly. You know how a board game looks. You know how the players concentrate on the game. Then, as you read details about the chess game in "The Homecoming," you are ready to make a **prediction,** a logical guess, about what might happen next.

What if your prediction turns out to be wrong? No problem. Part of the fun of reading is adjusting your predictions as you get more details. As you read, use story clues and your own knowledge to make predictions along the way.

DIRECTIONS: *You have prior knowledge about people who give unwanted advice. You have prior knowledge about characters in stories and movies who look strange. You know what happens when someone gets very hungry. Start with your prior knowledge. Combine it with a detail from the story. Then, make a prediction on the following chart. One entry has been modeled for you.*

Prior Knowledge About Board Games	Detail From Story	Prediction
They take hours to play. +	The men play for seven days. =	There is something magical about this game.
1. About people who give unwanted advice _____ _____ +	_____ _____ =	_____ _____
2. About characters who look strange or magical _____ +	_____ =	_____
3. About someone who is hungry _____ +	_____ =	_____

"The Homecoming" by Laurence Yep
Literary Analysis: Plot

The **plot** of "The Homecoming" is the arrangement of events in the story. The elements of plot include:

- **Exposition:** introduction of the setting, characters, and basic situation
- **Conflict:** the story's central problem
- **Rising action:** events that increase the tension
- **Climax:** high point of the story when the story's outcome becomes clear
- **Falling action:** events that follow the climax
- **Resolution:** the final outcome

All the events in a plot follow one after another in a logical way. Like most stories, "The Homecoming" centers on a conflict or struggle. You keep reading because you want to find out who will win the conflict or how the problem will be solved. At the climax of the story, you know who or what will win. The problem is solved. The story ends.

A. DIRECTIONS: *The following questions focus on the exposition, the rising action, and the falling action in "The Homecoming." Answer each question in the space provided.*

1. The exposition introduces the setting, characters, and basic situation. Here is one exposition detail:

   Exposition detail: The woodcutter will be an important character.

   On the lines, write another exposition detail.

   Exposition detail: _____

   _____

2. The events in the rising action come before the climax. There are many events in the rising action of "The Homecoming." Here is one event in the rising action:

   Rising action event: The woodcutter leaves the village.

   On the following lines, write two additional events that happen in the rising action.

   Rising action events:

   a. _____

   _____

   b. _____

   _____

3. In "The Homecoming," there are many events in the falling action. Here is one:

   Falling action event: The woodcutter goes home.

   What is another event that happens in the falling action?

   Falling action event: _____

   _____

Name _____ Date _____

"The Homecoming" by Laurence Yep
Vocabulary Builder

Word List

charitable   distracted   escorting   fascinating   murmured   recognize

A. DIRECTIONS: *In each question below, think about the meaning of the underlined word from the Word List. Then answer the questions.*

1. Listening to music <u>distracted</u> you from studying for a spelling test. Is your teacher likely to accept that as a good reason for your getting a poor grade? Why or why not?

   Answer: _____

   Explanation: _____

2. You see your friend standing across the street, so you wave to him. He doesn't <u>recognize</u> you. What could be the explanation?

   Explanation: _____

3. Six small boats are <u>escorting</u> a ship. Why might the small boats be doing this?

   Answer: _____

   Explanation: _____

4. Would you be ashamed if you acted in a <u>charitable </u>way toward a friend? Why?

   Answer: _____

   Explanation: _____

5. The speaker <u>murmured</u> when he spoke. Was he easy to hear? Why or why not?

   Answer: _____

   Explanation: _____

6. There is a <u>fascinating</u> show on television. Would you like to watch it? Why or why not?

   Answer: _____

   Explanation: _____

B. WORD STUDY: *The Latin suffix -able means "having qualities of." Think about the meaning of each underlined word that ends with* -able. *Then, answer the questions.*

1. What qualities might make a person <u>likeable</u>?

   _____

2. If you eat a <u>sizeable</u> meal, how might you feel?

   _____

3. If someone's mood is very <u>reasonable</u>, how might he behave?

   _____

"The Homecoming" by Laurence Yep
Enrichment: Folk Tales

"The Homecoming" follows a basic formula for a certain kind of folk tale. The formula goes like this: A character, usually a human being, has a problem or weakness. Because of this problem, the character goes on a journey. On the journey, the character meets a supernatural figure such as a talking animal. The supernatural figure uses a magical charm or object to help the human. Sometimes, instead of helping, the supernatural figure plays a trick on the human to teach the person a lesson. At the end of the folk tale, something important about the character's situation has changed.

A. DIRECTIONS: *Refer to "The Homecoming" to answer the questions below.*

1. Which character has a problem? _____

2. What is the problem? _____

3. Why does the character go on a journey? _____

   _____

4. What supernatural being does the character meet? _____

   _____

5. What is the magic charm or object? _____

6. How does the folk tale end? _____

   _____

B. DIRECTIONS: Get together with a partner and plan an original folk tale. Use the formula described above or change it slightly. On the lines below, or on a separate sheet of paper, jot down ideas or outline the plot for your folk tale. Then tell your folk tale to another pair of students. Listen while they tell you their story.

_____

_____

_____

_____

_____

_____

_____

_____

_____

"**Stray**" by Cynthia Rylant
"**The Homecoming**" by Laurence Yep
Integrated Language Skills: Grammar

Common and Proper Nouns; Possessives

Nouns may be either common or proper. Some nouns are made up of more than one word.

- A **common noun** names any one of a group of people, places, things, or ideas.
  Examples: girl, city, dogs, chairs, freedom, computer room, teacher, ice cream

- A **proper noun** names a particular person, place, or thing. A proper noun always begins with a capital letter. *Do not confuse a proper noun with a common noun that is capitalized because it is the first word of a sentence.*
  Examples: Doris, Mr. Amos Lacey, North Carolina, "The Homecoming," Asian American Museum, United States of America

The **possessive** of a noun shows ownership or possession. An **apostrophe,** which looks like a comma that has jumped up into the space above the line, is used to form the possessive.

- To form the possessive of a singular noun (naming one person, place, thing, or idea), add an apostrophe and an **s.**
  Examples: Doris's dog, West Virginia's farmland, the computer room's radiator

- To form the possessive of a plural noun that ends in **s,** add only the apostrophe.
  Examples: five minutes' time, the Beckmans' address, the girls' team

- To form the possessive of a plural noun that does *not* end in **s,** add an apostrophe and an **s.**
  Examples: children's stories, mice's cheese, the women's meeting

Never use an apostrophe to form the plural of a noun. Remember: An apostrophe, when used with a noun, shows ownership.

Incorrect: The birds' left their eggs behind in the nest.

Correct: The birds' eggs were left behind in their nest.

A. Directions: *Underline each noun in the sentences below. Above each noun, write C if it is a common noun and P if it is a proper noun. Add another line under the possessive nouns.*

1. Cynthia Rylant discovered that her life's story interested children.

2. Rylant spent part of her childhood in West Virginia's hills.

3. Like the main character in "Stray," Rylant loves animals.

4. Laurence Yep was born and raised in San Francisco, California.

5. Yep began writing stories in high school.

Name _____ Date _____

"Stray" by Cynthia Rylant
"The Homecoming" by Laurence Yep

Integrated Language Skills: Support for Writing a News Report

You are going to write a news report. Use the chart below to take notes for your news report. Describe the character, tell the story, and explain what happened.

Headline (Title)_____
Lead sentence (Capture attention!) _____   _____
Who? _____   _____
What? _____   _____
When? _____   _____
Where? _____   _____
Why? _____   _____
How? _____   _____

Use your notes to write a news report that sums up the basic facts. Include facts and quotes. Remember to focus on what happened.

Unit 1 Resources: Fiction and Nonfiction
© Pearson Education, Inc. All rights reserved.
58

"**Stray**" by Cynthia Rylant
"**The Homecoming**" by Laurence Yep

Integrated Language Skills: Support for Extend Your Learning

Research and Technology: "Stray"

Owning a pet can be very rewarding, but it can also be a lot of work. It is important to know how to properly care for an animal. Use the chart below to collect information you find on the Internet and from library resources. You will use the information to put together a brochure for new pet owners.

	Notes	Source
General feeding instructions		
Early training tips		
Keeping dogs happy and healthy		

Research and Technology: "The Homecoming"

Supernatural or magical characters often live forever. The chess players in "The Homecoming" are one type of supernatural character called **Chinese immortals.** Use the chart below to collect information for a brochure about Chinese immortals. You will find information about them from library and Internet sources.

	Notes	Source
Common characteristics		
History of folk tales		

"**The Homecoming**" by Laurence Yep
Open-Book Test

Short Answer *Write your responses to the questions in this section on the lines provided.*

1. Think about how the woodcutter acts on his way out of the village at the beginning of "The Homecoming." What clues help the reader predict what he will do when he sees the men playing chess?

   _____

   _____

   _____

2. In "The Homecoming," the woodcutter's wife says he is "too easily distracted." Why is it not a good idea for students to get distracted in class?

   _____

   _____

3. In "The Homecoming," the woodcutter's wife knows her husband takes too much of an interest in other people's business. Explain why she warns him not to talk to anyone when he goes to get firewood.

   _____

   _____

4. Events in the rising action increase tension. The chess game is part of the rising action in "The Homecoming." Think about what the woodcutter does during the chess game. Explain how the woodcutter's actions make the reader fear for him.

   _____

   _____

   _____

5. In the left column of the chart are examples of how the chess players treat the woodcutter in "The Homecoming." In the right column, write why they treat him this way. Then, on the lines below, explain how they view the woodcutter.

How Chess Players Treat Woodcutter	Why They Act This Way
Ignore him	
Do not feed him	

   _____

   _____

6. Explain how the peach stone is important to the climax, or high point, of "The Homecoming."

_____

_____

_____

_____

7. A certain type of folk tale focuses on a human being with a weakness. This character meets a supernatural figure on a journey. The supernatural figure uses a magic charm either to help the character or to teach a lesson. How would prior knowledge about such folk tales help the reader predict the woodcutter's fate in "The Homecoming"?

_____

_____

_____

8. In "The Homecoming," the fat man tells the woodcutter, "It may already be too late." In what way is it too late for the woodcutter?

_____

_____

_____

9. The woodcutter does not "recognize one person" in his village when he returns in "The Homecoming." Think about the meaning of the word *recognize*. Identify three people the woodcutter would expect to recognize in his village.

_____

_____

_____

10. The woodcutter does not remember his wife's warning until the resolution of "The Homecoming." Why does the author wait for this point to have him remember? Explain your answer.

_____

_____

_____

Essay

Write an extended response to the question of your choice or to the question or questions your teacher assigns you.

11. A busybody is someone who is unusually interested in other people's business, like the woodcutter in "The Homecoming." In an essay, tell what you think the story is saying about busybodies. Consider how people feel about the woodcutter and what happens to him. Use examples from the story to support your ideas.

12. In an essay, discuss whether or not the woodcutter has learned his lesson by the end of "The Homecoming." Use examples from the story to support your ideas.

13. In an essay, tell what "The Homecoming" might be saying about traditional Chinese beliefs and values. Use examples from the story to support your ideas.

14. **Thinking About the Big Question: How do we decide what is true?** In "The Homecoming," the woodcutter ignores clues that could help him understand the truth of what is happening. In an essay, discuss how the woodcutter's personality blinds him to what is really happening at the chess game. Use examples from the story to support your response.

Oral Response

15. Go back to question 1, 4, 6, or 8 or to the question your teacher assigns to you. Take a few minutes to expand your answer and prepare an oral response. Find additional details in "The Homecoming" that support your points. If necessary, make notes to guide your response.

"The Homecoming" by Laurence Yep
Selection Test A

Critical Reading *Identify the letter of the choice that best answers the question.*

____ 1. Why do the villagers laugh at the woodcutter?
   A. They know he is a big liar.
   B. He gets angry easily.
   C. His wife bosses him around.
   D. He minds everybody's business.

____ 2. To predict what will happen in this story, what do you combine?
   A. what you like about reading folk tales with what you want to know
   B. what you know with what is important to learn
   C. what you already know with story clues
   D. what the author believes with what you believe

____ 3. In "The Homecoming," the woodcutter meets two strangers in the mountains. What game are the strangers playing?
   A. checkers
   B. chess
   C. backgammon
   D. ping-pong

____ 4. Which one of the following story clues tells you that the two strangers are not what they seem?
   A. They play the game skillfully, even though they wear blindfolds.
   B. They pay no attention to the woodcutter's advice.
   C. Their robes change color as they play the game.
   D. They play the game, night and day, for seven days.

____ 5. In the plot of a story, events that increase tension happen in the *rising action*. At the *climax*, the story's outcome becomes clear. The events that follow the climax are called the *falling action*. Finally, you have the *resolution* or *conclusion*. In "The Homecoming," the woodcutter tries to advise the game players in the
   A. rising action.
   B. climax.
   C. falling action.
   D. resolution.

_____ 6. What action causes the woodcutter to lose everything?

    A. He lights a lantern covered with stars.

    B. He moves a golden disk to a new place on the game board.

    C. He sucks on a peach stone.

    D. He tears a page from the clan book.

_____ 7. The fat man says to the woodcutter, "It may already be too late." What does he mean?

    A. The woodcutter may always be an annoying person.

    B. The woodcutter must warn his village that a landslide is about to happen.

    C. If the woodcutter doesn't get home before nightfall, his wife will be upset.

    D. A great deal of time has already passed.

_____ 8. At the end of the story, the woodcutter remembers, too late, his wife's warning. What warning did she give him as he left the village?

    A. Don't talk to anyone.

    B. Remember your starving children.

    C. Stay away from other villages.

    D. Don't go beyond the ridgetop.

_____ 9. Which of the following events occurs during the resolution of the story?

    A. The woodcutter realizes that thousands of years passed while he was away.

    B. The funny old man and the fat man share the peach.

    C. The funny old man and the fat man follow the woodcutter's advice.

    D. The woodcutter's wife dies.

_____ 10. To predict what happens at the end of the story, what prior knowledge would you find most useful?

    A. knowing how people change magically in the myths of many countries

    B. knowing what kinds of tricks are played on humans in Chinese folk tales

    C. understanding other science-fiction stories about creatures with artificial intelligence

    D. knowing about sword fighting in Japanese ghost stories

Vocabulary and Grammar

_____ 11. Which sentence uses the underlined vocabulary word incorrectly?

    A. I didn't <u>recognize</u> you in your clown costume.

    B. My teacher decided to <u>recognize</u> the student who had improved the most.

    C. When you <u>recognize</u> like that, you deserve to stay after school.

    D. Doctors <u>recognize</u> the signs of some illnesses before they become dangerous.

___ 12. The woodcutter gets _____ by others and doesn't finish his
work.

    A. surprised

    B. tired

    C. sad

    D. distracted

___ 13. How many nouns (common and proper) are in the following sentence?

        On Friday, Samuel took his two children to the circus.

    A. two

    B. three

    C. four

    D. five

___ 14. Which sentence uses an apostrophe *incorrectly*?

    A. The childrens' playground needs some work.

    B. After the girls' soccer game, we had a picnic.

    C. He remembered his wife's warning when it was too late.

    D. The teacher's book contained the country's legends.

Essay

15. Two important elements of a story's plot are the climax and the resolution. The climax is the high point of a story, when the story's outcome becomes clear. The resolution, or conclusion, is the final outcome of the story. Describe either the climax or the resolution of "The Homecoming," and give examples from the story to support the plot element.

16. "The Homecoming" is a story that teaches several lessons. Here are some of them: Don't talk to strangers. Concentrate on your own work. Mind your own business. Don't hang around people who ignore you. Don't eat the remains of food that others have thrown away. Which lesson in the story do you think is most important? Choose one of the lessons, tell what it is, and explain how the woodcutter learned it. Finally, tell why you think that is the most important lesson.

17. **Thinking About the Big Question: How do we decide what is true?** In "The Homecoming," the woodcutter ignores clues that show the chess game is a very unusual one. Consider what the villagers say about the woodcutter and what the woodcutter thinks about himself. In an essay, discuss how the woodcutter's personality keeps him from understanding what is really happening. Use examples from the story to support your response.

"**The Homecoming**" by Laurence Yep
Selection Test B

Critical Reading *Identify the letter of the choice that best completes the statement or answers the question.*

_____ 1. The villagers laugh at the woodcutter because he
   A. talks constantly and boasts about how much he knows.
   B. is impatient and gets angry when his neighbors do things wrong.
   C. has a wife who always tells him what to do and when to do it.
   D. is easily distracted and gives unsolicited advice.

_____ 2. The villagers' comment that the woodcutter "knew a little of everything and most of nothing" means that the woodcutter
   A. deserves to be admired for having so many different skills.
   B. is disliked for pretending to know little while actually knowing a great deal.
   C. knows too much to be happy living for the rest of his life in their village.
   D. is being mocked for interfering in their affairs while ignoring his own.

_____ 3. The woodcutter's wife tells him he must leave the village because
   A. she fears that the villagers will attack him.
   B. she wants him to bring back firewood as quickly as possible.
   C. he must take the palm leaf fans into town.
   D. this is the first test he must pass successfully.

_____ 4. What prior knowledge tells you that the woodcutter is going to get into trouble when he goes into the mountains?
   A. You know that people don't change their habits easily.
   B. You know that husbands and wives often have different opinions.
   C. You know that desperate people often do desperate things.
   D. You know that people deserve what happens to them.

_____ 5. In "The Homecoming," the game that fascinates the woodcutter and two players is
   A. checkers.
   B. chess.
   C. backgammon.
   D. memory.

_____ 6. When you use prior knowledge to make a prediction, you start with
   A. what you liked most in your reading.
   B. what you think is most important to learn.
   C. what you already know before you read.
   D. the author's opinions and yours.

_____ 7. What clue indicates that the funny old man and the fat man are more than they seem?
   A. They play the game with supernatural skill.
   B. They pay no attention to the woodcutter.
   C. Their robes change color as they play the game.
   D. They play the game all day and all night.

Name _____ Date _____

____ 8. The woodcutter tries to advise the game players in the story's
  A. exposition.   C. falling action.
  B. rising action.   D. resolution.

____ 9. At the end of the story, the schoolteacher says that the two game players must
  have been saints. What qualities do these saints possess?
  A. They play tricks on their victims.
  B. They live forever.
  C. They are humans who act like gods.
  D. They are creatures with artificial intelligence.

____ 10. To predict what happens at the end of this story, it would be most useful to have
  prior knowledge about
  A. autobiographies.
  B. Chinese folk tales.
  C. science fiction for young people.
  D. Japanese ghost stories.

____ 11. The magic object that changes everything for the woodcutter is
  A. a lantern covered with stars.   C. a peach stone.
  B. a golden disk.   D. a clan book.

____ 12. Which of the following occurs during the resolution of the story?
  A. The woodcutter remembers his wife's warning.
  B. The funny old man and the fat man have something to eat.
  C. The funny old man and the fat man finally accept the woodcutter's suggestions.
  D. The woodcutter's wife dies.

____ 13. As the woodcutter goes home, one sign that much time has passed is that
  A. the river has changed course.
  B. the woodcutter has become an old man.
  C. the trees look as if they have been rearranged.
  D. the woodcutter's children have grown up.

____ 14. Too late, the woodcutter remembers his wife's warning, which was
  A. Don't talk to anyone.
  B. Remember your starving children.
  C. Stay out of trouble.
  D. Don't go too far into the mountains.

Vocabulary and Grammar

____ 15. In the following passage from "The Homecoming," what is the best meaning of
  escorting?
      "What are you doing?" he asked.
      His wife folded her arms as they walked along. "Escorting you."
  A. honoring   C. accompanying
  B. touring with   D. protecting

____ 16. Which sentence uses the vocabulary word *recognize* incorrectly?
   A. I almost didn't recognize you with your new haircut.
   B. If you are going to recognize like that, you deserve to stay after school.
   C. The teacher will recognize students who have improved since the last grading period.
   D. A doctor can recognize the symptoms of many illnesses before they become dangerous.

____ 17. The woodcutter is _____ when he fails to concentrate on cutting wood.
   A. worried
   B. changed
   C. distracted
   D. excited

____ 18. How many nouns are in the following sentence?
   The children's father, Samuel, looked up from the table where he had been speaking with Mrs. Young.

   A. five
   B. six
   C. seven
   D. eight

____ 19. Which sentence uses an apostrophe *incorrectly*?
   A. The two Chinese immortals' lunch was one ripe peach.
   B. He remembered his wife's warning when it was too late.
   C. The mens' chess pieces were disks painted in gold.
   D. The schoolteacher's clan book mentioned the village's woodcutter.

Essay

20. The six elements of plot are exposition, conflict, rising action, climax, falling action, and resolution. Choose and define one of these elements. In an essay, describe the part of "The Homecoming" that demonstrates this plot element. Use examples from the story to support your explanation.

21. "The Homecoming" is a story that teaches a lesson. Write an essay explaining what lesson the woodcutter learned, and tell how he learned it. Do you think that this lesson is important for everyone in all situations? Why or why not? Use details from the story to support your answer.

22. **Thinking About the Big Question: How do we decide what is true?** In "The Homecoming," the woodcutter ignores clues that could help him understand the truth of what is happening. In an essay, discuss how the woodcutter's personality blinds him to what is really happening at the chess game. Use examples from the story to support your response.

Study these words from "The Drive-In Movies." Then, complete the activities.

Word List A

brew [BROO] *n.* liquid containing several things mixed together
   She made a <u>brew</u> with sugar, water, salt, and lemons.

disgusting [dis GUS ting] *adj.* very unpleasant
   After I left my shoes out in the rain, they smelled <u>disgusting</u>.

evident [EV uh duhnt] *adj.* clear or obvious
   It was <u>evident</u> from her smile that she was happy.

migrated [MY gray tid] *v.* moved from one place to another
   The ants <u>migrated</u> from the counter to the windowsill.

nightfall [NITE fawl] *n.* time when it gets dark and night begins
   At <u>nightfall</u>, the sun set, and soon it grew dark.

plucked [PLUHKT] *v.* pulled out
   Emily <u>plucked</u> burrs from her dog's coat after he rolled in the grass.

remedy [REM uh dee] *n.* cure
   I needed a <u>remedy</u> for my headache, so I took an aspirin.

snails [SNAYLZ] *n.* small, slimy, shelled animals with no legs
   After a rainfall, our yard is filled with <u>snails</u> tucked into their shells.

Word List B

applied [uh PLYD] *v.* put something into direct contact with something else
   I <u>applied</u> the final coat of paint to the ceiling.

buffed [BUHFT] *v.* polished with a dry cloth
   I <u>buffed</u> the floor until it shone.

chrome [KROHM] *n.* type of shiny, silver-colored metal
   I bought a shiny new toaster made of <u>chrome</u>.

dedicated [DED uh kay tid] *adj.* giving a lot of time and energy to
   Lisa was <u>dedicated</u> to winning the soccer championship this year.

glinting [GLIN ting] *v.* sparkling; shining
   The shiny, brand-new dime was <u>glinting</u> in the sunlight.

involved [in VOLVD] *adj.* being part of or mixed up with
   Jen was glad she had gotten <u>involved</u> with helping the homeless.

vigorously [VIG uh rus lee] *adv.* forcefully, powerfully
   Delores shook the man's hand so <u>vigorously</u> that his body shook.

waxing [WAKS ing] *v.* putting on polish or a protective coat of wax
   My brother likes <u>waxing</u> the car because the wax makes it waterproof.

Unit 1 Resources: Fiction and Nonfiction
69

"The Drive-In Movies" by Gary Soto
Vocabulary Warm-up Exercises

Exercise A *Fill in each blank in the paragraph below with an appropriate word from Word List A. Use each word only once.*

It was after [1] _____ and pretty dark. I knew that was when my least

favorite garden creatures, [2] _____, all [3] _____

to my yard. It was [4] _____ that there were snails in my yard

because all my plants had leaves with big holes. Fortunately, I had a well-known

[5] _____ for my problem. I [6] _____ some things off my

kitchen shelf. Then I made a [7] _____ of many strange ingredients and

set it out around my yard. I knew the [8] _____, smelly mixture I had

made would drive the creatures away.

Exercise B *Decide whether each statement below is true or false. Then, circle T or F. Explain your answer.*

1. <u>Waxing</u> the car makes it very dirty.
   T / F _____

2. In order for something to be <u>glinting</u>, there should be sunlight.
   T / F _____

3. If you <u>applied</u> shampoo to your hair, your hair would be clean.
   T / F _____

4. People who are <u>dedicated</u> to their job don't care much about it.
   T / F _____

5. You can get <u>involved</u> in an argument by minding your own business.
   T / F _____

6. <u>Chrome</u> refers to the parts of a car that are made of plastic.
   T / F _____

7. If you do something <u>vigorously</u>, you are likely to get tired.
   T / F _____

8. If you <u>buffed</u> your doorknobs, they would feel greasy.
   T / F _____

Unit 1 Resources: Fiction and Nonfiction
70

Name _____ Date _____

"The Drive-In Movies" by Gary Soto
Reading Warm-up A

Read the following passage. Pay special attention to the underlined words. Then, read it again, and complete the activities. Use a separate sheet of paper for your written answers.

When I was little, I loved going to the drive-in movies. In the summer, my parents would often take us on Friday nights. It was a good <u>remedy</u> for the heat and three whiny children on a summer evening. The cure made us all happy.

Part of the excitement was that the drive-in didn't begin until after <u>nightfall</u>, so we got to stay up later than usual. In the summer, it got dark very late, past our bedtime.

If the theater was busy, there would be a long line of cars at the entrance, moving as slowly as <u>snails</u>. It seemed to take forever for it to be our turn to enter.

Once my dad had paid, we would park. It was <u>evident</u>, or obvious, who liked to park where. The teenagers always parked in the back, where it was darkest. Older people liked the front. Families with small children liked the middle, where it was easier to leave the drive-in if the kids acted up.

My brother, sister, and I took turns going to the refreshment stand. We got to buy popcorn, a treat, and a drink to share. I always hated it when my brother went, because he would bring back a <u>brew</u> made up of several things he had mixed together. "It's lemonade, fruit punch, and root beer," he would say. Whatever it was, it was always <u>disgusting</u>. Everyone but him thought it was horrible.

When it was my turn, I always got caramel corn and peanuts, mixed together. As I watched the movie I reached way down into the bag. I <u>plucked</u> out the peanuts with my fingers. For some reason, they always <u>migrated</u> from the top of the bag to the bottom. Sitting in the back seat of the car, eating peanuts and popcorn and watching a movie, I was about as happy as I had ever been.

1. Circle the word that means the same thing as <u>remedy</u>. Then, name two things for which you might need a *remedy*.

2. Underline the words that are clues to the meaning of <u>nightfall</u>. Write a sentence describing something you do after *nightfall*.

3. Underline the words that compare the cars to <u>snails</u>. What are some other things that move like *snails*?

4. Circle the word that means the same thing as <u>evident</u>. Write a sentence about something that seems *evident* to you.

5. Underline the words that tell you what was in the brother's <u>brew</u>. Describe *brew* in your own words.

6. Circle the word that tells you what <u>disgusting</u> means. What is something that you think is *disgusting*?

7. Circle the words that tell how the narrator <u>plucked</u> the peanuts from the bag. Name two other things that might get *plucked* out of a bag at the movies.

8. Underline the words that tell you where the peanuts <u>migrated</u>. Write a sentence using the word *migrated*.

"The Drive-In Movies" by Gary Soto
Reading Warm-up B

Read the following passage. Pay special attention to the underlined words. Then, read it again, and complete the activities. Use a separate sheet of paper for your written answers.

Have you ever thought about <u>waxing</u> the family car? Giving it a protective coating makes the car look nice and helps keep it from rusting. Waxing might seem difficult, but it's really not that hard. In fact, it can be a fun chore to do on a sunny Saturday morning. Here is all the information you will need to get started.

First, get out the wax and dab it onto your car, using only small amounts at a time. If you have <u>applied</u> it correctly, the wax will be easy to rub in. Put on too much, though, and you could have a problem. Once you have applied the wax, rub it <u>vigorously</u> all over. Rubbing gently will not do the trick. You will know you are doing it right if your arm starts to ache a little. Don't forget to put it on the <u>chrome</u>, because waxing really makes that metal shine!

Once you have <u>buffed</u> every inch of the car, you're done. This step is important, because rubbing gently with a dry cloth after waxing really makes the car shine. In fact, if you have buffed properly, the car should be <u>glinting</u> in the sunlight. The shine might even hurt your eyes!

If you are <u>dedicated</u> to keeping the car looking nice, you will work at getting it done. That means waxing the car once a week, or at least twice a month. Sometimes it might be hard to get started, but you will find that once you get <u>involved</u> with the job the time will pass quickly. Then, before you know it, you will be finished.

1. Write two steps, according to the passage, that are part of <u>waxing</u> a car.

2. Underline the words that tell you what <u>applied</u> means. Then, list two things that could be *applied* to a minor cut.

3. Circle the word that means the opposite of <u>vigorously</u>. Then, write a sentence describing something else you might do *vigorously*.

4. Where might you find <u>chrome</u> on a car?

5. Name two things that might need to be <u>buffed</u> besides a car.

6. Write a sentence that describes something <u>glinting</u> in the sunlight.

7. What do you have to do if you're <u>dedicated</u> to keeping the family car looking nice?

8. What activities do you enjoy getting <u>involved</u> in? Name two.

Name _____ Date _____

Writing About the Big Question

How do we decide what is true?

Big Question Vocabulary

confirm	decision	determine	evidence	fact
fantasy	fiction	investigate	opinion	prove
realistic	study	test	true	unbelievable

A. *Use one or more words from the list above to complete the following sentences.*

1. If someone is nice to you only when he or she has something to gain, you may _____ that that person is not really nice.

2. If someone's words do not match his or her actions, those words are
_____.

3. We can use evidence to _____ what is fact and what is
_____.

4. Sometimes it is possible to _____ your opinions to see whether or not they are true.

B. *Respond to each item. Use at least two Big Question vocabulary words in each answer.*

1. Describe a time when somebody you thought was a good person did something that was not nice.

_____

_____

2. After the issue was resolved, did you determine that the person was a good person or not? Explain.

_____

_____

C. *Complete the sentence below. Then, write a short paragraph connecting this situation to the Big Question.*

A truly "extra good" person is _____

Is it true that somebody can be "extra good"? Or does everyone have a good side and a bad side? How do you know?

_____

_____

_____

"The Drive-In Movies" by Gary Soto
Reading: Read Ahead to Verify Predictions

Predictions are reasonable guesses about what is most likely to happen next. Your predictions should be based on details in the literature and your own experience. After you have made a prediction, **read ahead to check your prediction.** Making and checking predictions improves your understanding by helping you notice and think about important details.

For example, at the beginning of "The Drive-In Movies," you might wonder if Gary's mom is going to take her children to the movies. You read the story clue that Mom might be tired from working all week. You know that when parents are tired they might want to get to bed early. You might predict that the children won't get to the movies. You keep reading and you find out at the end of the story if your prediction is right or wrong.

DIRECTIONS: *As you read "The Drive-In Movies," use the chart below to help you predict events in the story. First, read the question in column 1. Fill in column 2 with a story clue. In column 3, note information from your own experience. Then make a prediction in column 4. Finally, read to see if your prediction is correct. If your prediction is correct, write the letter* C *in the narrow column. If it is wrong, write the letter* W.

1. Question	2. Story Clue	3. What You Know from Experience	4. Prediction	C or W
Will Rick help?				
Will a good job be done on the car?				
How will Mom react to the way the car looks?				
Will Gary enjoy the movies?				

"The Drive-In Movies" by Gary Soto
Literary Analysis: Narrator and Point of View

The **narrator** is the voice that tells a true or imagined story. **Point of view** is the perspective from which the story is told. These two points of view are the most commonly used:

- **First-person point of view:** The narrator participates in the action of the story and refers to himself or herself as "I." Readers know only what the narrator sees, thinks, and feels.

  One Saturday I decided to be extra good.

- **Third-person point of view:** The narrator does not participate in the action of the story. A third-person narrator can tell things that the characters do not know.

  Rick, Gary, and Debra wanted their mother to love each of them best.

Most true stories about a person's life are told in first-person point of view.

A. DIRECTIONS: *If the sentence is spoken by a first-person narrator, write* FP *on the line. If the sentence is spoken by a third-person narrator, write* TP *on the line.*

____ 1. My knees hurt from kneeling, and my brain was dull from making the trowel go up and down, dribbling crumbs of earth.

____ 2. His knees hurt from kneeling, and his brain was dull from making the trowel go up and down, dribbling crumbs of earth.

____ 3. His brother joined him with an old gym sock, and their sister, happy not to join them, watched while sucking on a cherry Kool-Aid ice cube.

____ 4. My brother joined me with an old gym sock, and our sister watched us while sucking on a cherry Kool-Aid ice cube.

B. DIRECTIONS: *In the space provided below, rewrite the following paragraph with Mom as the first-person narrator. The first sentence is done for you.*

Mom came out and looked at the car. She saw that the waxed side was foggy white. The other side hadn't even been done. She said, "You boys worked so hard." She turned on the garden hose and washed off the soap her sons had not been able to get off. Even though she was tired from working all week, she took her children to the drive-in that night. She knew that Gary had worked most of Saturday. He had been extra good and he especially deserved a treat.

I went out to look at my car.

_____

_____

_____

"The Drive-In Movies" by Gary Soto
Vocabulary Builder

Word List

evident   migrated   prelude   pulsating   vigorously   winced

A. DIRECTIONS: *In each item below, think about the meaning of the underlined word. Look for clues in the rest of the sentence. Then, answer the question.*

1. When the band plays the <u>prelude</u> to your favorite march, is the musical piece ending? Why or why not?

    _____

2. If wild geese have <u>migrated</u> to your town for the winter, are they likely to stay all year? Why or why not?

    _____

3. My dad <u>winced</u> when he buttoned his shirt collar. Was the collar too loose? Why or why not?

    _____

4. If the identity of the thief is <u>evident</u> to everyone, will the police know who robbed the bank? Why or why not?

    _____

5. Which part of the human body is always <u>pulsating</u>, the kidneys or the heart? Explain your answer, using a synonym for *pulsating*.

    _____

6. John wanted to get someplace quickly. Would he walk <u>vigorously</u>? Why or why not?

    _____

B. WORD STUDY: The Latin prefix *pre-* means "before." Read each sentence. Decide whether it makes sense. If it does, write *Correct*. If it doesn't make sense, revise it so that it does.

1. After I wore my new jeans, I washed them to *preshrink* the fabric.

    _____

2. The United States Constitution ends with a *preamble*.

    _____

3. Early in the day, you can *precook* the main course and then reheat it in the microwave just before dinner is served.

    _____

"The Drive-In Movies" by Gary Soto
Enrichment: Comic Movies

In "The Drive-In Movies," Gary Soto refers to seeing the comedy *Cinderfella.* According to Soto, the movie made him laugh as a child when an actor put golf tees up his nose. Many people laugh when actors do things that are foolish. For example, someone might slip on a banana peel or drop a tray of food. That kind of comedy is called "physical comedy." Other movies are funny because the actors say clever things that make you smile or laugh out loud. That kind of comedy is called "verbal comedy."

DIRECTIONS: *Think of the comedies you have seen at the movies or on television. Which were your favorites? What were your favorite parts? On the chart below, list at least three comedies you have seen. Briefly describe the parts you thought were funniest. Then identify those parts as "physical" or "verbal" comedy.*

Title of Comedy	Funniest Part	Physical or Verbal?
1.		
2.		
3.		

"The Drive-In Movies" by Gary Soto
Open-Book Test

Short Answer *Write your responses to the questions in this section on the lines provided.*

1. The narrator of "The Drive-In Movies" says that the cartoons were a "prelude of what was to come." Explain what he means.

   _____

   _____

   _____

2. In "The Drive-In Movies," the narrator starts the day by making breakfast for his mother. How does this action help the reader predict how the narrator will spend the rest of the day?

   _____

   _____

   _____

   _____

3. Why does the narrator of "The Drive-In Movies" not cry when the bee stings him?

   _____

   _____

   _____

4. In "The Drive-In Movies," the narrator writes that his mother "winced at the grille" before returning to the house. Explain what the meaning of the word *winced* tells you about the grille.

   _____

   _____

   _____

5. Near the end of "The Drive-In Movies," the narrator and his brother cannot get the white fog off the car. They are nearly in tears. The narrator thinks about what his mother will do. What prediction does the reader most likely make at this point?

   _____

   _____

   _____

6. Think about what the family members in "The Drive-In Movies" do for one another. In each oval of the web, write an event that shows how the members of the family help each other. Then, on the lines below, describe their relationship.

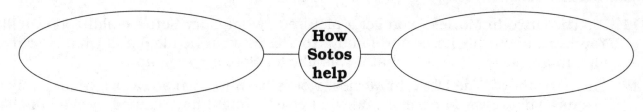

How Sotos help

_____
_____
_____
_____

7. Think about the kind of life the narrator and his family live. Why would going to the drive-in movies be so important to him? Use details from the story to support your response.

_____
_____
_____
_____

8. A first-person narrator participates in the action of the story and refers to himself or herself as "I." Give one statement from the story that shows that "The Drive-In Movies" is a first-person narrative.

_____
_____

9. Imagine that "The Drive-In Movies" uses a third-person narrator. Give one example of what a third-person narrator could include that Gary cannot.

_____
_____
_____

10. At the end of "The Drive-In Movies" the narrator falls asleep. Explain how he might feel about all his hard work when he wakes up. Does he think it was worth it?

_____
_____
_____
_____

Essay

Write an extended response to the question of your choice or to the question or questions your teacher assigns you.

11. In "The Drive-In Movies," you get a picture of what Gary Soto's childhood was like. You learn about his home and family. You learn what he liked and what he did not like. In an essay, describe what it was like for Soto growing up.

12. The narrator of "The Drive-In Movies" works hard to earn a reward. In an essay, discuss what reward he earns and what else he might have gained from all his hard work. Use details from the story to support your answer.

13. "The Drive-In Movies" is written from the point of view of the author, Gary Soto. How would the story be different if it were written by a neighbor who observed the events described in the story? In an essay, discuss the differences. Then explain which version you prefer and why.

14. **Thinking About the Big Question: How do we decide what is true?** In "The Drive-In Movies," the narrator believes certain things are true about his mother. In an essay, discuss two things he believes about his mother. Consider why he thinks each thing is true. Explain why he is or is not correct in his thinking.

Oral Response

15. Go back to question 3, 5, 9, or 10 or to the question your teacher assigns to you. Take a few minutes to expand your answer and prepare an oral response. Find additional details in "The Drive-In Movies" that support your points. If necessary, make notes to guide your response.

"The Drive-In Movies" by Gary Soto
Selection Test A

Critical Reading *Identify the letter of the choice that best answers the question.*

____ 1. The narrator of "The Drive-In Movies" tells the story from the first-person point of view. Who is the narrator?
   A. Mom
   B. Gary
   C. Rick
   D. another person

____ 2. Why does the narrator of "The Drive-In Movies" decide to be extra good on Saturday?
   A. He wants to go to the movies that night.
   B. He is going to ask for a bigger allowance.
   C. He wants to be a good example for his brother.
   D. He feels sorry for his mother because she works so hard.

____ 3. In "The Drive-In Movies," which of the following jobs does the narrator *not* do?
   A. fix his mother's breakfast
   B. weed the garden
   C. take out garbage
   D. wash clothes

____ 4. What does the narrator of "The Drive-In Movies" do when the bee stings his foot?
   A. He pulls out the sting and packs his foot with mud.
   B. He cries until his mother looks out of the window.
   C. He hobbles inside the house and gets ice cubes for his foot.
   D. He wraps his foot in a old gym sock.

____ 5. "The Drive-In Movies" is a story told by a first-person narrator. Which quality is special to first-person narration?
   A. It tells a true story.
   B. The person telling the story is in the story.
   C. It includes conversations, thoughts, and feelings.
   D. It tells a story that comes from the imagination.

___ 6. Which of the following words best describes the narrator in "The Drive-In Movies"?
A. lazy
B. hardworking
C. silly
D. impatient

___ 7. As you read "The Drive-In Movies," what should you do after you make a prediction?
A. read another story by the same author
B. read ahead to check your prediction
C. read again what you have already read
D. discuss your prediction with classmates

___ 8. In "The Drive-In Movies," what is one reason that the car-wax job turns out badly?
A. The boys don't polish hard enough.
B. The sun was too hot on the car.
C. The boys run out of wax.
D. The boys use white wax on a blue car.

___ 9. Which of the following statements shows that "The Drive-In Movies" is a first-person narrative?
A. The lawn was tall but too wet to mow.
B. I was sweaty hot.
C. The paint was coming off.
D. She turned on the garden hose and washed the car.

___ 10. In "The Drive-In Movies," when Mom sees the work the boys have done, how does she seem to feel?
A. sad
B. annoyed
C. angry
D. grateful

___ 11. The following passage comes near the end of "The Drive-In Movies." What does it lead you to predict?

> I blamed Rick and he blamed me. Debra stood at the window, not wanting to get involved. Now, not only would we not go to the movies, but Mom would surely snap a branch from the plum tree and chase us around the yard.

A. Debra will be blamed, too.
B. They will not go to the movies.
C. The day will end happily.
D. Mom will come out to play with the children.

___ 12. At the end of "The Drive-In Movies," why do you think the narrator rubs his "watery eyes"?
   A. He's watching a sad movie on TV.
   B. He's trying to stay awake.
   C. He can't see well enough.
   D. Some dust got into his eyes.

Vocabulary and Grammar

___ 13. In which sentence is the underlined vocabulary word used incorrectly?
   A. The birds <u>migrated</u> to Florida for the warm weather.
   B. The national anthem is the <u>prelude</u> to many sporting events.
   C. The children <u>winced</u> in happiness over the new puppy.
   D. It's <u>evident</u> from your improved test scores that you studied hard.

___ 14. Which of the following sentences uses the correct form of a plural noun?
   A. I set the boxes of cereal in front of her.
   B. A bee stung the bottom of my feets.
   C. My brother joined me with an old gym sock.
   D. We returned outside with tasty sandwichs.

Essay

15. As you read "The Drive-In Movies," how well were you able to predict what was going to happen? In an essay, tell about two events in the story that surprised you. How do you feel about those surprises?

16. In "The Drive-In Movies," the narrator is the author, Gary Soto. In the story, you get a picture of the type of child he was. In an essay, name three of his qualities, such as the quality of being a hard worker. Give an example of an action from the story for each quality you name.

17. **Thinking About the Big Question: How do we decide what is true?** In "The Drive-In Movies," the narrator believes his mother will take him to the movies if she is in a good mood and pleased with his work. He also believes she will punish him for the bad wax job on the car. Consider why he thinks each thing is true. In an essay, explain why he is or is not correct in his thinking.

"The Drive-In Movies" by Gary Soto
Selection Test B

Critical Reading *Identify the letter of the choice that best completes the statement or answers the question.*

____ 1. On the Saturday morning described in "The Drive-In Movies," why does the narrator decide to work especially hard?
   A. He wants to go to the movies that night.
   B. He needs a bigger allowance.
   C. He wants to set a good example for his brother and sister.
   D. He feels sorry for his mother because she works so hard.

____ 2. What might the following passage from "The Drive-In Movies" lead you to predict?
   > One Saturday I decided to be extra good. When she came out of the bedroom tying her robe, she yawned a hat-sized yawn and blinked red eyes at the weak brew of coffee I had fixed for her. I made her toast with strawberry jam spread to all the corners and set the three boxes of cereal in front of her. If she didn't care to eat cereal, she could always look at the back of the boxes as she drank her coffee.

   A. Whatever the narrator does is going to turn out badly.
   B. The narrator's mother will go back to bed.
   C. The narrator will keep trying to be good all day.
   D. Mom will take advantage of the narrator's decision by giving him many jobs to do.

____ 3. The narrator of "The Drive-In Movies" does not cry when the bee stings him because
   A. the sting feels like a pin prick.
   B. he is afraid that his brother and sister will laugh at him.
   C. he does not want to make trouble for his mother.
   D. he likes to pretend that pain doesn't bother him.

____ 4. "The Drive-In Movies" is told from the first-person point of view. The narrator is
   A. Mom
   B. Gary
   C. Rick
   D. Debra

____ 5. Which quotation from "The Drive-In Movies" **best** shows the perspective of the narrator?
   A. More ticks had migrated to his snout.
   B. The paint was coming off.
   C. My arms ached from buffing, which though less boring than weeding, was harder.
   D. The waxed side of the car was foggy white.

____ 6. In "The Drive-In Movies," Rick probably comes out to help his brother because
   A. waxing the car is his job and his brother doesn't know how to do it.
   B. he doesn't want his brother to take all the credit.
   C. he feels a little guilty that he's done no work that day and wants to help.
   D. he realizes that waxing the car is a two-person job.

_____ 7. When she sees the work the boys have done that morning, the mother in "The Drive-In Movies" seems to feel
   A. appreciative.
   C. annoyed.
   B. sad.
   D. worried.

_____ 8. In "The Drive-In Movies," the boys' experience with waxing the family car shows that
   A. they do not work hard enough.
   B. they do not have the proper tools and know-how.
   C. the wax they use is the wrong kind for the job.
   D. they fear their mother even though they love her.

_____ 9. Imagine that a third-person narrator tells this story of "The Drive-In Movies." What new information could a third-person narrator include that Gary cannot?
   A. how other family members feel and what they think
   B. what Gary does that day
   C. what the mother ate for breakfast
   D. how the car looks

_____ 10. You can tell from "The Drive-In Movies" that the narrator is a person
   A. with great energy and determination.
   B. who avoids hard work whenever possible.
   C. who does not understand that children need time to play on Saturdays.
   D. who has little sympathy for others.

_____ 11. Which of the following does the first-person narrator of "The Drive-In Movies" not know?
   A. how the other kids in his family feel about going to movies
   B. which jobs Gary thinks are easy and which he thinks are hard
   C. why Debra tries to be good on this Saturday
   D. how Mom really feels about how the car looks after the wax job

_____ 12. What does the following passage lead you to predict about how "The Drive-In Movies" will end?

   I blamed Rick and he blamed me. Debra stood at the window, not wanting to get involved. Now, not only would we not go the movies, but Mom would surely snap a branch from the plum tree and chase us around the yard.

   A. Debra will be the only one who goes to the movies with Mom.
   B. Mom will take them all to the movies.
   C. Mom will tell the narrator to take care of the other kids, and she will go to the movies by herself.
   D. The children will not go to the movies and Mom will punish the boys.

_____ 13. Read the following statement from "The Drive-In Movies." How do you predict the narrator will feel at the drive-in?

   My knees hurt from kneeling, and my brain was dull from making the trowel go up and down. . . . I dug for half an hour. . . .

   A. tired
   C. upset
   B. relaxed
   D. angry

Vocabulary and Grammar

___ **14.** What is the meaning of the word *evident* in this passage from "The Drive-In Movies"?
But the beauty was <u>evident</u>. The shine, hurting our eyes and glinting like an armful of dimes, brought Mother out.
   A. startling
   B. an introduction
   C. clear to see
   D. disappointing

___ **15.** Some might correctly say that the *prelude* to summer is
   A. autumn
   B. winter
   C. spring
   D. a symphony

___ **16.** In "The Drive-In Movies," the narrator writes that his mother "winced at the grille and returned inside the house." The meaning of the word *winced* tells you
   A. she hopes that the boys will work on the grille next.
   B. the grille is the best-looking part of the car.
   C. there's something wrong with the grille.
   D. she is looking for things to complain about.

___ **17.** Which of the following sentences correctly changes every singular noun to the correct form for the plural noun?
   A. After lunch, we returned outside with tasty sandwichs.
   B. After our lunchs, we returned outside with tasty sandwichs.
   C. After our lunch, we returned outside with a tasty sandwich.
   D. After our lunches, we returned outside with tasty sandwiches.

Essay

18. First-person narrators can reveal a great deal about the kind of people they are without actually describing themselves directly. In an essay, describe three qualities that the narrator of "The Drive-In Movies" reveals about himself. Give examples from the story that show how the narrator demonstrates these qualities.

19. In the happy ending to "The Drive-In Movies," Mom rewards the narrator's good behavior. Do you like the way the story ends? If so, tell in an essay why you like the ending. If not, tell why you don't like the ending and suggest a different ending.

20. **Thinking About the Big Question: How do we decide what is true?** In "The Drive-In Movies," the narrator believes certain things are true about his mother. In an essay, discuss two things he believes about his mother. Consider why he thinks each thing is true. Explain why he is or is not correct in his thinking.

"The Market Square Dog" by James Herriot
Vocabulary Warm-up Word Lists

Study these words from "The Market Square Dog." Then, complete the activities.

Word List A

appealing [uh PEEL ing] *adj.* likeable or of interest
  The thought of joining the soccer team was very <u>appealing</u> to Jen.

bruised [BROOZD] *adj.* having a dark mark on the skin from falling or being hit
  After the rock fell on me, I was <u>bruised</u> for days.

healed [HEELD] *adj.* better; well
  I didn't go back to school until my wound was completely <u>healed</u>.

injured [IN jerd] *v.* hurt or harmed
  Roberto <u>injured</u> himself cooking dinner when the knife slipped.

meantime [MEEN tym] *n.* time in-between other things
  Selena couldn't wait for summer, but in the <u>meantime</u> she studied hard.

stitched [STICHT] *v.* sewed up a wound
  The doctor <u>stitched</u> up the large cut on Roberto's hand.

surgery [SER jer ee] *n.* an operation
  After he broke his leg, Donald had to have <u>surgery</u>.

various [VAIR ee us] *adj.* several and different
  Anil looked at the <u>various</u> kinds of bread for sale in the grocery store.

Word List B

attractive [uh TRAK tiv] *adj.* pretty; pleasant to look at
  Sam thought that Kayla's silk floral dress was quite <u>attractive</u>.

classified [KLAS uh fyd] *v.* sorted into groups
  The students were <u>classified</u> according to their ages.

devoured [di VOW erd] *v.* ate quickly and hungrily
  After two days of not eating, Chang <u>devoured</u> his food.

fringed [FRINJD] *adj.* bordered by feathers, hair, threads, or other fiber
  The bird had a <u>fringed</u> tail.

hesitation [hez uh TAY shuhn] *n.* a pause before doing something
  There was a moment of <u>hesitation</u>, but then he dove into the icy water.

response [ri SPONS] *n.* an answer or reply
  When I called, there was no <u>response</u>.

squatting [SKWAHT ing] *v.* crouching, sitting with knees bent very low
  The three men were <u>squatting</u> around the fire, trying to keep warm.

stray [STRAY] *n.* a lost or ownerless cat or dog
  The <u>stray</u> looked as if it hadn't eaten in days.

Unit 1 Resources: Fiction and Nonfiction

Name _____ Date _____

"The Market Square Dog" by James Herriot
Vocabulary Warm-up Exercises

Exercise A *Fill in each blank in the paragraph below with an appropriate word from Word List A. Use each word only once.*

Ernesto was at home recovering from [1] _____. The doctors had

[2] _____ his wound together, but the site was still aching and

[3] _____. They said it would be a week before he was completely

[4] _____. In the [5] _____, Ernesto was very bored.

He considered [6] _____ things to do, like watching TV or playing

chess, but none of them seemed very [7] _____. He wished he had

never [8] _____ himself in the first place.

Exercise B *Answer the questions with complete explanations.*

Example: If someone was <u>squatting</u>, what might they be doing?
If someone was <u>squatting</u>, they might be talking to a child or petting a small animal.

1. Do you consider <u>fringed</u> items <u>attractive</u>? Why or why not?
_____

2. If a man <u>devoured</u> his food, what reason might there be?
_____

3. Do you think it is wise to have a moment of <u>hesitation</u> before making a big decision? Explain.
_____

4. What would your <u>response</u> be if you found out that someone had <u>classified</u> you as boring?
_____

5. What would you do if you saw a <u>stray</u> on the street?
_____

"The Market Square Dog" by James Herriot
Reading Warm-up A

Read the following passage. Pay special attention to the underlined words. Then, read it again, and complete the activities. Use a separate sheet of paper for your written answers.

Every year, thousands of kids in the United States get injured, or hurt, playing sports. It could be something as simple as a bruised shin that turns dark purple the next day. Or it might be a deep cut that needs to be stitched, or sewn together, at the hospital. More seriously hurt kids could even require surgery. That is a concern. There are always risks when an operation is involved.

There are various ways that kids can get injured during sports. Whatever happens, though, the sad fact is that many injuries are preventable. Being prepared is the best defense against getting hurt. It is never too early to start preparing.

It is important for kids to get ready before playing a sport. This means wearing the right clothing or equipment to protect bones from breaking. It also means stretching and warming up properly. Equally important is keeping kids informed. They should know the rules of the game and what is expected of them. They should also know what is okay or not okay to do before they begin to play.

There's yet another good way to prevent kids from getting hurt. What's that? It's making sure that previously injured kids are completely healed before they play again. Getting back in the game might be appealing to injured kids. They want to play. However, they may not realize that returning before they have recovered can be risky. Not allowing enough time for recovery can lead to problems later on. No one wants that.

Advancements in science and technology may soon make it easier to keep kids from getting hurt during sports. In the meantime, however, a little prevention can go a long way. It can help keep kids off crutches and out of the emergency room.

1. Circle the word that means the same thing as injured. Write a sentence about how a person might get *injured*.

2. Underline the words that describe what bruised means. Then, describe how someone might get *bruised*.

3. Circle the phrase that means the same thing as stitched. Then, describe why someone might have to get *stitched*.

4. Circle the phrase that helps you to know what surgery means. Would it be scary to have *surgery*? Explain.

5. Write a sentence describing three of the various ways kids might get hurt playing sports.

6. Circle the word that tells what healed means. Tell why it's important to be completely *healed* before playing sports again.

7. Underline the words that tell what might be appealing to injured kids. Write a sentence telling what *appealing* means.

8. Scientific advancements may soon make it rare to get hurt playing sports. What should people do in the *meantime*?

Name _____ Date _____

"The Market Square Dog" by James Herriot
Reading Warm-up B

Read the following passage. Pay special attention to the underlined words. Then, read it again, and complete the activities. Use a separate sheet of paper for your written answers.

Jenny saw the cat first on a warm Monday afternoon, squatting on the steps of an abandoned building. She was pretty sure the cat was a stray. It did not look owned. It had no collar, and, while it did not look ill or starving, it did not look well cared for either.

Something about the cat appealed to her. It was not that the cat was attractive. In fact, the cat was almost ugly, with strange, fringed paws and a dirty white coat. It had more to do with the cat's dignity, the way it appeared to watch the world with amusement.

After a week, Jenny broke down and bought the cat some food. She placed it in a small dish near the steps and then stepped back, not sure of what the cat's response would be. After a few seconds' hesitation, the cat came forward and sniffed the bowl. Then the food was devoured, eaten faster than Jenny had thought possible. She realized that the cat must have been starving, and for the rest of the day, she was angry with herself for not feeding the cat sooner.

Jenny decided that her feelings for the cat could not really be classified. What could she call them? On the one hand, she told herself, she was just being kind to an animal. On the other hand, she knew, deep down inside, that she was falling in love with the little creature.

Finally, one very rainy afternoon, Jenny came by with food, only to find the cat huddled in the building doorway. It was meowing piteously, all its dignity gone. Jenny could stand it no longer. "You belong to me," she whispered, and then gathered the cat in her arms. Together, they went home, and when they walked through the front door and the cat sprang out of her arms and into a cozy chair, they both knew it was just settling down where it had always belonged.

1. Where was the cat squatting? Describe how a *squatting* cat might look.

2. Underline the words that tell you what stray means. Write a sentence telling where you might find a *stray*.

3. Circle the word that means the opposite of attractive. Then, write a sentence describing what kinds of pets you find *attractive*.

4. Write a sentence describing how fringed paws on a cat probably look.

5. What was the cat's response to the food? Did the *response* surprise you? Why or why not?

6. Underline the words that help you know what hesitation means. Why do you think the cat had some *hesitation* about the food?

7. Circle the word that means almost the same thing as devoured. Then, explain the difference between the two words.

8. Why couldn't Jenny's feelings for the cat be classified? How would you have *classified* them?

Name _____ Date _____

"**The Market Square Dog**" by James Harriot
Writing About the Big Question

How do we decide what is true?

Big Question Vocabulary

confirm	decision	determine	evidence	fact
fantasy	fiction	investigate	opinion	prove
realistic	study	test	true	unbelievable

A. *Use one or more words from the list above to complete the following sentences.*

1. To _____ that information is true, we can _____ the facts.

2. When making a _____, it is important to have _____ information.

3. Sometimes people's beliefs about what is _____ cannot be _____.

4. People may have _____ that are not _____.

B. *Respond to each item. Use at least one Big Question vocabulary word in each answer.*

1. Describe a situation in which you determined that something everyone thought was true was really fiction.

_____

_____

2. How did the evidence change what you did?

_____

_____

C. *Complete the sentence below. Then, write a short paragraph connecting this situation to the Big Question.*

In order to be a truly great pet, a dog needs to be _____

_____

_____

_____

_____

_____

_____

Name _____ Date _____

"The Market Square Dog" by James Herriot
Reading: Read Ahead to Verify Predictions

Predictions are reasonable guesses about what is most likely to happen next. Your predictions should be based on details in the literature and your own experience. After you have made a prediction, **read ahead to check your prediction.** Making and checking predictions improves your understanding by helping you to notice and think about important details.

For example, at the beginning of "The Market Square Dog," you might wonder what will become of the little dog. You read the story clue that the dog runs away whenever someone gets near him. You know that a dog that fears people will have trouble finding a home. You might predict that this dog is in danger of being injured by a vehicle. You keep reading, and you find out if your prediction is right or wrong.

DIRECTIONS: *As you read "The Market Square Dog," use the following chart to help you predict events in the story. First, read the question in column 1. Fill in column 2 with a story clue. In column 3, note information from your own experience. Then make a prediction in column 4. Finally, read to see if your prediction is correct. If your prediction is correct, write the letter C in the narrow column. If it is wrong, write the letter W*

1. Question	2. Story Clue	3. What You Know from Experience	4. Prediction	C or W
Will the dog be caught?				
Will the dog survive the accident?				
Will the dog's owners claim him at the kennels?				
Will the dog find a good home?				

"The Market Square Dog" by James Herriot
Literary Analysis: Narrator and Point of View

The **narrator** is the voice that tells a true or imagined story. **Point of view** is the perspective from which the story is told. These two points of view are the most commonly used:

- **First-person point of view:** The narrator participates in the action of the story and refers to himself or herself as "I." Readers know only what the narrator sees, thinks, and feels.

  I knew he would make a perfect pet for anyone.

- **Third-person point of view:** The narrator does not participate in the action of the story. A third-person narrator can tell things that the characters do not know.

  He worried about what had become of the dog. He wondered if it had been hit by a car.

Most true stories about a person's life are told in the first person.

A. DIRECTIONS: *If the sentence is spoken by a first person narrator, write* FP *on the line. If the sentence is spoken by a third-person narrator, write* TP *on the line.*

_____ 1. I always think a dog looks very appealing sitting up like that.

_____ 2. He always thought a dog looked very appealing when it sat up like that.

_____ 3. I visited the kennels often, and each time the shaggy little creature jumped up to greet me, laughing into my face, with his mouth open, his eyes shining.

_____ 4. "Well, you certainly took me in," he said, not minding in the least that Funny Phelps had played a joke on him.

_____ 5. "Well, you certainly took me in," I said.

B. DIRECTIONS: *In the space provided below, rewrite the following paragraph with the policeman as the first-person narrator. The first sentence is done for you.*

The policeman told the vet he had arrested the dog. The vet was surprised. He asked if he could see the dog. The policeman said that he would take the vet to the dog. They walked to a pretty cottage and saw the dog curled up in a big new doggy bed. Two small girls were sitting by him, stroking his coat. The policeman laughed and told the vet that this was his house and that he had taken the dog as a pet for his two daughters. He said they had wanted a dog and he thought this one would be just right for them.

It was hard for me not to laugh when I told the vet I'd arrested the dog he had operated on. _____

_____

_____

_____

_____

Name _____ Date _____

"The Market Square Dog" by James Herriot
Vocabulary Builder

Word List

anxiously   bewildered   classified   custody   devoured   trotted

A. DIRECTIONS: *In each item below, think about the meaning of the underlined word. Look for clues in the other sentences. Then, answer the question.*

1. When the children at the party saw the girl go by on her skateboard, they <u>trotted</u> after her. Do you think they will catch up with her? Why or why not?

   _____

   _____

2. Your family <u>anxiously</u> watches television for news of the hurricane. Are they worried about where it will strike? Why or why not?

   _____

   _____

3. We hear that the person suspected of breaking into our car was taken into <u>custody</u> yesterday. Will we feel that the car is safer tonight? Why or why not?

   _____

   _____

4. The horse <u>devoured</u> the bucket of oats. Did the horse seem hungry or annoyed before he did that? Explain.

   _____

   _____

5. The children seemed <u>bewildered</u> by the puzzle. Will they be able to solve it quickly? Why or why not?

   _____

   _____

6. Ms. Snow, the librarian, <u>classified</u> the book as nonfiction. Did that action suggest that she thought it was a good book? Why or why not?

   _____

   _____

B. WORD STUDY: The Old English prefix *be-* often means "to make." Read each sentence. Decide whether it makes sense. If it does, write *Correct.* If it doesn't make sense, revise it so that it does.

1. Please clean the floor so that it is *besmeared* with mud.

   _____

2. For the drama, Harry was *bewigged* with gray hair so he'd resemble an old wise man.

   _____

3. On that beautiful, clear day, the island was totally *befogged*.

   _____

Unit 1 Resources: Fiction and Nonfiction
© Pearson Education, Inc. All rights reserved.
94

"The Market Square Dog" by James Herriot
Enrichment: Veterinarians

The narrator in "The Market Square Dog" is a veterinarian. To become a doctor who cares for animals, one must attend a four-year veterinary school. All veterinary students have strong backgrounds in science. In college, they have to complete pre-veterinary courses in biology and chemistry. There are few veterinary schools, so there is a great deal of competition to get into a veterinary program. It helps to have prior experience in an animal-related job. Many applicants have worked on farms, in animal shelters, or in a veterinarian's office as an assistant.

Not all trained veterinarians provide pet health care in small-animal hospitals. Some veterinarians care for and treat farm animals. Others work in animal shelters, zoos, or with organizations that study and protect wild animals.

A. DIRECTIONS: *Answer the following questions about preparing to become a veterinarian. For each question, circle the letter of the best answer.*

1. For how many years do students attend veterinary school?
   A. one year
   B. two years
   C. four years
   D. six years
2. Which of the following courses is the most likely to be a required part of pre-veterinary study?
   A. American history
   B. astronomy
   C. chemistry
   D. geology
3. Which of the following summer or part-time jobs would be most helpful in preparing someone for veterinary studies?
   A. working for the local parks department
   B. working in a bookstore
   C. volunteering at a library
   D. volunteering at an animal shelter

B. DIRECTIONS: *Imagine that you are interviewing college graduates who want to get into veterinary school. Write three questions that you would ask them to find out if they are suited for careers as veterinarians. Write your questions on a separate sheet of paper. After you complete your questions, exchange papers with a classmate. Answer each other's questions. Then discuss your answers to see if you can improve upon your answers.*

"The Drive-In Movies" by Gary Soto
"The Market Square Dog" by James Herriot
Integrated Language Skills: Grammar

Singular and Plural Nouns

A **singular noun** names one person, place, or thing.
    Plural nouns name more than one person, place, or thing.

- To form the plural of most nouns, add **s** to the singular form of the noun.

cake	Add *s*	cakes
market	Add *s*	markets
shark	Add *s*	sharks

- When nouns end in **-y** after a vowel, add **s**.

day	Add *s*	days
toy	Add *s*	toys
turkey	Add *s*	turkeys

- When nouns end in **-s, -ss, -x, -sh,** or **-ch**, add **es**.

bus	Add *es*	buses
dress	Add *es*	dresses
box	Add *es*	boxes
wish	Add *es*	wishes
lunch	Add *es*	lunches

A. DIRECTIONS: *Write the plural form of each singular noun on the line provided. Use a dictionary to help you spell the word correctly.*

1. fox _____
2. dish _____
3. cross _____
4. mark _____
5. key _____
6. lake _____
7. couch _____

8. Saturday _____
9. pet _____
10. stray _____
11. hippopotamus _____
12. sandwich _____
13. class _____
14. wax _____

Name _____ Date _____

"The Drive-In Movies" by Gary Soto
"The Market Square Dog" by James Herriot
Integrated Language Skills: Support for Writing

For your autobiographical narrative, begin by making a timeline. Use the graphic organizer below to list chronologically a few important events in your life. On the diagonal lines, write a few words about big events or periods of time that you remember well. For example, you might write "moved to new school."

Timeline

Birth   Now

Choose an event from the timeline for your autobiographical narrative and write the event on the Event line below. Then list details about the event on the Details lines. Number the details in the order they occurred. Use your numbered list to help you write your autobiographical narrative.

Event _____

Details _____

_____

_____

_____

_____

_____

_____

_____

_____

_____

_____

_____

_____

Name _____ Date _____

"The Drive-In Movies" by Gary Soto
"The Market Square Dog" by James Herriot
Integrated Language Skills: Extend Your Learning

Listening and Speaking

1. Use the space below to write a few details you and your partner might include in your invented dialogue.

_____

_____

_____

_____

_____

_____

_____

_____

2. Use this space to jot down details about each character's traits, goals, and feelings. These notes will help you write stage directions to show how each character should speak. For example, you might write

   Gary Soto: *(speaking softly)* That was hard work.

   Character #1: (Name: _____)

   _____

   Character #2: (Name: _____)

   _____

Name _____ Date _____

"The Market Square Dog" by James Herriot
Open-Book Test

Short Answer *Write your responses to the questions in this section on the lines provided.*

1. The narrator of "The Market Square Dog" is James Herriot. From what point of view is the story told? Explain how you know.

   _____

   _____

2. The dog runs away from the vet at the market in "The Market Square Dog." Why doesn't the reader know where the dog has gone?

   _____

   _____

   _____

3. What shared qualities bring the country veterinarian and the policeman together in "The Market Square Dog"? Support your answer with details from the story.

   _____

   _____

   _____

4. How would "The Market Square Dog" be different if it were told from a third-person point of view? Give an example from the selection that shows something the reader would not learn from a third-person narrator.

   _____

   _____

   _____

5. At the beginning of "The Market Square Dog," the reader might predict that the appealing animal will find a good home. Then, something happens that makes the reader fear for the dog. Identify this event and explain why it puts the prediction in doubt.

   _____

   _____

6. In "The Market Square Dog," the veterinarian looks at the dog lying on the back seat of the car. Explain why it is significant to Herriot that the injured dog is able to manage a brief tail wag.

   _____

   _____

   _____

7. The narrator of "The Market Square Dog" says that he and his wife "kept glancing anxiously at the little dog" after his operation. Explain what the word *anxiously* tells about the couple's feelings for the dog.

_____

_____

_____

8. Fill in the boxes to tell how the market square dog behaves toward people at the market and at the kennels. Then, on the lines below, explain why his behavior changes.

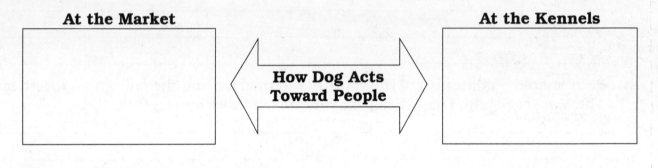

At the Market

At the Kennels

How Dog Acts Toward People

_____

_____

_____

9. Suppose the reader predicts that the market square dog will find a good home. Explain at what point in the story this prediction can be confirmed.

_____

_____

_____

10. What is it about the policeman that makes Herriot confident that the market square dog has found a good home? Support your answer with details from the story.

_____

_____

_____

_____

Essay

Write an extended response to the question of your choice or to the question or questions your teacher assigns you.

11. The dog in "The Market Square Dog" finds a new home with the policeman. Think about the dog's behavior and personality. Then, consider what type of home would be best for him. In an essay, explain whether the policeman's home will be the right place for the dog.

12. In an essay, discuss whether the narrator of "The Market Square Dog" is well suited to be a country veterinarian. Include examples from the story to support your ideas.

13. What are two main points that the author of "The Market Square Dog" wants to convey to the reader? In an essay, explain how the author develops each of these points in the story.

14. **Thinking About the Big Question: How do we decide what is true?** In "The Market Square Dog," what does the narrator decide is true about the dog and about the policeman? Explain how he comes to these conclusions and why he is so good at deciding what is true.

Oral Response

15. Go back to question 3, 5, 6, or 10 or to the question your teacher assigns to you. Take a few minutes to expand your answer and prepare an oral response. Find additional details in "The Market Square Dog" that support your points. If necessary, make notes to guide your response.

"**The Market Square Dog**" by James Herriot
Selection Test A

Critical Reading *Identify the letter of the choice that best answers the question.*

____ 1. Herriot writes "The Market Square Dog" in the first person. Who narrates, or tells, the story?
A. the dog
B. a farmer
C. a veterinarian
D. a policeman

____ 2. In "The Market Square Dog," what is the dog doing when the vet first notices him?
A. He is chasing a stick someone has thrown.
B. He is sitting up, begging for food.
C. He is being chased by children.
D. He is hiding behind a farmer.

____ 3. Which of the following best describes the dog in "The Market Square Dog"?
A. He is a cross-bred of a sheepdog and a terrier.
B. He is a purebred terrier.
C. He is a thin, smooth-coated racing dog.
D. He is a large sheepdog.

____ 4. Near the beginning of "The Market Square Dog," why can't the policeman catch the dog?
A. The dog won't let the policeman get close to him.
B. He is afraid the dog will bite him.
C. The dog probably belongs to someone.
D. He doesn't have a leash to put on the dog.

____ 5. The dog is so appealing at the beginning of "The Market Square Dog" that you might predict he will easily find a home. As you read on, you change that prediction. What is the first event that most likely makes you change, or at least doubt, this prediction?
A. The narrator notices the dog begging in the market.
B. The dog is badly injured when he is hit by a car.
C. The dog is taken to the kennels.
D. The policeman says that the dog has been arrested.

_____ 6. How does the vet help the dog in "The Market Square Dog"?

    A. He fixes his broken leg.

    B. He finds a good home for the dog.

    C. He takes the dog into his own home as a gift to Helen.

    D. He teaches the dog a new trick.

_____ 7. When he is at the police kennels, the dog in "The Market Square Dog" becomes very friendly and active. Why do you think this happens?

    A. He knows this is his new home.

    B. He is kept in a cage.

    C. He wants someone to take him home.

    D. The policemen are teaching him tricks.

_____ 8. In "The Market Square Dog," there is evidence that the vet and the policeman are alike in two ways. Which two qualities do both characters have?

    A. curiosity and a good memory

    B. interest in dogs and sympathy for them

    C. a love of the city and ability to work hard

    D. courage and ability to take a joke

_____ 9. In "The Market Square Dog," what reason does the policeman give for the dog's absence in the kennel?

    A. The dog escaped.

    B. The policeman's daughters are taking the dog for a walk.

    C. The dog has been adopted by a farmer.

    D. The dog has been arrested for begging.

_____ 10. At which point in the story can you confirm a prediction that the policeman will adopt the dog?

    A. The dog is begging at the market.

    B. The policeman brings the injured dog to the vet.

    C. The policeman is pleased at the dog's recovery.

    D. Mr. Herriot sees the dog in the policeman's home.

_____ 11. The narrator of "The Market Square Dog" uses "I" to tell the story. He can tell you only what he sees, thinks, knows, and feels. What, therefore, can he *not* tell you?

    A. where the dog came from

    B. how the vet feels about animals

    C. who Helen is

    D. why the dog is classified as a stray

Vocabulary and Grammar

____ 12. The vocabulary word *anxiously* means "in a worried way." Which of the following words is most nearly opposite in meaning to *anxiously*?

A. eagerly

B. angrily

C. nervously

D. calmly

____ 13. Which sentence uses an underlined vocabulary word in an *incorrect* way?

A. The babysitter has <u>custody</u> of my sister when Mom is at work.

B. I cook <u>anxiously</u> because I love to eat.

C. The pony <u>trotted</u> to us so we could feed him an apple.

D. We waited <u>anxiously</u> to hear if the storm warning had been canceled.

____ 14. How many plural nouns does the following sentence include?

The dogs in the kennels hopped up on benches to get a better look at the policeman who brought them their food.

A. one

B. two

C. three

D. four

____ 15. Which plural noun below has been formed incorrectly?

A. marketes

B. sandwiches

C. daughters

D. strays

Essay

16. In an essay, tell what you found out about the job of a country vet in "The Market Square Dog." Describe what you would like and what you would dislike if you had that job.

17. In an essay, discuss why you think the dog in "The Market Square Dog" has trouble finding a new owner. Talk about the dog's appearance and his personality. Then describe the type of family that would make the best new home for this dog.

18. **Thinking About the Big Question: How do we decide what is true?** In "The Market Square Dog," the narrator decides what is true about the dog and about the policeman. Explain what he decides about each and how he comes to these conclusions.

"The Market Square Dog" by James Herriot
Selection Test B

Critical Reading *Identify the letter of the choice that best completes the statement or answers the question.*

____ 1. The first-person narrator of "The Market Square Dog" is
  A. a stray dog.
  B. a farmer.
  C. a veterinarian.
  D. a policeman.

____ 2. When the narrator first notices the dog in "The Market Square Dog," the dog
  A. is chasing a stick thrown by the policeman.
  B. is sitting up, begging for food.
  C. is being chased by children around the market stalls.
  D. is trotting among the market square crowd.

____ 3. The first-person narrator of "The Market Square Dog" would *not* be able to know
  A. where the dog came from.
  B. how the vet feels about animals.
  C. how to treat a dog's broken leg.
  D. why the dog is classified as a stray.

____ 4. Why is the policeman unable to catch the dog at the beginning of "The Market Square Dog"?
  A. The dog stays just out of the policeman's reach.
  B. The policeman says he has no time to chase dogs.
  C. The dog has a collar and tags and is not a stray.
  D. The policeman's loud voice frightens away the dog.

____ 5. Which quotation from "The Market Square Dog" most clearly shows the perspective of the narrator?
  A. Anything could have happened to him.
  B. "We can still have our picnic," she said.
  C. "I'll take you to him," the policeman replied.
  D. "What's your name?" I asked.

____ 6. Which clue best leads you to predict that the dog in "The Market Square Dog" will find a home?
  A. The dog is unwilling to be caught by the policeman or the vet.
  B. Mr. Herriot describes the dog as having two friendly brown eyes and a wonderfully attractive face.
  C. A market stallholder throws a bun to the dog.
  D. Mr. Herriot, a country veterinarian, and Helen, his wife, are dressed up and going to the races.

_____ 7. Which story event in "The Market Square Dog" best confirms a prediction that the dog will find a new home?
A. The dog's previous owner cannot be found.
B. The dog is injured by a car.
C. The Yorkshire terrier and sheepdog leave the kennels.
D. Mr. Herriot sees the dog curled up in its new doggy bed.

_____ 8. In "The Market Square Dog," when the policeman and the vet see that the badly injured dog can manage a brief tail wag, they know that
A. the dog will never walk again.
B. the dog is still alive.
C. the dog is afraid.
D. the dog's begging days are over.

_____ 9. How do the vet and his wife help the dog in "The Market Square Dog"?
A. They set his broken leg.
B. They find a home for him.
C. They find its rightful owner.
D. They teach it not to fear humans.

_____ 10. When he is at the police kennels, the dog in "The Market Square Dog"
A. is fed regularly.
B. is recovering from his injuries.
C. responds to the kindness of people.
D. all of the above

_____ 11. In "The Market Square Dog," the country vet and the policeman are initially brought together because they share
A. the same profession.
B. an interest in dogs and sympathy for them.
C. a devotion to work and love of family.
D. a joke.

_____ 12. Which detail is a good predictor that the policeman will adopt the dog?
A. The dog has an attractive face.
B. The policeman takes the injured dog to the vet.
C. The policeman, pleased with the dog's recovery, takes good care of him at the kennel.
D. The policeman has two daughters, a home, and a job.

_____ 13. In "The Market Square Dog," the policeman tells the vet that the dog has been arrested because
A. the dog has snarled at the policeman's daughter.
B. the policeman is playing a joke on the vet.
C. the dog has no owner.
D. the dog stole the golden retriever's food.

___ 14. One of the main points that the author of "The Market Square Dog" makes is that
   A. a vet's wife works hard.
   B. a stray dog cannot survive on its own.
   C. people and pets depend on each other.
   D. country people prefer working dogs.

Vocabulary and Grammar

___ 15. The word most nearly opposite in meaning to *anxiously* is
   A. anxiety.   C. nervously.
   B. calmly.   D. eagerly.

___ 16. How many singular nouns and plural nouns does the following sentence include?
   The picnic basket for two people contained forks, dishes, napkins, chicken sandwiches, eggs, scones, and a chocolate cake.

   A. one singular noun, eight plural nouns
   B. two singular nouns, seven plural nouns
   C. four singular nouns, six plural nouns
   D. three singular nouns, three plural nouns

___ 17. In which sentence is the underlined vocabulary word used incorrectly?
   A. Because the dog was a stray, the police took custody of him.
   B. The amused children laughed anxiously at the clown's funny tricks.
   C. We trotted cheerfully all over town even though our feet were beginning to hurt.
   D. The kitten cried whenever her mother trotted off to hunt for food.

___ 18. Which plural noun is spelled incorrectly?
   A. coaches   C. trayes
   B. sandwiches   D. foxes

___ 19. What is the meaning of *anxiously* in the following sentence?
   Helen kept glancing anxiously at the little injured dog sleeping beside us.
   A. lovingly   C. quickly
   B. eagerly   D. worriedly

Essay

20. What kind of person is the country veterinarian in "The Market Square Dog"? In an essay, describe the vet. Explain how and why he is well suited to his job.

21. After you read the first few paragraphs of "The Market Square Dog," you may have predicted how the story would end. As you read, new details and events may change or confirm your original prediction. In an essay, explain two predictions you made while reading "The Market Square Dog." Which details or events caused you to make those predictions? How were your predictions changed or confirmed?

22. **Thinking About the Big Question: How do we decide what is true?** In "The Market Square Dog," what does the narrator decide is true about the dog and about the policeman? Explain how he comes to these conclusions and why he is so good at deciding what is true.

"Why Monkeys Live in Trees" by Julius Lester
"The Case of the Monkeys that Fell from the Trees" by Susan E. Quinlan
Vocabulary Warm-up Word Lists

Study these words from the selections. Then, complete the activities.

Word List A

behavior [bee HAY vyuhr] *n.* the way someone acts
    Jessica was exhibiting some strange <u>behavior</u>, singing in her sleep.

bellowed [BEL ohd] *v.* shouted or roared
    Lin <u>bellowed</u> at the kids to come back, but they didn't listen to her.

determine [di TER min] *v.* find out
    I wanted to <u>determine</u> where my sister was going every day after school.

evidence [EV uh dens] *n.* information and facts that help prove something
    I gathered the <u>evidence</u> I would need to prove him guilty.

incidents [IN suh dents] *n.* events; things that happen
    The strange <u>incidents</u> began after the spaceship landed.

individual [in duh VIJ oo uhl] *adj.* single and separate
    Each <u>individual</u> witness was interviewed separately.

involved [in VAHLVD] *adj.* taking part in
    I was <u>involved</u> in the school play and really enjoyed it.

suspiciously [suh SPISH uhs lee] *adv.* in a way that seems bad or strange
    After he returned from his trip, Bob began acting <u>suspiciously</u>.

Word List B

complicated [KAHM pli kay tid] *adj.* having a lot of parts or steps; difficult
    The problem was too <u>complicated</u> to solve quickly.

nonetheless [nuhn thuh LESS] *adv.* in spite of
    Jerry was angry, but <u>nonetheless</u> he had a big smile.

researchers [REE serch erz] *n.* people who study things in depth
    The <u>researchers</u> were looking for ways to make our jobs easier.

tolerate [TAHL uh rayt] *v.* to put up with something; be able to deal with something
    He could only <u>tolerate</u> loud noises in small doses.

toxic [TAHK sik] *adj.* poisonous
    Until he got sick, he didn't realize the mushrooms were <u>toxic</u>.

uncommon [uhn KAHM uhn] *adj.* rare, unusual
    It was <u>uncommon</u> to see Jane and Mandy get along.

unlimited [un LIM uh tid] *adj.* without end, having no boundaries
    Shawn got excited when he saw the <u>unlimited</u> supply of candy.

vary [VAIR ee] *v.* change; make different
    I like to <u>vary</u> my clothes by wearing a different color every day.

"Why Monkeys Live in Trees" by Julius Lester
"The Case of the Monkeys that Fell from the Trees" by Susan E. Quinlan
Vocabulary Warm-up Exercises

Exercise A *Fill in each blank in the paragraph below with an appropriate word from Word List A. Use each word only once.*

It was a series of strange [1] _____ that got Detective Gumshoe

[2] _____ in the case. His job was to gather [3] _____

that would help [4] _____ who the criminal was. Detective Gumshoe

began by examining everyone's actions and [5] _____. Was anyone

acting [6] _____, or peculiar? Finally, one day he spotted an

[7] _____ holding something tightly to his chest. It was hidden beneath

his jacket. "Stop! Thief!" the detective [8] _____, but the man just kept

running.

Exercise B *Answer the questions with complete explanations.*

Example: Would a <u>complicated</u> story be easy to follow? Why or why not?
It probably would not be easy to follow because <u>complicated</u> means involving many steps.

1. What are two things <u>researchers</u> of animal behavior might study?

_____

2. If an event such as an eclipse was <u>uncommon</u>, would you expect to see it often? Why or why not?

_____

3. If you could have an <u>unlimited</u> amount of anything, what would it be? Why?

_____

4. If the doctor told you to <u>vary</u> your diet, would you eat the same things every day? Explain.

_____

5. What is one thing you just can't <u>tolerate</u>, and why?

_____

6. If someone ate something <u>toxic</u>, would you <u>nonetheless</u> expect him or her to feel great? Explain.

_____

"Why Monkeys Live in Trees" by Julius Lester
"The Case of the Monkeys that Fell from the Trees" by Susan E. Quinlan
Reading Warm-up A

Read the following passage. Pay special attention to the underlined words. Then, read it again, and complete the activities. Use a separate sheet of paper for your written answers.

At first, I didn't think much about it, but then the incidents began piling up. Strange occurrences began happening almost daily. Food was missing from the kitchen, or messes were made in various rooms in the house. I was determined to get to the bottom of it all because I wanted to know who was involved. Who had a part in these crimes?

I began by examining everyone's behavior. How was everyone acting? Was any individual in the house acting suspiciously, or rather, was any person who lived here acting more strangely than usual?

Unfortunately, I could not determine that anyone was. In fact, I just couldn't figure it out. Inez still went off to work every morning, while Ernesto stayed in his room most of the time and listened to music. Monica followed me around the house, begging me to play with her. There was nothing unusual about any of that. In short, things were just as they always were.

Still, slowly, I began to gather evidence, carefully writing down each clue I discovered. Then I created a profile of my suspect: He (or she) was small and very, very sneaky.

Days went by without a sign of my villain, but I didn't give up. I watched and waited patiently, until one day I caught him. A little monkey climbed in through the window and grabbed some bananas off the kitchen table. "Oh, no, you don't!" I bellowed after him. I began to give chase, but the monkey got away. When I told the kids, they just laughed. "Mom," they said, "monkeys are a part of life in Costa Rica. Now you can say you've finally settled in!"

1. Underline the words that explain what underlined incidents are. Then, write about two *incidents* that happened to you last week.

2. Underline the words that tell what involved means. Then, describe something you are *involved* in.

3. Circle the word that tells what behavior means. What two adjectives would you use to describe the narrator's *behavior*?

4. Underline the phrase that tells you what individual and suspiciously mean. Then, use both words together in a sentence.

5. Circle the words that tell what determine means. What does the narrator want to *determine*?

6. Underline the words that tell how the narrator gathers evidence. What does she use the *evidence* for?

7. Underline the sentence that explains why the narrator has bellowed at the monkey. Describe a situation in which you might *bellow* at someone.

"Why Monkeys Live in Trees" by Julius Lester
"The Case of the Monkeys that Fell from the Trees" by Susan E. Quinlan
Reading Warm-up B

Read the following passage. Pay special attention to the underlined words. Then, read it again, and complete the activities. Use a separate sheet of paper for your written answers.

For years, researchers have been studying why people eat the foods they do. They're curious about how humans came to realize that certain foods are healthful, while others are just plain toxic. How did they know to eat blueberries but not deadly nightshade? How were the edible parts of potatoes, which have poisonous leaves, first discovered? How did people avoid poisonous items yet still get all the nutrients they needed?

The answer, of course, is complicated. It is not just a simple theory that can be proved or disproved. There is no magic window onto the past that allows us to see how things happened. We have to figure it out using clues and logic.

Many experts suggest that people figured out what to eat through trial and error. This makes sense. Out of an almost unlimited number of possibilities, people ate what did not make them sick. In other words, if people could tolerate a certain food, it got added to the list. If not, it got rejected. Those who chose their foods wisely were more likely to survive. Eating something uncommon and therefore untested was definitely risky.

Nonetheless, around the world, humans still managed to create diets that contained a great variety of foods. That, perhaps, is part of the secret. It was not just enough to avoid foods that are known to be bad. There must have also been advantages to seeking out as many foods as possible. Perhaps those who ate a wider variety received more nutrients, lived longer, and had more children.

What lesson can we take from all this about our eating habits today? First of all, it's important to avoid things that we know are poisonous. Perhaps more important, though, is the idea that we need to vary our diet. Eating a wide variety of foods may be the only way to ensure that we get the nutrients we need.

1. Circle two words that help describe researchers. Then, write a sentence describing a *researcher*.

2. Circle the word that means the same thing as toxic. Then, use *toxic* in a sentence.

3. Circle the word that means the opposite of complicated. What makes something *complicated?*

4. Based on the passage, there is almost an unlimited number of what?

5. Based on the passage, what happened if people couldn't tolerate a food?

6. What was risky about eating an uncommon food?

7. In your own words, rewrite the sentence containing the word nonetheless. Then, write what *nonetheless* means.

8. Underline the words that help to explain what vary means. Why is it important to *vary* our diet?

Name _____ Date _____

"Why Monkeys Live in Trees" by Julius Lester
"The Case of the Monkeys That Fell From the Trees" by Susan E. Quinlan
Writing About the Big Question

How do we decide what is true?

Big Question Vocabulary

confirm	decision	determine	evidence	fact
fantasy	fiction	investigate	opinion	prove
realistic	study	test	true	unbelievable

A. *Use one or more words from the list above to complete the following sentences.*

1. Although some fiction can be mostly _____, other fiction has _____ elements to it.

2. Often, we can learn _____ lessons about life from good fiction.

3. Nonfiction books can be a good source to _____ what is true.

4. Nonfiction resources like encyclopedias and dictionaries can help us find _____ to support statements in research papers.

B. *Respond to each item. Use at least two Big Question vocabulary words in each answer.*

1. Discuss one true thing that you learned by reading a fictional book.

   _____

   _____

   _____

2. How do facts in nonfiction sources help you when you are writing a research paper?

   _____

   _____

   _____

C. *Complete the sentence below. Then, write a short paragraph connecting this situation to the Big Question.*

In this story, make-believe monkeys who live in trees might _____

_____

_____

_____

_____

_____

Name _____ Date _____

"Why Monkeys Live in Trees" by Julius Lester

"The Case of the Monkeys That Fell from the Trees" by Susan E. Quinlan

Literary Analysis: Fiction and Nonfiction

Fiction is writing that tells about imaginary people, animals, or events. A work of fiction contains one or more made-up elements, such as a leopard that speaks. Some writers create works of fiction that are realistic. Although they may *seem* real, these works contain invented characters, settling, or plots.

Nonfiction is writing that tells about real people, animals, places, events, or ideas. For example, a science article that explains the eating habits of jungle animals is a work of nonfiction. In nonfiction, everything must be true. It must contain facts and details from the real world.

DIRECTIONS: *Each passage below comes from one of the selections about monkeys, either "Why Monkeys Live in Trees" or "The Case of the Monkeys That Fell from the Trees." Read each passage. On the first line following the story, tell whether the passage comes from a work of fiction or nonfiction. Then, on the following lines, explain how you know if it is fiction or nonfiction.*

1. At that exact moment, one of Leopard's children ran up to him.

   "Daddy! Daddy! Are you going to be in the contest?"

   "What contest?" Leopard wanted to know. If it was a beauty contest, of course he was going to be in it.

   This passage comes from a work of _____. I know this because _____

   _____

2. Normally, howling monkeys are skilled, nimble climbers. They often leap ten feet or more between tree limbs, and they almost never fall.

   This passage comes from a work of _____. I know this because _____

   _____

3. King Gorilla had the animals pick numbers to see who would go in what order. To everybody's disappointment, Hippopotamus drew Number 1.

   This passage comes from a work of _____. I know this because _____

   _____

4. Again, Glander found an answer in his field records. Howlers had fed in 331 of the trees in the study area, but they made only one stop in 104 of these trees.

   This passage comes from a work of _____. I know this because _____

   _____

Unit 1 Resources: Fiction and Nonfiction

113

Name _____ Date _____

"Why Monkeys Live in Trees" by Julius Lester
"The Case of the Monkeys That Fell From the Trees" by Susan E. Quinlan
Vocabulary Builder

Word List

> abruptly   bellowed   distress   incidents   reflection   regally

A. DIRECTIONS: *Follow each instruction below to write a sentence. Use at least one word from the Word List in each sentence.*

1. Write a sentence about something that happens without warning.

   _____

   _____

2. Write a sentence about someone who has just received bad news.

   _____

   _____

3. Write a sentence about something you might see in a mirror.

   _____

   _____

4. Write a sentence about related events.

   _____

   _____

5. Write a sentence about someone calling to a lost pet.

   _____

   _____

6. Write a sentence about a formal action by a king.

   _____

   _____

B. DIRECTIONS: *Circle the word that is closest in meaning to the word in CAPITAL LETTERS.*

1. INCIDENTS
   A. discussions   B. projects   C. questions   D. happenings

2. BELLOWED
   A. tumbled   B. hollered   C. swerved   D. gobbled

3. DISTRESS
   A. suffering   B. noise   C. relaxation   D. pleasure

4. ABRUPTLY
   A. mysteriously   B. roughly   C. unexpectedly   D. silently

Name _____ Date _____

"Why Monkeys Live in Trees" by Julius Lester
"The Case of the Monkeys That Fell From the Trees" by Susan E. Quinlan

Integrated Language Skills: Support for Writing to Compare Literary Works

Before you write your paragraph comparing and contrasting the monkeys in these two selections, complete the graphic organizer below. In the left and right columns, note how the monkeys in each selection are different. In the center column, note how the monkeys in both selections are similar.

Monkeys in "Why Monkeys Live in Trees"	How Monkeys Are Similar in Both Selections	Monkeys in "The Case of the Monkeys That Fell From the Trees"

Use your notes to write a paragraph comparing and contrasting the monkeys in "Why Monkeys Live in Trees" and "The Case of the Monkeys That Fell From the Trees."

"Why Monkeys Live in Trees" by Julius Lester
"The Case of the Monkeys That Fell From the Trees" by Susan E. Quinlan
Open-Book Test

Short Answer *Write your responses to the questions in this section on the lines provided.*

1. Leopard in "Why Monkeys Live in Trees" likes to gaze at his reflection. What trait does this reveal about him? Explain.

   _____

   _____

2. In "Why Monkeys Live in Trees," King Gorilla tests each of the animals in a contest. Explain why all of the animals before Monkey fail.

   _____

   _____

3. The monkeys in "Why Monkeys Live in Trees" try to pull a trick on the other animals. They almost get away with it. Explain why the author wrote about monkeys instead of some other animal. Think about what type of character would be able to pull such a trick.

   _____

   _____

4. Scientists in "The Case of the Monkeys That Fell From the Trees" observed monkeys eating leaves from poisonous trees without any signs of distress. What signs of distress might they have expected to see?

   _____

   _____

5. Near the end of "The Case of the Monkeys That Fell From the Trees," the author suggests that "the monkeys' poisoned-filled pantry has a silver lining." Explain what she means.

   _____

   _____

   _____

6. The author of "The Case of the Monkeys That Fell From the Trees" shows how scientists do their work. Name one important quality a scientist must possess. Use examples from the essay to support your answer.

   _____

   _____

   _____

Unit 1 Resources: Fiction and Nonfiction
116

7. A work of fiction contains at least one made-up element. In a work of nonfiction, everything must be true. Compare "Why Monkeys Live in Trees" and "The Case of the Monkeys That Fell From the Trees." Write each of these items in the correct place on the diagram: *scientists; gorilla as king; trees.* Then, on the line below, explain how the information tells you which selection is fiction.

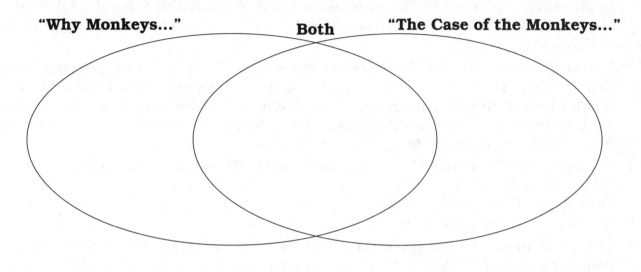

"Why Monkeys..."   **Both**   **"The Case of the Monkeys..."**

_____

8. Young animals are mentioned in both "Why Monkeys Live in Trees" and "The Case of the Monkeys That Fell From the Trees." Explain how the behavior of the young animals tells you whether each selection is fiction or nonfiction.

_____

_____

9. Identify one sentence from "Why Monkeys Live in Trees" that indicates it is a work of fiction. Then, identify one sentence from "The Case of the Monkeys That Fell From the Trees" that indicates it is a work of nonfiction. Explain your answers.

_____

_____

_____

10. The authors of "Why Monkeys Live in Trees" and "The Case of the Monkeys That Fell From the Trees" had very different reasons for writing. Which author wrote to share interesting facts about monkeys—the author of the work of fiction or of nonfiction? Explain why the type of writing fits the purpose.

_____

_____

_____

Essay

Write an extended response to the question of your choice or to the question or questions your teacher assigns you.

11. Nonfiction is writing that tells about real people, animals, places, events, and ideas. In an essay, explain why "The Case of the Monkeys That Fell From the Trees" is a work of nonfiction. Use details from the selection to explain why it fits the definition of nonfiction.

12. The monkeys in "Why Monkeys Live in Trees" and "The Case of the Monkeys That Fell From the Trees" are typical monkeys in some ways but not in others. Think about where each group of monkeys lives, what each group eats, and what unusual skills or behaviors each group displays. Then, in an essay, explain how each group of monkeys compares to the typical monkey.

13. In some ways, Leopard in "Why Monkeys Live in Trees" is like the scientists in "The Case of the Monkeys That Fell From the Trees." In an essay, explain how they are similar. Then, discuss whether Leopard would make a good scientist. Use information from both selections in your answer.

14. **Thinking About the Big Question: How do we decide what is true?** In an essay, respond to one of the following. Use examples from the selection to support your response.
    - In "Why Monkeys Live in Trees," the animals do not realize what the monkeys are doing to win the contest. They seem to have a hard time deciding what is true, and only Leopard is able to find out the truth. What does this reveal about the others and Leopard?
    - How do the Glanders go about trying to decide what is true in "The Case of the Monkeys That Fell From the Trees"? Explain what their behavior tells about them and whether you trust their conclusions.

Oral Response

15. Go back to question 3, 5, 6, or 10 or to the question your teacher assigns to you. Take a few minutes to expand your answer and prepare an oral response. Find additional details in "Why Monkeys Live in Trees" or "The Case of the Monkeys That Fell From the Trees" that will support your points. If necessary, make notes to guide your response.

"Why Monkeys Live in Trees" by Julius Lester
"The Case of the Monkeys That Fell from the Trees" by Susan E. Quinlan
Selection Test A

Critical Reading *Identify the letter of the choice that best answers the question.*

____ 1. In "Why Monkeys Live in Trees," why do the animals have a contest?
    A. to see who can climb a pile of dirt
    B. to see who can find a pot of gold
    C. to see who can chase Monkey the farthest
    D. to see who can eat a mound of dust

____ 2. In "Why Monkeys Live in Trees," how do the monkeys trick the other animals?
    A. by helping Monkey eat the pepper
    B. by hiding the pot of gold in the grass
    C. by hiding the pot of gold in a tree
    D. by making Hippopotamus eat the pepper

____ 3. Which word best describes the monkeys in "Why Monkeys Live in Trees"?
    A. lazy
    B. clever
    C. giving
    D. frightening

____ 4. How do you know that "Why Monkeys Live in Trees" is a work of fiction?
    A. The monkey characters are good climbers.
    B. The animal characters live in the jungle.
    C. The animal characters can talk.
    D. The monkey characters nibble on their food.

____ 5. In "The Case of the Monkeys That Fell from the Trees," what is surprising about the falling monkeys?
    A. They have lost their climbing skills.
    B. They do not go back into the trees after they fall.
    C. They will not allow the scientist to watch them.
    D. They eat large amounts of food before falling.

____ 6. In "The Case of the Monkeys That Fell from the Trees," what question do the scientists try to answer?
    A. Why do the monkeys fall?
    B. Where do the monkeys fall?
    C. When do the monkeys eat leaves?
    D. How hard do the monkeys hit the ground?

____ 7. Which is the best summary of the scientists' findings in "The Case of the Monkeys That Fell from the Trees"?

    A. All tropical leaves are poisonous.

    B. Some tropical leaves are poisonous and others are not.

    C. All howler monkeys use poisonous leaves for medicine.

    D. Some monkeys eat only the leaves that are poisonous.

____ 8. Which statement best describes "The Case of the Monkeys That Fell from the Trees"?

    A. Some parts are true and some are made up.

    B. It contains only one made-up element.

    C. It is a work of fiction.

    D. Everything in it is true and it is nonfiction.

____ 9. How are the monkeys alike in "Why Monkeys Live in Trees" and "The Case of the Monkeys That Fell from the Trees"?

    A. The monkeys in both selections play tricks on others.

    B. The monkeys in both selections fall out of trees.

    C. The monkeys in both selections eat small bites of food.

    D. The monkeys in both selections can talk.

____ 10. How is Leopard in "Why Monkeys Live in Trees" like the scientist in "The Case of the Monkeys That Fell from the Trees"?

    A. He is curious.

    B. He is impatient.

    C. He likes to look at himself.

    D. He lives in a tree.

____ 11. Which is a made-up element from "Why Monkeys Live in Trees"?

    A. A scientist studies monkeys.

    B. A monkey falls from a tree.

    C. Animals live in a jungle.

    D. A gorilla sits on a throne.

____ 12. Which statement describes both selections, "Why Monkeys Live in Trees" and "The Case of the Monkeys That Fell from the Trees"?

    A. Both selections contain made-up parts.

    B. Both selections answer scientific questions.

    C. Both selections contain only facts.

    D. Both selections include a mystery to be solved.

_____ **13.** Which fact is in both "Why Monkeys Live in Trees" and "The Case of the Monkeys That Fell From the Trees"?

    A. Monkeys can talk.

    B. Monkeys are skilled climbers.

    C. Monkeys enjoy playing games.

    D. Monkeys like pepper.

Vocabulary

_____ **14.** When Leopard looks at his <u>reflection</u>, what does he see?

    A. his image

    B. his number

    C. his leader

    D. his child

_____ **15.** Which sentence uses an underlined vocabulary word *incorrectly*?

    A. Hippopotamus <u>bellowed</u> when he tasted the pepper.

    B. The monkey fell <u>abruptly</u> from the tree.

    C. Leopard spied three <u>incidents</u> in the grass.

    D. After falling, the monkey showed signs of <u>distress</u>.

Essay

16. In an essay, identify which selection is fiction, "Why Monkeys Live in Trees" or "The Case of the Monkeys That Fell From the Trees." Tell which clues convince you that it is a work of fiction.

17. Use information from "Why Monkeys Live in Trees" and "The Case of the Monkeys That Fell From the Trees" to write a brief nonfiction essay about monkeys. Tell where the monkeys live, what they eat, and what special talents they have.

18. Thinking About the Big Question: How do we decide what is true? In an essay, respond to one of the following. Use examples from the selection to support your response.

- In "Why Monkeys Live in Trees," the monkeys play a trick to win the contest. The other animals fall for the trick. Only Leopard is not fooled and able to find out the truth. What does this reveal about the other animals and about Leopard?

- How do the Glanders decide what is true in "The Case of the Monkeys That Fell From the Trees"? Explain what their behavior tells about them and whether you trust their conclusions.

"Why Monkeys Live in Trees" by Julius Lester
"The Case of the Monkeys That Fell From the Trees" by Susan E. Quinlan
Selection Test B

Critical Reading *Identify the letter of the choice that best completes the statement or answers the question.*

____ 1. In "Why Monkeys Live in Trees," the animals have a contest to see who can
   A. climb a mound of black pepper.
   B. climb trees.
   C. chase Monkey to the top of a tree.
   D. eat a mound of black dust.

____ 2. In "Why Monkeys Live in Trees," the monkeys trick the other animals by
   A. helping Monkey eat the pepper.
   B. hiding the pepper in the tall grasses.
   C. hiding the pot of gold in a tree.
   D. burying the gold in a mound of pepper.

____ 3. Which word best describes the monkeys in "Why Monkeys Live in Trees"?
   A. vain
   B. mischievous
   C. independent
   D. clumsy

____ 4. In "Why Monkeys Live in Trees," why do most of the animals fail in the contest?
   A. They don't learn from the experiences of those whose turns came first.
   B. They try to trick each other.
   C. They are distracted by the monkeys' silly behavior.
   D. They don't follow King Gorilla's instructions.

____ 5. In "Why Monkeys Live in Trees," Monkey's trick depends on
   A. some advice given by Hippopotamus.
   B. the nearsightedness of Leopard.
   C. the carelessness of King Gorilla.
   D. the assistance of many monkeys that look exactly alike.

____ 6. Which sentence from "Why Monkeys Live in Trees" indicates that the story is a work of fiction?
   A. He opened his mouth wide, took a mouthful, and started chewing and swallowing.
   B. The monkeys ran in all directions.
   C. King Gorilla said that was okay.
   D. There were a hundred monkeys in the tall grasses and they all looked alike!

____ 7. In "The Case of the Monkeys That Fell From the Trees," why do the scientists think it is strange to see monkeys falling from trees in the rain forest?
   A. Monkeys usually do not climb trees.
   B. There are no trees in the rain forest.
   C. Monkeys do not live in the rain forest.
   D. Monkeys are skilled tree climbers.

_____ 8. In "The Case of the Monkeys That Fell From the Trees," the scientist concludes that a tropical forest contains
A. mostly poisonous leaves.
B. leaves that are only poisonous to howler monkeys.
C. a mixture of poisonous and nonpoisonous leaves.
D. no poisonous leaves.

_____ 9. How might howler monkeys, such as those in "The Case of the Monkeys That Fell From the Trees," help scientists in the future?
A. The monkeys might be trained to help scientists find poisonous leaves.
B. Knowing the eating habits of monkeys might help scientists find new medicines.
C. The monkeys might help scientists predict the weather.
D. Monkeys might give advice about when and where to plant certain trees.

_____ 10. The author probably wrote "The Case of the Monkeys That Fell from the Trees" to
A. persuade readers not to eat leaves in a tropical forest.
B. entertain readers with a funny story about monkeys.
C. share interesting facts about howler monkeys.
D. teach readers a lesson about taking risks.

_____ 11. In both "Why Monkeys Live in Trees" and "The Case of the Monkeys That Fell From the Trees," how are the monkeys alike?
A. All the monkeys play tricks on people who spy on them.
B. All the monkeys fall from trees.
C. All the monkeys are loud screamers.
D. All the monkeys eat small bits of harmful foods.

_____ 12. Which statement is *not* true about both Leopard in "Why Monkeys Live in Trees" and the scientist in "The Case of the Monkeys That Fell From the Trees"?
A. Both believe they are very handsome.
B. Both are watchful.
C. Both want to understand something.
D. Both spend a lot of time in the forest or jungle.

_____ 13. Which detail from the selections, "Why Monkeys Live in Trees" or "The Case of the Monkeys That Fell from the Trees," is a detail that indicates a work of fiction?
A. The only way the monkeys could escape was to climb to the very tops of the tallest trees.
B. King Gorilla sat at one end of the clearing on his throne.
C. The Glanders tagged the leaves with wire labels, noting the tree, the date, and the time that the sample was collected.
D. The scientists found no signs of disease or parasites.

_____ 14. In both "Why Monkeys Live in Trees" and "The Case of the Monkeys That Fell From the Trees," what do the monkeys do?
A. talk
B. prefer to live in tall grasses rather than trees
C. act in a way that is mysterious to those who are watching them
D. spend most of their time eating

____ 15. Which statement describes a work of fiction?
   A. It has at least three made-up elements.
   B. All of its elements must be made up.
   C. It has one or more made-up elements.
   D. All its details must be true.

____ 16. Which statement describes a work of nonfiction?
   A. All its details are not true.
   B. It presents and explains ideas that tell about real people, places, and events.
   C. It has at least three made-up elements.
   D. Nonfiction writing is found only in newspapers.

Vocabulary

____ 17. When Leopard in "Why Monkeys Live in Trees" gazes at his <u>reflection</u>, what does he gaze at?
   A. his image   C. his leader
   B. his number   D. his child

____ 18. What kind of <u>incidents</u> are described in "The Case of the Monkeys That Fell From the Trees"?
   A. contests between animals   C. places monkeys live
   B. events involving monkeys   D. tricks animals play

____ 19. In "Why Monkeys Live in Trees," the monkeys and King Gorilla express <u>distress</u> when
   A. Monkey wins the contest.   C. Hippopotamus sneezes.
   B. Leopard growls.   D. the contest begins.

Essay

20. In an essay, identify which selection—"Why Monkeys Live in Trees" or "The Case of the Monkeys That Fell From the Trees"—is a work of fiction. Explain what is not realistic about the work and why it fits the definition of fiction.

21. In some ways, the monkeys in "Why Monkeys Live in Trees" and "The Case of the Monkeys That Fell From the Trees," are typical monkeys. In other ways, they are not. In an essay, explain how this is so. Consider where each group of monkeys lives, what each group eats, and what unusual talents or behaviors each group has.

22. **Thinking About the Big Question: How do we decide what is true?** In an essay, respond to one of the following. Use examples from the selection to support your response.

   • In "Why Monkeys Live in Trees," the animals do not realize what the monkeys are doing to win the contest. They seem to have a hard time deciding what is true, and only Leopard is able to find out the truth. What does this reveal about the others and Leopard?

   • How do the Glanders go about trying to decide what is true in "The Case of the Monkeys That Fell From the Trees"? Explain what their behavior tells about them and whether you trust their conclusions.

Name _____ Date _____

Writing Workshop—Unit 1, Part 1
Description: Descriptive Essay

Prewriting: Gathering Details

Use the following sensory details chart to help you gather details about the sights, scents, textures, sounds, and tastes associated with your setting.

Sights	Scents	Textures	Sounds	Tastes

Drafting: Organizing Details

Use the following graphic organizer to list the details of your description in spatial order—moving from left to right, from front to back, or outward from the most important feature.

Left/Front/Most Important   **Right/Back/Least Important**

Writing Workshop—Unit 1, Part 1
Descriptive Essay: Integrating Grammar Skills

Revising for Errors with Possessive Nouns

Possessive nouns show ownership and are formed with apostrophes. Most errors occur when apostrophes are left out or placed incorrectly. Begin by deciding whether a noun is singular or plural. Then, follow the rule.

Type of Noun	Example	Rule for Forming Possessive	Correct Possessive Form
singular noun	cat	Add apostrophe -s	the cat's dish
singular noun ending in -s	dress	Add apostrophe -s	the dress's collar
plural noun ending in -s	boys	Add apostrophe	the boys' desks
plural noun that does not end in -s	mice	Add apostrophe -s	the mice's nest

Using Possessive Nouns

A. DIRECTIONS: *Choose the correct form of possessive noun for each sentence. Write the form on the line in the sentence.*

1. It's great to paddle a canoe out to Uncle _____ dock. (Wes's / Weses')

2. Imagine looking at the lake from _____ edge at sunset. (water's / waters')

3. The _____ calls tell each other where they are. (wood ducks' / wood duck's)

4. The _____ honking is a loud, harsh sound. (geeses's / geese's)

Fixing Errors in Possessive Nouns

B. DIRECTIONS: *On the lines, rewrite these sentences using the correct possessive noun.*

1. Mens's shouts came from across the lake.

_____

2. Charleys' dad and his friends were trying to get our attention.

_____

3. They wanted us to canoe across to see several bird's nests.

_____

4. The water level was too high after the three day's rain.

_____

5. Just then I saw a bass' sleek body near the water's surface.

_____

Unit 1: Fiction and Nonfiction
Benchmark Test 1

MULTIPLE CHOICE

Reading Skill: Predicting

1. What are the main things to consider when you predict what will happen in a story?
    A. the plot and the title of the work
    B. the names and personalities of the story characters
    C. the author and the setting of the work
    D. your prior knowledge and the details in the story

2. What is the best way to make predictions as you read a story?
    A. Make a prediction as you read, and then read further to see if it comes true.
    B. Make a prediction as you read, and then peek at the ending to see if you are right.
    C. Make just one or two predictions because making too many will spoil the story.
    D. Make a prediction when you read the title and stick with that prediction until the end.

3. Which of these details most clearly predicts that the film is about to start?
    A. Sharon buys a ticket and gives it to the usher, who rips it in half.
    B. Larry removes his coat and hat after finding his seat in the theater.
    C. The movie theater darkens, and the audience grows quiet.
    D. Sarah returns from the food concession and takes her seat.

Read this selection from a short story. Then, answer the questions that follow.

Lana sat in the chair nervously, waiting for Dr. Curry. Finally, the dentist came in, greeting her as he washed his hands. He made some adjustments to her chair, asked her to open her mouth, and then took a hand tool with a curved prong and began exploring Lana's mouth. "Ouch," she said when he touched one molar. "Oh, dear," Dr. Curry told her, "I'm afraid you have a big one right there." He turned to the counter for some preparation and soon was back with a hypodermic needle in his hand.

4. From the details in the selection, which of these predictions seems most likely to happen?
    A. The dentist will inject anesthetic in Lana's gums and then drill and fill her cavity.
    B. The dentist will inject anesthetic in Lana's gums and then pull her tooth out.
    C. The dentist will tell Lana that everything looks fine and then clean her teeth.
    D. The dentist will send Lana home with instructions to take better care of her teeth.

5. What prior knowledge is most helpful in making a prediction about what happens next?
    A. knowing the properties of dental anesthetics and laughing gas
    B. knowing typical procedures at a dentist's office
    C. knowing the fears some people have about going to the dentist
    D. knowing the products people use in caring for their teeth

Reading Skill: Analyze Structural Features

6. Which of the following would be the suffix of the domain name for the official U.S. Department of State Web site?
   A. .org
   B. .edu
   C. .gov
   D. .com

7. What do you call the address of a Web site?
   A. a link
   B. an icon
   C. the home page
   D. the URL

8. You find that a museum's Web page is all graphics. Which graphic would you click to learn the hours that the museum is open?
   A. a picture of a work of art
   B. a picture of a clock
   C. a picture of a public bus
   D. a picture of a dollar sign

Literary Analysis: Plot and Point of View

9. What part of a story introduces the characters and setting?
   A. exposition
   B. rising action
   C. falling action
   D. resolution

10. In what part of the story does the reader learn the final outcome?
    A. exposition
    B. rising action
    C. falling action
    D. resolution

11. What is the point of view of a story?
    A. the author's attitude toward his or her subject or audience
    B. the perspective from which the narrator tells the story
    C. the customs of the period in which the story takes place
    D. the main idea, insight, or message of the story

Read the story. Then, answer the questions that follow.

(1) The Alaska Gold Rush brought many newcomers north, hoping to strike it rich. (2) One of these newcomers was Art Calder. (3) Calder had arrived over a week earlier but was stuck in the tiny mining town of Nugget because of the bad weather. (4) Impatient to begin, Calder decided to go off on his own. (5) "It's forty below," an old timer told him, but Calder didn't care. (6) "What a fool!" the old timer muttered after Calder left. (7) "He'll never make it." (8) Meanwhile, Calder left with no companion except his sled dog. (9) The snow got worse and worse. (10) Even through all his layers, Calder's fingers

and feet were freezing. (11) He could not see a thing ahead of him and decided to turn back, but then he realized he could not see behind him either. (12) Panicking, he wondered if he could survive. (13) Then, suddenly, his sled dog pulled at him. (14) Realizing the dog knew more about Alaska than he did, he let himself be led back to Nugget. (15) As he entered the shelter and spotted the old timer, Calder admitted that he had been a fool.

12. Which part of the story is the exposition?
    A. sentences 1–2
    B. sentences 3–4
    C. sentences 5–7
    D. sentence 15

13. Around what conflict do the events of the story center?
    A. Calder's struggle with the Alaskan wilderness
    B. the sled dog's problems with Calder
    C. Calder's argument with the old timer about leaving
    D. Calder's drive to be rich and famous

14. Where does the climax of the story take place?
    A. sentence 3–4
    B. sentences 8–9
    C. sentences 11–14
    D. sentences 14–15

15. From what point of view is the story narrated?
    A. first person
    B. third person, limited to the thoughts and experiences of one character
    C. second person
    D. third person, providing the thoughts and experiences of all characters

16. Read this brief selection from an autobiography. Which pronouns indicate the selection has a first-person point of view?

    In the 1950s I left Puerto Rico with my father and mother, and we came to live with my uncle in New York City. My uncle had an apartment in the Bronx, but he traveled to his job in Manhattan every day on the subway.

    A. *I, my,* and *he*
    B. *I, my,* and *we*
    C. *I, we,* and *his*
    D. *we, he,* and *his*

17. What is the difference between fiction and nonfiction?
    A. In fiction, everything must be made up; in nonfiction, some things must be true.
    B. In fiction, at least one thing must be made up; in nonfiction, everything must be true.
    C. In fiction, everything must be true; in nonfiction, some things can be made up.
    D. In fiction, at least one thing is true; in nonfiction, everything must be made up.

18. Which of these is an example of nonfiction?
    A. a short story
    B. a novel
    C. a folk tale
    D. a biography

Vocabulary: Prefixes and Suffixes

19. Using your knowledge of the suffix -*ation*, what is the most likely meaning of *accusation* in the following sentence?

    Luis denied her accusation.

    A. a type of communication
    B. a charge of wrongdoing
    C. a display of affection
    D. an urgent request

20. Using your knowledge of the suffix -*able*, what is the most likely meaning of *memorable* in the following sentence?

    The concert was a memorable occasion.

    A. worth remembering   C. making memories weaker
    B. not worth remembering   D. making memories clearer

21. Using your knowledge of the prefix *pre*-, what is the most likely meaning of *precaution* in the following sentence?

    She took the precaution of locking the windows.

    A. care taken after the fact   C. lack of care
    B. care taken in advance   D. insufficient care

22. Using your knowledge of the prefix *be*-, what is the most likely meaning of *befriend* in the following sentence?

    We will befriend the new student.

    A. introduce to a friend   C. find friends for
    B. give friendly advice to   D. treat as a friend

23. What does the prefix *pre-* mean?
    A. before
    B. after
    C. back
    D. again

24. To which of the following words could you successfully add the suffix *-ation*?
    A. efficient
    B. color
    C. jealous
    D. glamour

Grammar: Nouns

25. Which statement is true about common and proper nouns?
    A. A proper noun is more specific than a common noun.
    B. A proper noun is more polite than a common noun.
    C. A common noun usually begins with a capital letter.
    D. A proper noun usually does not begin with a capital letter.

26. How many proper nouns are in this sentence?

    Last Labor Day, Marcos and his cousin visited the Grand Canyon.

    A. one
    B. two
    C. three
    D. four

27. Which sentence below uses correct capitalization?
    A. Did Sue see the Golden Gate Bridge or any museums when she visited San Francisco?
    B. Did Sue see the golden gate Bridge or any museums when she visited San francisco?
    C. Did Sue see the Golden Gate Bridge or any Museums when she visited San Francisco?
    D. Did sue see the golden gate bridge or any museums when she visited san Francisco?

28. How do you form the plural of most nouns?
    A. add *-ies* or *-ed*
    B. add *-s* or *-es*
    C. change the last *a* or *o* to an *e* or *i*
    D. add *-s* or *-x*

29. Which of these sentences uses plural nouns correctly?
    A. The womens put the chocolate mouses in boxes and wrapped them for their familyes.
    B. The womans put the chocolate mices in boxes and wrapped them for their families.
    C. The women put the chocolate mice in boxies and wrapped them for their familys.
    D. The women put the chocolate mice in boxes and wrapped them for their families.

30. Which rule should you follow to form possessive nouns?
  A. To form the possessive of most singular nouns, add just an apostrophe to the noun.
  B. To form the possessive of plural nouns that end in *s*, add an apostrophe and *s*.
  C. To form the possessive of plurals that do not end in s, add an apostrophe and *s*.
  D. Do not use apostrophes to form the possessive of most nouns.

31. Which of these sentences uses possessive nouns correctly?
  A. The two sisters' gift to the charity's drive was a pile of hand-sewn children's clothing.
  B. The two sister's gift to the charitys' drive was a pile of hand-sewn childrens' clothing.
  C. The two sister's gift to the charity's drive was a pile of hand-sewn children's clothing.
  D. The two sister's gift to the charitys' drive was a pile of hand-sewn childrens' clothing.

ESSAY

Writing

32. Think of the plot of a book or story that you really liked. Then, on your paper or a separate sheet, write an imaginary news report about the events of the book or story.

33. Think of an event or experience that was very important to your life. Then, on this paper or a separate sheet, jot down your ideas for a brief autobiographical narrative about the event or experience. Use this paper or a separate sheet.

34. Think of a place that you consider very beautiful or very ugly. Then, describe it in a brief descriptive essay. Write your essay on your paper or on a separate sheet.

Unit 1: Fiction and Nonfiction Skills Concept Map—2

How do we decide what is true?

Literary Analysis:
Nonfiction

Words you can use to discuss the Big Question

| nonfiction narrative | has | an author's perspective | and | tone |

(demonstrated in this selection)

Selection name:

(demonstrated in this selection)

Selection name:

Reading Skills and Strategies:
Fact and Opinion

To understand the difference between **fact and opinion** → look for → **words or phrases that indicate an opinion** → and → **check facts by using resources**

(demonstrated in this selection)

Selection name:

Informational Text:
Atlas Entry

You can use **details** → to → make and support assertions

Basic Elements of Fiction and Nonfiction

• Characters
• Setting
• Plot
• Point of View

Types of Fiction and Nonfiction

• Novels and Novellas
• Essays
• Biographies and Autobiographies

Comparing Literary Works:
Symbols

often → have more than one meaning

often → are used to make a point

(demonstrated in these selections)

Selection names:

1.
2.

Student Log

Complete this chart to track your assignments.

Writing	Extend Your Learning	Writing Workshop	Other Assignments

Vocabulary Warm-up Word Lists

Study these words from "My Papa, Mark Twain." Then, complete the activities.

Word List A

charming [CHAHR ming] *adj.* delightful, pleasing
　　He's a <u>charming</u> fellow; everyone likes him right away.

desperate [DES per it] *adj.* willing to do nearly anything to fix a problem
　　I grew <u>desperate</u> when I couldn't find my homework.

fled [FLED] *v.* escaped, ran away
　　The mouse <u>fled</u> when it saw the cat.

humor [HYOO mer] *n.* the funny side of something
　　Everyone laughed when Neal fell in the lake, but he didn't see any <u>humor</u> in it.

rudely [ROOD lee] *adv.* crudely, not politely
　　If you keep speaking so <u>rudely</u> to him, the coach will take you off the team.

seldom [SEL dum] *adv.* not very often, rarely
　　Since we got our new car, we <u>seldom</u> take the bus.

snatched [SNACHT] *v.* grabbed quickly
　　Kirk <u>snatched</u> the sandwich away before his brother could eat it.

style [STYL] *n.* the way in which something is said, made, or done
　　The writer's <u>style</u> is full of humor and word play.

Word List B

acquaintance [uh KWAYN tuhns] *n.* someone you know, but not that well
　　He's just an <u>acquaintance</u>; I wouldn't call him a good friend.

author [AW ther] *n.* writer of a book or article
　　The <u>author</u> gave away copies of the book she had just written.

biography [by AHG ruh fee] *n.* a book that tells about the life of a person
　　I read a <u>biography</u> to find out more about George Washington's life.

enable [en AY buhl] *v.* make possible, allow
　　This key will <u>enable</u> you to enter the house.

reveal [ri VEEL] *v.* bring out into the open or make known
　　At the end of the show, the magician will <u>reveal</u> how he performed his tricks.

recognition [rek uhg NI shuhn] *n.* fame and attention
　　The fireman got a lot of <u>recognition</u> after saving the children from the burning store.

sympathetic [sim puh THET ik] *adj.* feeling or understanding for a person or situation
　　I was <u>sympathetic</u> when Tim told me about losing his lunch; I know what it's like to be hungry.

variety [vuh RY i tee] *n.* a group or selection of different things
　　The story had a <u>variety</u> of Halloween costumes—superheroes, monsters, even animals.

"My Papa, Mark Twain" by Susy Clemens
Vocabulary Warm-up Exercises

Exercise A *Fill in each blank in the paragraph below with an appropriate word from Word List A. Use each word only once.*

Hannah's favorite lunchroom activity was teasing her best friend Seth. "One day you'll get in trouble for your bad behavior. You always act so [1] _____,"

she said. "Why can't you be [2] _____ like me?" Seth

[3] _____ paid attention to Hannah's teasing but, when dessert

came, he [4] _____ the cupcake Hannah wanted off the tray. "I

guess 'charming' just isn't my [5] _____," Seth said as he quickly

[6] _____ with the cupcake. Hannah didn't find any

[7] _____ in this action. She was [8] _____ to get the

cupcake back and made a mad dash after him.

Exercise B *Write a complete sentence to answer each question. For each item, use a word from Word List B to replace the underlined word or phrase without changing its meaning.*

1. What is one way a pop star can gain a lot of <u>fame and attention</u>?

   _____

2. Name a situation in which you might meet <u>someone for the first time</u>.

   _____

3. Where could you find a <u>book that tells the story of a famous person's life</u>?

   _____

4. Name one device that would <u>make it possible</u> for you to cook a hot dog.

   _____

5. How can you <u>bring out into the open</u> the secret identity of a masked superhero?

   _____

6. Where can you go to find a <u>selection of different things</u> to buy?

   _____

7. Does your teacher <u>show understanding</u> if you turn in your homework late?

   _____

8. How might a <u>writer</u> find ideas for a book?

   _____

"My Papa, Mark Twain" by Susy Clemens
Reading Warm-up A

Read the following passage. Pay special attention to the underlined words. Then, read it again, and complete the activities. Use a separate sheet of paper for your written answers.

It can be difficult having a famous father. I know that might seem hard to believe, but it's true. My dad is a movie star. He's good-looking, famous, and <u>charming</u>. Everyone wants to be in the same room with him. Everyone likes it when he's around. He plays all the mighty heroes and adventurers in the movies. He's always beating up the bad guys and is <u>seldom</u> defeated. After all, heroes rarely lose. When he does lose, the kids in my class are sure to give me a hard time.

"Hey Will, what happened to your father?" was the first thing I heard when I walked into the school cafeteria on the Monday after *Revenge of the Creatures* came out.

"That monster tossed your dad around like a marshmallow," my friend Jake said. "I thought your dad's <u>style</u> was playing the tough guy. He didn't look too tough in *Revenge of the Creatures*."

Jake laughed hysterically, and the rest of the table laughed too. I failed to find the <u>humor</u> in it. It just wasn't funny. Don't these guys know that movies aren't real?

I wanted to run away, but if I <u>fled</u>, I knew that it would just make it worse. I was <u>desperate</u> to come up with something snappy to say back to Jake, but I couldn't think of anything. Angrily, I <u>snatched</u> my lunch out of my backpack and sat down to eat. I was mad at my dad for making a movie in which he didn't win, and I was mad at Jake for acting so <u>rudely</u>.

After a few minutes, Jake came over and apologized. I forgave him. Sometimes, though, I do wish my father just went in to an office like everybody else's dad.

1. Underline a sentence that proves that the narrator's father is <u>charming</u>. When is it important to be *charming*?

2. Underline the nearby word that has a similar meaning to <u>seldom</u>. List something you *seldom* do.

3. Circle the words that identify Will's father's <u>style</u>. Describe the *style* of your favorite movie star.

4. Circle words that tell you that Jake *did* find <u>humor</u> in the situation. What is something you find *humor* in?

5. Underline the words that have nearly the same meaning as <u>fled</u>. Name a situation from which people have *fled*.

6. Write a sentence describing a time when someone might feel <u>desperate</u>.

7. Using a synonym for <u>snatched</u>, write a sentence describing Will's action of taking his lunch out of his backpack.

8. Write a sentence giving an example of how Jake was acting <u>rudely</u>. What is the opposite of behaving *rudely*?

Name _____ Date _____

"**My Papa, Mark Twain**" by Susy Clemens
Reading Warm-up B

Read the following passage. Pay special attention to the underlined words. Then, read it again, and complete the activities. Use a separate sheet of paper for your written answers.

Samuel Clemens, otherwise known as Mark Twain, earned <u>recognition</u> as one of America's finest writers. A master writer, Clemens deserved this fame. He was an expert at creating <u>sympathetic</u> characters. Huck Finn and Tom Sawyer are just two examples of characters that were easy for people to relate to and understand.

If you open a <u>biography</u> of the <u>author</u>, you will discover that the writer's life was almost as interesting as those of his characters. It will <u>enable</u> you to gain a greater appreciation for his work. Samuel Clemens was born in Missouri and grew up in the Midwest. This became the setting for many of his works. Studying his biography will <u>reveal</u> how heavily books like *The Adventures of Tom Sawyer* draw upon Clemens's experiences in the place where he grew up.

As an adult, Clemens held a <u>variety</u> of jobs. He worked as a printer's assistant. He worked as a riverboat pilot and as a miner. He worked as a reporter. His jobs took him all over the country. San Francisco, Nevada, and Philadelphia were just a few of the places he called home.

One interesting fact from Clemens's biography is his connection with Halley's comet. Halley's comet is a space object that makes a huge orbit around the sun. The orbit takes about seventy-six years. It showed up on the night Clemens was born in 1835. The next time it came back was on the night he died in 1910.

For many, that night was a very sad moment. You didn't have to be a friend or <u>acquaintance</u> of Clemens to mourn the man and his work. Few authors have written so many great books in a lifetime.

1. Underline the nearby word that has a similar meaning to <u>recognition</u>. Write a sentence using the word ***recognition***.

2. Underline the phrase that helps explain the word <u>sympathetic</u>. Name a character from a story or movie for whom you feel ***sympathetic***.

3. Would a fictional story written by Clemens be a <u>biography</u>? Explain.

4. Circle the nearby word that has a similar meaning to <u>author</u>. Which ***author*** does this sentence tell about?

5. Rewrite this sentence replacing the word <u>enable</u> with a word or phrase of similar meaning.

6. In your own words, explain what Clemens's biography will <u>reveal</u> about the setting of his books.

7. Write a sentence listing the <u>variety</u> of jobs Clemens held.

8. Who do you think would be sadder at Clemens's death: a friend or an <u>acquaintance</u>? Explain.

Name _____ Date _____

"My Papa, Mark Twain" by Susy Clemens
Writing About the Big Question

How do we decide what is true?

Big Question Vocabulary

confirm	decision	determine	evidence	fact
fantasy	fiction	investigate	opinion	prove
realistic	study	test	true	unbelievable

A. *Use one or more words from the list above to complete the following sentences.*

1. Often people form an _____ about another person that is not
   _____.

2. It is not _____ to think you know somebody with whom you have
   very little personal contact.

3. To make a _____ about a person, you must get to know him or her.

4. Impressions that we have about public figures may be wrong because they are not
   based on _____.

B. *Answer the questions. Use at least one Big Question vocabulary word in each
answer.*

1. What opinion might somebody form about you when he or she first met you?

   _____

   _____

   _____

2. What part of that opinion would be realistic? What would be false?

   _____

   _____

   _____

C. *Complete the sentence below. Then, write a short paragraph connecting this situation
to the Big Question.*

   To find out what a person is really like, you must _____

   _____

   _____

   _____

   _____

   _____

"My Papa, Mark Twain" by Susy Clemens
Reading: Recognize Clues That Indicate Fact or Opinion

Nonfiction works often include an author's opinion as well as facts. A **fact** is information that can be proved. An **opinion** is a person's judgment or belief. **Recognizing clues that indicate an opinion** will help you evaluate a work of nonfiction. To do this:

- Look for phrases that indicate an opinion, such as *I believe* or *in my opinion*.
- Look for words that indicate a personal judgment, such as *wonderful* or *terrible*.
- Be aware of words such as *always, nobody, worst,* and *all* that might indicate a personal judgment or viewpoint.

Fact: Susy Clemens wrote a biography of her father when she was thirteen.

Opinion: It is obvious from her biography that Susy loved her father all her life.

DIRECTIONS: *Read the following passages from Susy Clemens's description of* The Prince and the Pauper *in "My Papa, Mark Twain." Underline details that indicate an opinion, personal judgment, or viewpoint. On the lines below each passage, rewrite the passage to include only facts. The first one has been done for you.*

1. Papa's appearance has been described many times, but <u>very incorrectly</u>.

   Fact: Papa's appearance has been described many times.

2. One of papa's latest books is "The Prince and the Pauper" and it is unquestionably the best book he has ever written, . . .

   Fact: _____

   _____

3. I have wanted papa to write a book that would reveal something of his kind sympathetic nature, and "The Prince and the Pauper" partly does it.

   Fact: _____

   _____

4. The book is full of lovely charming ideas, and oh the language! It is perfect.

   Fact: _____

   _____

5. I never saw a man with so much variety of feeling as papa has; now "The Prince and the Pauper" is full of touching places, but there is always a streak of humor in them somewhere.

   Fact: _____

   _____

Name _____   Date _____

"My Papa, Mark Twain" by Susy Clemens
Literary Analysis: Author's Perspective

An **author's perspective** is the viewpoint from which he or she writes. This perspective is based on the writer's beliefs and background. The author's perspective reveals his or her own feelings or personal interest in a subject.

Many authors have written a biography of Mark Twain. Most of them include details that reveal their perspective, feelings, or personal interest. For instance, a biographer who dislikes Twain might include details that reveal these feelings. Twain's daughter Susy adored her father. She includes the kind of details that reveal her love for him.

A. DIRECTIONS: *Read the following passage from "My Papa, Mark Twain." Then, answer the questions.*

> We know papa played "Hookey" all the time. And how readily would papa pretend to be dying so as not to have to go to school! Grandma wouldn't make papa go to school, so she let him go into a printing office to learn the trade. He did so, and gradually picked up enough education to enable him to do about as well as those who were more studious in early life.

1. What situation or event does the author describe?

   _____

   _____

2. How does the author feel about her father's dislike of school?

   _____

   _____

3. Underline the parts of the passage that reveal the author's perspective on the results of her father's education.

B. DIRECTIONS: *Write a brief letter that Grandma (Mark Twain's mother) might write to a relative. In the letter, show Grandma's perspective on her son's reluctance to attend school.*

   _____

   _____

   _____

   _____

   _____

   _____

   _____

   _____

"My Papa, Mark Twain" by Susy Clemens
Vocabulary Builder

Word List

absent-minded   consequently   impatient   incessantly   peculiar   striking

A. DIRECTIONS: *For each item below, follow the instructions and write a sentence. Be sure that you use the Word List words correctly and that your sentence expresses the meaning of each word.*

1. Use *absent-minded* and *consequently* in a sentence about homework.

   _____

   _____

   _____

2. Use *striking* and *incessantly* in a sentence about a fireworks display.

   _____

   _____

   _____

3. Use *impatient* in a sentence about standing in a long line of customers at a store.

   _____

   _____

4. Use *peculiar* in a sentence about a strange costume.

   _____

   _____

B. WORD STUDY: The Latin root *-sequ-* or *-sec-* means "to follow." Use context clues and what you know about this root to answer each question.

1. What is the correct *sequential* order of these months: May, February, March, September?

   _____

2. Which student would be most likely to attend a *secondary* school, a 5-year-old or a 16-year-old? Explain.

   _____

3. Would a *sequacious* person tend to be a leader or a follower? Explain.

   _____

"My Papa, Mark Twain" by Susy Clemens
Enrichment: Expressing Facts and Opinions

Susy Clemens's perspective on Mark Twain was that he could do no wrong. It would have been difficult for her to describe him in a way that included only facts. Try writing your own description of someone you admire.

A. DIRECTIONS: *Think of someone you admire a great deal, such as a family member, a friend, or a national hero you have seen on TV. Then, answer these questions.*

1. Whom have you chosen? _____

2. What is your opinion of this person? _____

3. What character traits and achievements support your opinion of this person?

   _____

   _____

   _____

   _____

4. What are some facts about this person? Include only details that can be checked or proved. For example, you might list age, height, eye and hair color, and where the person lives.

   _____

   _____

   _____

   _____

B. DIRECTIONS: *On the following lines, describe your subject in two ways. In the first paragraph, write sentences that include only facts. In the second paragraph, combine facts and opinions to show your perspective on the person.*

Paragraph 1 (Only the facts): _____

_____

_____

_____

Paragraph 2 (Facts and opinions): _____

_____

_____

_____

_____

"My Papa, Mark Twain" by Susy Clemens
Open-Book Test

Short Answer *Write your responses to the questions in this section on the lines provided.*

1. In "My Papa, Mark Twain," Susy Clemens writes that her father was absentminded. What would an absentminded person do with an umbrella on a rainy day?

   _____

   _____

2. A fact is information that can be checked and proved. An opinion is a person's judgment or belief. In "My Papa, Mark Twain," Susy Clemens writes, "Our burglar alarm is often out of order." Explain why this statement is a fact or why it is an opinion.

   _____

   _____

3. In "My Papa, Mark Twain," Twain goes down and opens a window. Consequently, the alarm bell rings. Use the word *consequently* to describe another situation in the biography.

   _____

   _____

   _____

4. In "My Papa, Mark Twain," Susy Clemens includes a description of Twain's problems with a burglar alarm. Consider what Twain does not understand about the situation. Then, explain what Susy wants to reveal about her father by including this description.

   _____

   _____

5. Explain why Susy Clemens includes the paragraph about pet cats in "My Papa, Mark Twain."

   _____

   _____

   _____

6. In writing about her father's story, Susy Clemens says, "I think that one of the most touching scenes in it is where the pauper is riding on horseback with his nobles. . . ." Explain why this statement is an opinion. Identify the phrase that indicates an opinion and the one that indicates a personal judgment.

   _____

   _____

   _____

7. In each of the two detail boxes, write a detail from "My Papa, Mark Twain" showing Susy's opinion of *The Prince and the Pauper.* Then, use these details to write a sentence in the third box describing Susy's perspective of her father's writing.

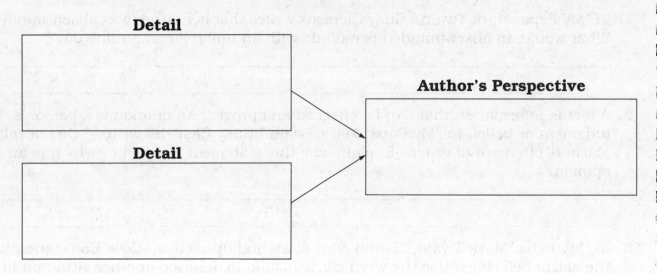

Detail

Detail

Author's Perspective

8. What reason might Susy Clemens have had for writing "My Papa, Mark Twain"? Use details from the biography to support your answer.

_____

_____

_____

9. Think about what Susy Clemens knows about Mark Twain that others do not. What perspective, or viewpoint, can she bring to "My Papa, Mark Twain" that another author could not? Use details from the biography in your answer.

_____

_____

_____

_____

10. Suppose that a biographer not related to Mark Twain wrote about him. Explain how that biography would show a different attitude toward the subject than "My Papa, Mark Twain."

_____

_____

_____

_____

Essay

Write an extended response to the question of your choice or to the question or questions your teacher assigns you.

11. In "My Papa, Mark Twain," Susy Clemens tells what it is like to have Mark Twain as a father. In an essay, discuss whether you think Twain is a good father. Consider how Susy describes him and how she feels about him. Think about what kind of relationship they have. Use details from the biography to support your ideas.

12. In "My Papa, Mark Twain," Susy Clemens writes about her father's bad qualities as well as his good ones. In an essay, describe Mark Twain's good points and faults as Susy Clemens sees them. Include examples from the biography in your answer.

13. Suppose that Mark Twain had written this selection about himself. In an essay, explain how his version might differ from "My Papa, Mark Twain" and how it might be similar.

14. **Thinking About the Big Question: How do we decide what is true?** In "My Papa, Mark Twain," the reader gets Susy Clemens's perspective of her father. A loving daughter might be partial to her father. In an essay, discuss what parts of the biography you believe and what parts you doubt. Use details from the biography to support your ideas about what you think is true.

Oral Response

15. Go back to question 5, 8, 9, or 10 or to the question your teacher assigns to you. Take a few minutes to expand your answer and prepare an oral response. Find additional details in "My Papa, Mark Twain" that support your points. If necessary, make notes to guide your response.

Name _____ Date _____

"My Papa, Mark Twain" by Susy Clemens
Selection Test A

Critical Reading *Identify the letter of the choice that best answers the question.*

____ 1. In "My Papa, Mark Twain," what does Susy Clemens's perspective, or viewpoint, reveal?
    A. what she thinks about herself and her sister
    B. information about the main problems of her time
    C. how much she knows about her father's books
    D. her feelings about and personal interest in her father

____ 2. Which detail from "My Papa, Mark Twain" most clearly reveals that this biography was written by Mark Twain's daughter?
    A. Clara and I are sure that Papa played a trick on Grandma.
    B. He smokes a great deal.
    C. Some of the simplest things he can't understand.
    D. He doesn't like to go to church at all.

____ 3. In "My Papa, Mark Twain," Susy Clemens describes how her father looks. Which detail is in her description?
    A. beautiful black hair
    B. kind brown eyes
    C. a sad, care-worn face
    D. a wonderfully shaped head

____ 4. Which phrase best describes Mark Twain as Susy Clemens presents him?
    A. strict and proper
    B. youthful and athletic
    C. quiet and shy
    D. humorous and kind

____ 5. A fact is information that can be checked and proved. An opinion is a person's judgment or belief. Which detail from "My Papa, Mark Twain" is a fact?
    A. A mugwump is pure from the marrow out.
    B. He doesn't wear a beard.
    C. He is the loveliest man I ever saw or ever hope to see.
    D. It is unquestionably the best book he has ever written.

_____ 6. Which detail from "My Papa, Mark Twain" is most clearly an opinion?
   A. We consist of Papa, Mamma, Jean, Clara, and me.
   B. The switch hovered in the air.
   C. She let him go into a printing office to learn the trade.
   D. It is a wonderfully beautiful and touching little scene.

_____ 7. In "My Papa, Mark Twain," why do you think Susy Clemens includes the description of Twain's problems with the burglar alarm?
   A. It shows that Twain has a good imagination.
   B. It shows that he does not have a logical mind.
   C. It shows why Twain's wife had to work so hard.
   D. It shows that he understands and fixes problems of every kind.

_____ 8. Which pair of phrases indicates an opinion in the following passage from "My Papa, Mark Twain"?
   I think that one of the most touching scenes in it is where the pauper is riding on horseback with his nobles in the "recognition procession" and he sees his mother . . .
   A. I think/most touching
   B. is where/the pauper is riding
   C. on horseback/with his nobles
   D. in the "recognition procession"/he sees his mother

_____ 9. What does Susy Clemens's perspective add to "My Papa, Mark Twain" that another author's could not add?
   A. a list of Mark Twain's books
   B. personal details about Mark Twain and his family
   C. the names of Mark Twain's family members
   D. a description of Mark Twain's appearance

Vocabulary and Grammar

_____ 10. Which word or phrase is closest in meaning to *consequently* as it is used in this sentence?
   Papa went down and opened the window; <u>consequently</u> the alarm bell rang.
   A. finally
   B. as a result
   C. to begin with
   D. surprisingly

_____ **11.** Which sentence uses a personal possessive pronoun?

    A. I just went down to see if it would ring!

    B. The old lady whirled around and snatched her skirts out of danger.

    C. I know you not, woman.

    D. He told us the other day.

_____ **12.** How many personal possessive pronouns are used in this sentence?

    He has got a temper, but we all of us have in this family.

    A. none

    B. one

    C. two

    D. three

Essay

13. Use information from "My Papa, Mark Twain" to write an essay telling whether you would like or dislike having Mark Twain as a father.

14. Susy Clemens includes Mark Twain's bad qualities (as she sees them) as well as his good qualities in her biography. In an essay, describe Mark Twain as Susy Clemens sees him.

15. Thinking About the Big Question: How do we decide what is true? In "My Papa, Mark Twain," the reader learns what Susy Clemens thinks and feels about her father. However, a loving daughter might not be the most trustworthy biographer. In an essay, discuss the parts of the biography you believe and the parts you doubt. Use details from the biography to support your ideas about what you think is true.

Name _____   Date _____

"My Papa, Mark Twain" by Susy Clemens
Selection Test B

Critical Reading *Identify the letter of the choice that best completes the statement or answers the question.*

____ 1. Which detail from "My Papa, Mark Twain" shows most clearly that it was written from the perspective of Twain's daughter?
   A. Clara and I are sure that papa played the trick on Grandma about the whipping that is related in *The Adventures of Tom Sawyer.* . . .
   B. . . . *The Prince and the Pauper* is full of touching places, but there is always a streak of humor in them somewhere.
   C. His complexion is very fair, and he doesn't wear a beard.
   D. He has beautiful gray hair, not any too thick or any too long. . . .

____ 2. In "My Papa, Mark Twain," what does Susy Clemens mean when she writes the following?

   I never saw a man with so much variety of feeling as papa has.

   A. She never met her father.
   B. Mark Twain never showed his feelings.
   C. Mark Twain could express many different emotions in his writing.
   D. She never saw her father laugh.

____ 3. In "My Papa, Mark Twain," the number of cats in the Twain home is a detail that supports the idea that
   A. Twain is very absent-minded.
   B. Twain does not care about keeping a neat home.
   C. Twain loves animals.
   D. Twain was writing a book about cats.

____ 4. In "My Papa, Mark Twain," Susy Clemens reveals her unique perspective on the subject of her father when she
   A. tells the names of the family cats.
   B. says she has read many of her father's books.
   C. tells who is in her family.
   D. reveals personal stories about her father at home.

____ 5. According to the information Susy Clemens presents in "My Papa, Mark Twain," her father could best be described as
   A. strict, proper, and predictable.
   B. practical, energetic, and lively.
   C. quiet, shy, and serious.
   D. humorous, absent-minded, and affectionate.

____ 6. Which of these details from "My Papa, Mark Twain" is the clearest statement of fact?
   A. He hasn't extraordinary teeth.
   B. I shall have no trouble in not knowing what to say about him.
   C. Our burglar alarm is often out of order.
   D. A mugwump is pure from the marrow out.

___ 7. In "My Papa, Mark Twain," what does Susy Clemens tell you about Mark Twain in this passage?

> . . . he could listen to himself talk for hours without getting tired, of course he said this in joke, but I've no dought it was founded on truth.

A. Twain was a good and sympathetic listener.
B. Twain enjoyed talking more than listening to others.
C. Twain liked to make fun of people.
D. Twain preferred writing to speaking.

___ 8. Which of the following sentences from "My Papa, Mark Twain" is an opinion?
A. We consist of Papa, Mamma, Jean, Clara, and me.
B. It is a wonderfully beautiful and touching little scene. . . .
C. The switch hovered in the air.
D. Grandma wouldn't make Papa go to school, so she let him go into a printing office to learn the trade.

___ 9. In "My Papa, Mark Twain," Twain's problem with the burglar alarm shows that
A. Twain has trouble understanding how such devices work.
B. Twain is not concerned about keeping his house secure from burglary.
C. Twain has a good imagination.
D. Twain is very helpful with chores around the home.

___ 10. In "My Papa, Mark Twain," what excuse does Susy Clemens give for her father's not being able to understand how the burglar alarm works?
A. He has no mechanical ability.
B. He cannot be bothered with unimportant things.
C. He has the mind of a writer and cannot understand simple things.
D. Her mother takes care of things like that.

___ 11. Which clue indicates that the following passage from "My Papa, Mark Twain" is an opinion?

> One of papa's latest books is *The Prince and the Pauper* and it is unquestionably the best book he has ever written, some people want him to keep to his old style, . . .

A. One of papa's latest books
B. unquestionably the best
C. some people
D. his old style

___ 12. If a biographer who is not related to Mark Twain wrote about him, what would probably be the biggest difference between that description and Susy Clemens's description in "My Papa, Mark Twain"?
A. It would have more details based on Internet research.
B. It would contain both negative and positive criticism of Twain's books.
C. It would contain more information about the narrator.
D. It would not reveal such a loving attitude toward Twain.

Vocabulary and Grammar

____ 13. The word most nearly opposite to the word *extraordinary* is
    A. exceptional.
    B. wonderful.
    C. readily.
    D. usual.

____ 14. Which of the following sentences contains a personal possessive pronoun?
    A. I have just opened the window to see.
    B. "Why, Youth," mamma replied. "If you've opened the window, why of course the alarm will ring!"
    C. The old lady whirled around and snatched her skirts out of danger.
    D. We know papa played "Hookey" all the time.

____ 15. How many personal pronouns are in the following sentence?
    All his features are perfect except that he hasn't extraordinary teeth.

    A. one
    B. two
    C. three
    D. none

____ 16. What is the meaning of *incessantly* as used in this sentence?
    During the storm, the waves crashed incessantly against the dock.

    A. forgetfully
    B. continually
    C. softly
    D. exceptionally

Essay

17. In "My Papa, Mark Twain," Susy Clemens creates a vivid portrait of her father. Write an essay that tells the good points and the faults that Clemens reveals about her father.

18. Write an essay about Susy Clemens's perspective of her relationship with her father, Mark Twain. Include facts about the relationship as well as Susy Clemens's opinions that are included in "My Papa, Mark Twain."

19. **Thinking About the Big Question: How do we decide what is true?** In "My Papa, Mark Twain," the reader gets Susy Clemens's perspective of her father. A loving daughter might be partial to her father. In an essay, discuss what parts of the biography you believe and what parts you doubt. Use details from the biography to support your ideas about what you think is true.

Study these words from "Stage Fright." Then, complete the activities that follow.

Word List A

awed [AWD] *v.* amazed
The crowd was <u>awed</u> when the hitter slammed a five-hundred foot home run.

audience [AW dee uhns] *n.* people gathered to watch something
The movie drew a large <u>audience</u> on its first day in the theaters.

auditorium [aw di TAWR ee uhm] *n.* a large room where people come to see something
There weren't enough seats in the <u>auditorium</u> for all the people.

appreciation [uh pree shee AY shun] *n.* thankfulness
To show my <u>appreciation</u> for helping me study, I thanked my tutor again and again.

horrible [HAWR uh buhl] *adj.* awful, terrible
The medicine tasted so <u>horrible</u> that Nancy spit it out right away.

kindness [KYND nes] *n.* friendliness, helpfulness
She showed her <u>kindness</u> by giving us an umbrella when we were caught in the rain.

memory [MEM uh ree] *n.* ability to remember things
Shelly's <u>memory</u> is so good she can remember something you said last year.

speech [SPEECH] *n.* text meant to be read aloud in front of a group of people
After winning the election, the candidate gave a <u>speech</u> thanking those who voted for him.

Word List B

agony [A guh nee] *n.* extreme suffering or pain
My tooth was causing such <u>agony</u> that I ran to the dentist's office.

applause [uh PLAWZ] *n.* clapping
The team heard lots of <u>applause</u> from the crowd after winning the big game.

lecture [LEK cher] *n.* talk given by a teacher or instructor to share information
The science teacher was giving a <u>lecture</u> to help people learn about chemistry.

manuscript [MAN yoo skript] *n.* written text that hasn't yet been printed as a book
The writer had finished working on the <u>manuscript</u> for his next novel.

occasion [uh KAY zhuhn] *n.* an event, a time when something happens
On the <u>occasion</u> of his fiftieth birthday, Granddad threw a party for the whole family.

seasick [SEE sik] *adj.* nauseous and dizzy from the rolling, tossing motion of a boat
On a transatlantic voyage, a storm at sea made many passengers <u>seasick</u>.

sympathy [SIM puh thee] *n.* a feeling of understanding for another person
I knew Tyrell felt bad about finishing last so I tried to show him my <u>sympathy</u>.

theater [THEE uh ter] *n.* place where performances are held or movies are shown
Hurry, I want to get to the <u>theater</u> before the movie starts.

Unit 1 Resources: Fiction and Nonfiction
152

Name _____ Date _____

Vocabulary Warm-up Exercises

Exercise A *Fill in each blank in the paragraph below with an appropriate word from Word List A. Use each word only once.*

The senator gave a dynamic [1] _____ in front of a large

[2] _____ of students. He spoke in the town's high-school

[3] _____. Many students and teachers thought he sounded

[4] _____ because of his sore throat. Others didn't mind. They were

[5] _____ by the amazing things that he said. The senator is known for

not using notes; instead, he speaks from [6] _____. Afterward, he

thanked the school for its [7] _____ in inviting him to speak. The

listeners clapped in [8] _____ of his thoughtful words.

Exercise B *Revise each sentence so that the underlined vocabulary word is used in a logical way. Be sure to keep the vocabulary word in your revision.*

Example: I always feel <u>seasick</u> when I ride in a car.
   I always feel <u>seasick</u> when I ride in a boat.

1. I don't like watching movies on TV; I prefer the small screen of a <u>theater</u>.

   _____

2. Tim didn't want to go to the <u>lecture</u> because he hates talking for long periods.

   _____

3. The novel is still a <u>manuscript</u>; it is already printed.

   _____

4. This candy is so good that I'm not saving it for a special <u>occasion</u>.

   _____

5. Marvin did so well in the race that he needed some <u>sympathy</u>.

   _____

6. The performance was so bad that the singer received lots of <u>applause</u>.

   _____

7. The pain medicine made the <u>agony</u> of my twisted ankle much worse.

   _____

"**Stage Fright**" by Mark Twain
Reading Warm-up A

Read the following passage. Pay special attention to the underlined words. Then, read it again, and complete the activities. Use a separate sheet of paper for your written answers.

I was nervous when the principal asked me to give a underline{speech}. I would have to write something to be read aloud at an assembly. The assembly was being held for Ms. Hagerty, a teacher who was leaving the school after many years. At the assembly, many people would speak about how much we would miss her.

It wasn't hard to find speakers; everyone loved Ms. Hagerty. She was known for her kindness and would do anything to help a student learn. She spent hours each week tutoring students after classes ended. Students and teachers had long been awed by her teaching skills. They were amazed at her ability to make almost any difficult subject easy to understand.

The assembly was being held in the auditorium, a large hall that was perfect for putting on plays and concerts. The audience was going to be huge—at least three or four hundred people.

The point of my speech was to express my appreciation for Ms. Hagerty. I wanted to show how thankful I was that she had been my teacher. To write it, I reached back into my memory, trying to recall all the great things she had done for me. It wasn't hard. She had helped me many, many times over the years.

Even though I wasn't used to speaking in front of people, giving the speech wasn't hard. There was one bad moment at first when I dropped the microphone. It made a horrible screeching sound that hurt everyone's ears. I picked it up again and calmed down. Then I talked about all the wonderful things that Ms. Hagerty had done. "We will miss her," I said. The audience seemed to agree. They clapped loudly when I finished speaking.

1. Underline the words that tell what a underline{speech} is. Then, tell what sort of person might have to give lots of *speech*es.

2. Underline an example of Ms. Hagerty's underline{kindness}. Then, write what *kindness* means.

3. Circle the nearby word that has a similar meaning to underline{awed}. Describe something that would leave you *awed*.

4. Underline the words that tell what an underline{auditorium} is used for. Describe the last time you were in an *auditorium*.

5. Underline the words that explain what the underline{audience} would be like. Then, tell what *audience* means.

6. In your own words, explain what the speech writer wants to show underline{appreciation} for.

7. Write a sentence telling why the speech writer reached back into underline{memory}.

8. Circle the words that show what made the underline{horrible} sound. Write about a *horrible* sound you heard recently.

"Stage Fright" by Mark Twain
Reading Warm-up B

Read the following passage. Pay special attention to the underlined words. Then, read it again, and complete the activities. Use a separate sheet of paper for your written answers.

Have you ever felt <u>seasick</u>? Have you ever had the horrible illness that many people feel on a boat? If so, then you might know what it feels like to have stage fright. Many performers, actors, singers, and dancers say that the <u>agony</u> of being seasick and the pain of having stage fright are very much alike.

The difference for people who perform in a <u>theater</u> is that they can avoid getting on a boat. They can't avoid stepping up on stage, however; and if they freeze, they won't hear <u>applause</u>. Instead, they'll hear hisses and jeers. Few people have <u>sympathy</u> for performers who fail. They can't understand a performer's troubles. They don't understand that stage fright can happen to anyone, even those who perform all the time.

Still, stage fright can be worse for those who aren't used to appearing in public. Writers, for example, spend much of their time alone. They're not often asked to speak in front of a room full of strangers. When they are—to read from an unpublished <u>manuscript</u>, for example—stage fright can easily set in. Even teachers can suffer stage fright. A professor giving a <u>lecture</u> on a subject he knows very well may suddenly freeze.

Luckily, stage fright is not impossible to cure. Experts have plenty of advice for people who need to get up on stage. The most important thing is to practice your performance ahead of time. If you are comfortable with your performance, you will probably do it well. Another tip is to try to relax before performing. There are many ways to do this, including yoga and listening to music. Also, experts say, there will be an <u>occasion</u> when stage fright shows up, no matter how a person prepares. When that happens, performers should try to welcome it. Saying "Hooray, I've got stage fright again" can help a person get over the fear.

1. Underline the words that tell where people feel <u>seasick</u>. What might you do if you feel *seasick*?

2. Circle the words that tell what is similar to the <u>agony</u> of being seasick. Then, tell what *agony* is.

3. Write a sentence telling what kind of people might perform in a <u>theater</u>.

4. Circle the words that tell who might not hear <u>applause</u>. Then, tell what *applause* means.

5. Underline words that tell why people don't have <u>sympathy</u> for some performers. Then, tell what *sympathy* means.

6. Based on the passage, what can writers often do with an unpublished <u>manuscript</u>? Tell what *manuscript* means.

7. Circle the words that tell what a professor might give a <u>lecture</u> about. Name a *lecture* would you like to attend.

8. Underline the words that tell what happens on the <u>occasion</u> mentioned in this sentence. Then, tell what *occasion* means.

"Stage Fright" by Mark Twain
Writing About the Big Question

How do we decide what is true?

Big Question Vocabulary

confirm	decision	determine	evidence	fact
fantasy	fiction	investigate	opinion	prove
realistic	study	test	true	unbelievable

A. *Use one or more words from the list above to complete the following sentences.*

1. Sometimes what somebody shows on the outside is not a _____ reflection of how they are feeling.

2. To get a _____ idea of how someone is feeling, you should ask him or her.

3. If you think it is _____ for an actor to be calm in front of a large audience, you may be right. He may be acting.

4. An actor in a play is creating a _____ for the audience.

B. *Respond to each item. Use at least two Big Question vocabulary words in each answer.*

1. How could you confirm that a friend is feeling okay when you think she might be feeling bad but hiding it?

   _____

   _____

   _____

2. In what circumstance might you make the decision to hide your true feelings?

   _____

   _____

   _____

C. *Complete the sentence below. Then, write a short paragraph connecting this situation to the Big Question.*

   If a friend needed help hiding his or her true feelings, _____

   _____

   _____

   _____

"Stage Fright" by Mark Twain
Reading: Recognize Clues That Indicate Fact or Opinion

Nonfiction works often include an author's opinion as well as facts. A **fact** is information that can be proved. An **opinion** is a person's judgment or belief. **Recognizing clues that indicate an opinion** will help you evaluate a work of nonfiction. To do this:

- Look for phrases that indicate an opinion, such as *I believe* or *in my opinion.*
- Look for words that indicate a personal judgment, such as *wonderful* or *terrible.*
- Be aware of words such as *always, nobody, worst,* and *all* that might indicate a personal judgment or viewpoint.

Fact: "Stage Fright" is a speech that Mark Twain gave after his daughter's first singing recital.

Opinion: "Stage Fright" is a funny description of Mark Twain's first stage appearance.

DIRECTIONS: *Read the following passages from Mark Twain's "Stage Fright." Underline details that indicate an opinion, personal judgment, or viewpoint. On the lines below each passage, rewrite the passage to include only facts. The first one has been done for you.*

1. If there is an <u>awful, horrible</u> malady in the world, it is stage fright—and seasickness.

 Fact: Stage fright and seasickness are illnesses.

2. It was dark and lonely behind the scenes in that theater, . . .

 Fact: _____

 _____

3. Right in the middle of the speech I had placed a gem.

 Fact: _____

 _____

4. I had put in a moving, pathetic part which was to get at the hearts and souls of my hearers.

 Fact: _____

 _____

5. Well, after the first agonizing five minutes, my stage fright left me, never to return.

 Fact: _____

 _____

Name _____ Date _____

"**Stage Fright**" by Mark Twain
Literary Analysis: Author's Perspective

An **author's perspective** is the viewpoint from which he or she writes. This perspective is based on the writer's beliefs and background. The author's perspective reveals his or her own feelings or personal interest in a subject.

"Stage Fright" is a speech that Mark Twain gave after his daughter sang in public. In his speech, Twain gives an account of the first time he gave a lecture in front of an audience. "Stage Fright" reveals his perspective or feelings about his first appearance on the stage.

A. DIRECTIONS: *Read the following passage from "Stage Fright." Then, answer the questions.*

> Right in the middle of the speech I had placed a gem. I had put in a moving, pathetic part which was to get at the hearts and souls of my hearers. When I delivered it, they did just what I hoped and expected. They sat silent and awed. I had touched them.

1. What situation or event does Mark Twain describe?

   _____

   _____

2. When he gave the lecture, how did Twain feel about the middle part of his speech?

   _____

   _____

3. How do you think Twain felt later about that part of his speech?

   _____

   _____

4. Twain says that the audience "sat silent and awed." How do you think the audience really felt?

   _____

   _____

5. Underline the part of the passage that reveals the author's perspective on his first appearance as a lecturer.

B. DIRECTIONS: *Imagine that you were in Mark Twain's audience the first time he spoke in public. Write a brief letter to a friend telling about the event from your perspective.*

   _____

   _____

   _____

   _____

   _____

"Stage Fright" by Mark Twain
Vocabulary Builder

Word List

agonizing   awed   compulsion   hereditary   intently   sympathy

A. DIRECTIONS: *For each item below, follow the instructions and write a sentence. Be sure that you use the italicized Word List words correctly and that your sentence expresses the meaning of each word.*

1. Use *compulsion* in a sentence about people who participate in a dangerous sport.

   _____

   _____

2. Use *intently* in a sentence about how a cat hunts a mouse.

   _____

   _____

3. Use *sympathy* in a sentence about a bike accident.

   _____

   _____

4. Use *awed* in a sentence about a tornado.

   _____

   _____

5. Use *agonizing* in a sentence about a difficult event.

   _____

   _____

6. Use *hereditary* in a sentence about the color of a person's eyes.

   _____

   _____

B. WORD STUDY: The Latin root -*pel*- or -*pul*- means "to drive." Words containing this root include *repulse* ("to drive people away due to poor behavior") and *propel* ("to push forward"). Consider the meanings of these two words as you revise the following sentences so that they make sense.

1. A child might *repulse* neighbors with kindness and courtesy.

   _____

2. The strong wind hit us in the face and *propelled* us onward.

   _____

"**Stage Fright**" by Mark Twain
Enrichment: Being a Reporter

Mark Twain began his newspaper career when he was in his mid-twenties. Before that, he tried his hand at gold mining in the Nevada territory. Despite his failure to find gold, he managed to write humorous accounts of his experiences. His stories, signed "Josh," landed him a job with a frontier newspaper. When he was twenty-eight, Twain moved to San Francisco and worked as a reporter for *The Morning Call*. A year later, he visited the Hawaiian Islands. He sent back serious and comic accounts of his experiences there for publication in the *Sacramento Union*.

A. DIRECTIONS: *Choose four qualities or skills from those listed below. For each item, list one of these skills and explain why it is important for someone who wants to become a reporter to develop the skill. Explain what specific actions (if any) a person can take to develop each skill.*

- Interest in a wide range of topics
- Athletic ability
- Ability to see humor in everyday events
- Ability to write well
- Ability to draw and build models
- Ability to talk to other people and put them at ease

1. _____
   _____
   _____

2. _____
   _____
   _____

3. _____
   _____
   _____

4. _____
   _____
   _____

B. DIRECTIONS: *On a separate sheet of paper, write a news story about a real or imaginary experience. For example, the experience could be one that you had while taking a trip with your family. Don't forget to answer the questions **W**ho? **W**hat happened? **W**hen? **W**here? **W**hy? and **H**ow? in your news story.*

"Stage Fright" by Mark Twain
"My Papa, Mark Twain" by Susy Clemens
Integrated Language Skills: Grammar

Possessive Personal Pronouns

A pronoun takes the place of a noun. **Possessive personal pronouns** show ownership. They can modify nouns or be used by themselves. Notice that a possessive pronoun never uses an apostrophe (').

Possessive Pronouns Used Before Nouns	Possessive Pronouns Used By Themselves
my	mine
your	yours
our	ours
their	theirs
her	hers
his	his
its	its

A. DIRECTIONS: *Underline the possessive personal pronoun in each sentence.*

1. This is a photo of our family.
2. His gray hair is not too thick or any too long, but just right.
3. Mother liked to carry her little kitten on her shoulder.
4. It troubles me that so few people really know my Papa.

B. DIRECTIONS: *Rewrite each sentence to replace the noun with a possessive personal pronoun. Then, rewrite the sentence again to use a possessive personal pronoun by itself. The first one has been done for you.*

1. This backpack belongs to you.   This is your backpack.   The backpack is yours.
2. Kathy's home is on Grant Street.

   _____

   _____

3. The speech that I will make will be brief.

   _____

   _____

4. The cheers you heard came from us.

   _____

   _____

"**My Papa, Mark Twain**" by Susy Clemens
"**Stage Fright**" by Mark Twain

Integrated Language Skills: Support for Writing a Dramatic Scene

Before you write your script for a dramatic scene, decide which passage from the selection you will use. Choose a passage that mentions a situation with at least two characters. Imagine what might happen before, during, and after that situation. You may invent words and actions that build on what Mark Twain said in his speech or on what Susy Clemens wrote about her father.

What happens in the passage you have chosen?

_____

_____

List the characters in your scene.

_____

_____

Use the chart below to make notes on the dialogue and actions in your scene.

Character and Characters' Dialogue	Actions

When you write your scene, place each character's name at the left. Follow the name with a colon. Stage directions are words that tell about the actions. Put your stage directions in brackets before or after the lines of dialogue. Here is an example of the format.

Governor's wife: How can I help you, Mr. Twain? I want you to give a wonderful speech in this magnificent theater.

[Governor's wife gestures grandly toward the theater seats.]

Twain: [in a nervous, shaky voice] I'm afraid no one is going to laugh at my jokes.

Use your notes to write your dramatic scene based on the passage you chose.

Name _____ Date _____

"My Papa, Mark Twain" by Susy Clemens
"Stage Fright" by Mark Twain

Integrated Language Skills: Support for Extend Your Learning

Research and Technology

"My Papa, Mark Twain" by Susy Clemens

Which of Mark Twain's books and characters will you feature on your poster? First, find a list of Twain's books on the Internet or at the library. Use words such as "*Mark Twain*" along with *characters* to do a keyword search on the Internet. To find out more about each character, use the character's name in your keyword search. Be aware that some libraries list Twain's works under his real name, Samuel Clemens.

You may have space on your poster for three or four books and their characters. Use the graphic organizer below to make notes on the information you gather.

Book Title	Characters

"Stage Fright" by Mark Twain

You and your partner will decide how you will research stage fright. One of you could go to the library, while the other might do a keyword search on the Internet.

Use the graphic organizer below to guide your questioning and to make notes on the information you gather.

Questions About Stage Fright	Notes
What causes stage fright?	
How does a person with stage fright feel?	
What are some suggestions for coping with stage fright?	

Name _____   Date _____

"**Stage Fright**" by Mark Twain
Open-Book Test

Short Answer *Write your responses to the questions in this section on the lines provided.*

1. Mark Twain writes, "If there is an awful, horrible malady in the world, it is stage fright—and seasickness." Tell which phrase is an opinion and explain how you know.

   _____

   _____

   _____

2. The author of "Stage Fright" uses both fact and opinion. In the chart, put a check mark in the second or third column to tell if the sentence is a fact or an opinion. Then, explain the reason for your choice in the last column.

Sentence	Fact	Opinion	Explanation
I'm older than I look.			
It was on a little ship on which there were two hundred other passengers.			

3. In "Stage Fright," Twain has the governor's wife watch him *intently.* Think about why she does this. Now imagine a dog watching its owner *intently* while trying to learn a trick. How interested is the dog in learning the trick? Explain.

   _____

   _____

   _____

4. In "Stage Fright," Twain gets to the theater forty-five minutes before his lecture. Consider how he feels about the lecture. Explain why he gets to the theater so early.

   _____

   _____

   _____

5. In "Stage Fright," the audience is silent and "awed" by a moving part of Twain's speech. Explain how a person could be awed by the sight of a towering mountain.

   _____

   _____

   _____

6. In "Stage Fright," Twain touches the audience with the middle of his speech. Explain what happens next and how it ruins the moment.

_____

_____

_____

7. Twain writes in "Stage Fright" that he placed several friends around the auditorium. What purpose, other than pounding sticks on the floor, do the friends serve?

_____

_____

_____

8. An author's perspective, or viewpoint, reveals his or her own feelings. The author of "Stage Fright" writes, "My knees were shaking so that I didn't know whether I could stand up." Explain what this statement reveals about how Twain was feeling right before his first big lecture.

_____

_____

_____

_____

9. In "Stage Fright," what is Twain's perspective on the middle of his speech? Provide evidence from the selection to support your response.

_____

_____

_____

10. How would you describe Twain's perspective about himself throughout "Stage Fright"? Use examples from the speech to support your answer.

_____

_____

_____

_____

Essay

Write an extended response to the question of your choice or to the question or questions your teacher assigns you.

11. In "Stage Fright," Mark Twain remembers how frightened he was when he gave his first lecture. He also discusses how he feels about the experience forty years later. In an essay, explain Twain's perspective, or viewpoint, on the experience as he thanks the audience for attending his daughter's recital.

12. In "Stage Fright," Twain turns a frightening situation into a positive one. In an essay, discuss how Twain is able to manage this change. Explain why he expects to fail even though he is well prepared for his lecture. Then, explain how failure turns into success.

13. "Stage Fright" is a speech Twain gave after his daughter's first public singing recital. In an essay, discuss why Twain might have chosen to give the speech when he did. Consider why Twain would talk about stage fright at his daughter's recital and why he would do it after instead of before her performance. Use details from the speech to support your ideas.

14. **Thinking About the Big Question: How do we decide what is true?** In "Stage Fright," Twain talks about the frightening experience of his first lecture. In an essay, discuss what is true from the perspective of his audience. Consider whether the audience has any idea of what he is truly feeling. Also consider what clues they might have used to determine the truth.

Oral Response

15. Go back to question 4, 6, 9, or 10 or to the question your teacher assigns to you. Take a few minutes to expand your answer and prepare an oral response. Find additional details in "Stage Fright" that support your points. If necessary, make notes to guide your response.

Name _____ Date _____

"Stage Fright" by Mark Twain
Selection Test A

Critical Reading *Identify the letter of the choice that best answers the question.*

____ 1. In "Stage Fright," Mark Twain tells about the time when he first spoke in front of an audience. What kind of lecture did he give?
   A. a lecture about the flag
   B. a speech about exercise
   C. a humorous lecture
   D. a lecture about overcoming fear

____ 2. In "Stage Fright," what do the words *stage fright* mean?
   A. fear of being alone in a theater after dark
   B. fear of appearing before an audience
   C. a performer's fear that the show will be canceled
   D. fear of falling off the stage

____ 3. In "Stage Fright," why does Twain get to the theater forty-five minutes before his lecture?
   A. He feels nervous about getting there.
   B. He is so sick he needs to lie down.
   C. He wants to make some changes in his lecture.
   D. He has to tell his friends what he wants them to do.

____ 4. Which statement includes words that indicate an opinion, or someone's personal judgment or belief?
   A. It was dark and lonely behind the scenes in that theater.
   B. I managed to get started without it.
   C. By and by it lighted up, and the audience began to arrive.
   D. I recall the occasion of my first appearance.

____ 5. Which statement from "Stage Fright" best shows the perspective that only the author could know?
   A. It was on a little ship on which there were two hundred other passengers.
   B. They sat silent and awed.
   C. You know what happened.
   D. My knees were shaking so that I didn't know whether I could stand up.

____ 6. In "Stage Fright," what happens when Twain glances up at the box where the governor's wife is sitting?

    A. She laughs loudly.

    B. She starts to cry.

    C. She falls out of her seat.

    D. She gets up and walks out of the theater.

____ 7. In this sentence, which words are clues that indicate an opinion, not a fact?

    If there is an awful, horrible malady in the world, it is stage fright—and seasickness.

    A. If there is

    B. an awful, horrible malady

    C. in the world

    D. it is stage fright—and seasickness

____ 8. In "Stage Fright," which sentence shows Twain's perspective on the first public lecture he gave forty years earlier?

    A. He thinks he learned a great deal from it.

    B. He believes he was too hard on his performance.

    C. He is still disappointed that the audience did not respond to his jokes.

    D. He will never forget being so scared.

____ 9. Which experience is most like Twain's experience in "Stage Fright"?

    A. taking piano lessons

    B. trying out for the school play

    C. making a soccer goal

    D. reading a book

Vocabulary and Grammar

____ 10. What is the meaning of the word *intently* in this sentence?

    The baseball players watched intently, afraid they might miss the coach's signal.

    A. with a shared feeling of sadness

    B. with force

    C. firmly directed

    D. filled with fear

____ 11. Which sentence from "Stage Fright" uses a personal possessive pronoun?

    A. So I bound myself by a hard-and-fast contract so that I could not escape.

    B. They were to pound those clubs on the floor.

    C. She was going to deliver a gubernatorial laugh.

    D. I had put in a moving, pathetic part which was to get at the hearts and souls of my hearers.

____ **12.** Which sentence uses an underlined vocabulary word incorrectly?

    A. We stared <u>intently</u> at the sky as we watched for falling stars.

    B. She expressed her sincere <u>sympathy</u> with a joyful cheer.

    C. We were <u>awed</u> by the power of the waves crashing on the rocks.

    D. If you feel a <u>compulsion</u> to talk, you may have to stay after school.

Essay

13. In "Stage Fright," Mark Twain recalls a scary experience he had long ago. He tells how he felt about it then and how he feels about it now. In an essay, describe Twain's perspective on that event, forty years later.

14. Use information from the selection "Stage Fright " to write an essay telling how Mark Twain turned failure into success.

15. **Thinking About the Big Question: How do we decide what is true?** In "Stage Fright," Twain talks about the frightening experience of his first lecture. In an essay, discuss what his audience might have decided was true about his performance. Consider whether the audience has any idea of what he is feeling. Use examples from the selection to support your ideas.

"Stage Fright" by Mark Twain
Selection Test B

Critical Reading *Identify the letter of the choice that best completes the statement or answers the question.*

____ 1. In "Stage Fright," what kind of performance did Twain give in San Francisco forty years earlier?
   A. a patriotic lecture about the flag
   B. a speech about being a reporter in San Francisco
   C. a humorous lecture
   D. a speech about fear

____ 2. In "Stage Fright," the definition of *stage fright* is
   A. fear of being an audience member.
   B. fear of appearing before an audience.
   C. fear of riding in stage coaches.
   D. fear of falling off a stage.

____ 3. In "Stage Fright," why does Twain get to the theater forty-five minutes before his lecture?
   A. He is nervous about making his first public appearance as a lecturer.
   B. He is so sick that he needs to lie down before the lecture begins.
   C. He needs time to make some last-minute changes and rehearse them.
   D. He meets his friends and tells them how he wants them to pound on the floor.

____ 4. Which statement is an opinion?
   A. It was dark and lonely behind the scenes in that theater.
   B. I managed to get started without it.
   C. By and by it lighted up, and the audience began to arrive.
   D. I recall the occasion of my first appearance.

____ 5. Which statement is a fact?
   A. I'm older than I look.
   B. It was on a little ship on which there were two hundred other passengers.
   C. I was young in those days and needed the exercise.
   D. They sat silent and awed.

____ 6. Which statement from "Stage Fright" best shows the perspective of the narrator?
   A. My heart goes out in sympathy to anyone who is making his first appearance.
   B. It was dark and lonely behind the scenes in that theater.
   C. By and by it lighted up, and the audience began to arrive.
   D. They sat silent and awed.

____ 7. In "Stage Fright," when Mark Twain glances up at the box where the governor's wife is sitting, she
   A. laughs loudly.
   B. starts to cry.
   C. falls out of her seat.
   D. gets up and walks out of the theater.

___ 8. In "Stage Fright," Twain reveals his perspective on the content of his speech when he
A. describes how he expected his friends to help him.
B. describes the theater before it fills with people.
C. describes the "gem" in his speech as "moving and pathetic."
D. compares stage fright with seasickness.

___ 9. In this passage, which phrase most clearly signals an opinion?
   If there is an awful, horrible malady in the world, it is stage fright—and seasickness.
A. If there is
B. an awful, horrible malady
C. in the world
D. it is stage fright—and seasickness

___ 10. Throughout "Stage Fright," Twain's perspective on himself might best be described as
A. unconcerned, out of touch with his own feelings.
B. anxious, eager to improve.
C. mocking, making fun of himself.
D. confident, sure of his own abilities.

___ 11. Which sentence best reflects Twain's perspective in "Stage Fright" as he looks back forty years at his first public lecture?
A. He thinks it was an important learning experience that he had to get through.
B. He believes that he was too critical of his performance at that time.
C. He is still disappointed that the audience did not respond as he had expected.
D. He is still scared when he makes public appearances.

___ 12. At the end of "Stage Fright," you find that Twain is making this speech primarily to
A. compare his stage fright long ago with his daughter's fears.
B. thank the audience for helping his daughter.
C. thank the audience for helping him overcome his fear.
D. attempt a comeback as humorous lecturer.

___ 13. Mark Twain's experience in "Stage Fright" is most like the experience you might have if
A. you do not try out for the school play.
B. you are trying out for the school play.
C. you star in the school play, and the audience loves your performance.
D. the school play is called "Stage Fright."

Vocabulary and Grammar

___ 14. Which word best fits the meaning of *compulsion* when Twain says that "nothing short of compulsion would get me to the theater."
A. force
B. driving
C. carrying
D. argument

____ **15.** Which word means nearly the same as *intently* as it is used here?

We laughed and applauded intently, refusing to stop until the speaker came back on stage to tell more jokes.

    A. sympathetically
    B. half-heartedly
    C. earnestly
    D. fearfully

____ **16.** How many personal possessive pronouns are in this sentence?

It was dark and lonely behind the scenes in that theater, and I peeked through the little peek holes they have in theater curtains and looked into the big auditorium.

    A. none
    B. one
    C. two
    D. three

____ **17.** Which sentence uses a personal possessive pronoun?
    A. It was dark and lonely behind the scenes in the theater.
    B. I had touched them.
    C. I had a number of friends of mine in the audience.
    D. You know what happened.

Essay

18. In "Stage Fright," Mark Twain looks back on an experience he had long ago. Write an essay describing his perspective of his experience and what he learned from it.

19. When someone "snatches victory from the jaws of defeat," it means the person turns what seems like a certain failure into success. In an essay, describe how Mark Twain snatched victory from the jaws of defeat in "Stage Fright." Explain why, even though he was well prepared for the lecture, he expected to fail. Then, describe the point at which failure turned into success.

20. **Thinking About the Big Question: How do we decide what is true?** In "Stage Fright," Twain talks about the frightening experience of his first lecture. In an essay, discuss what is true from the perspective of his audience. Consider whether the audience has any idea of what he is truly feeling. Also consider what clues they might have used to determine the truth.

"Names/Nombres" by Julia Alvarez

Vocabulary Warm-up Word Lists

Study these words from "Names/Nombres." Then, complete the activities.

Word List A

attended [uh TEN did] *v.* went to; was present in a place
My best friend and I have <u>attended</u> the same school since kindergarten.

constantly [KAHN stunt lee] *adv.* happening all the time, without stopping
Jill was upset that her sister was <u>constantly</u> late for school.

desire [di ZYR] *n.* a strong wish for something
His one <u>desire</u> was to get the lead in the school play.

embarrassed [em BAR ruhst] *adj.* feeling awkward or uncomfortable
The dog's bad behavior at the contest <u>embarrassed</u> its trainer.

included [in KLOO did] *adj.* contained something or someone as a part of something else
Jenna felt <u>included</u> in the group after Sally invited her to the sleepover.

occasions [uh KAY zhuhns] *n.* events or happenings
There were many <u>occasions</u>, such as weddings, when the whole family got together.

pitied [PIT eed] *v.* felt sorry for
We <u>pitied</u> the victims of the hurricane who lost their homes.

recently [REE suhnt lee] *adv.* having happened only a short time ago
As <u>recently</u> as last week, Sunita still thought her family was moving.

Word List B

apparent [uh PA ruhnt] *adj.* obvious or clear
It was <u>apparent</u> to everyone that Nicole was happy about her grade.

combination [kahm bi NAY shun] *n.* mixture of two or more things
The <u>combination</u> of peanut butter and jelly is delicious.

complicated [KAHM pli kay tid] *adj.* made of many parts, difficult
The model ship was very <u>complicated</u> to put together.

exotic [eg ZAH tik] *adj.* strange and fascinating
Her accent and unusual clothes made her seem very <u>exotic</u>.

homesick [HOHM sik] *adj.* missing your home and family
Although Tom loved summer camp, he was often <u>homesick</u>.

originally [uh RIJ uh nuhl lee] *adv.* at first
<u>Originally</u>, we were going to the beach for vacation, but then we changed our minds.

predicted [pruh DIK tid] *v.* guessed what will happen in the future
The weatherman <u>predicted</u> that tomorrow it would rain.

reveal [ri VEEL] *v.* make known
It was finally time to <u>reveal</u> the secret he had kept hidden all these years.

Name _____ Date _____

"Names/Nombres" by Julia Alvarez
Vocabulary Warm-up Exercises

Exercise A *Fill in each blank in the paragraph below with an appropriate word from Word List A. Use each word only once.*

Alphonse's face was [1] _____ red because he was always

[2] _____. Everyone [3] _____ him because he was so

shy and self-conscious. [4] _____, however, he has given in to his secret

[5] _____ to be a mime. He has [6] _____ many special

[7] _____, like birthday parties, dressed as a mime and performed for

the people there. These days, when anyone makes a guest list, Alphonse is always

[8] _____.

Exercise B *Revise each sentence so that the underlined vocabulary word is used in a logical way. Be sure to keep the vocabulary word in your revision.*

Example: After she <u>revealed</u> her true identity, no one knew who she was.
Until she <u>revealed</u> her true identity, no one knew who she was.

1. He could not believe that he had correctly <u>predicted</u> his past.

   _____

2. Everyone thought the game was so easy to play because it was <u>complicated</u>.

   _____

3. After Josh's vacation to <u>exotic</u> places, he felt really <u>homesick</u>.

   _____

4. Jen <u>originally</u> wanted to be Persephone, after she changed her mind.

   _____

5. It was <u>apparent</u> that Malik was unhappy, so no one could tell.

   _____

6. I ordered a <u>combination</u>, since I wanted only pepperoni on my pizza.

   _____

"Names/Nombres" by Julia Alvarez
Reading Warm-up A

Read the following passage. Pay special attention to the underlined words. Then, read it again, and complete the activities. Use a separate sheet of paper for your written answers.

The people living in the United States come from various backgrounds, but many have one thing in common. At some point, a relative, drawn by the hope for a better life, decided to come here to live. It may have happened many generations ago. Or perhaps it happened more <u>recently</u>, in the past several decades. Maybe it was even your parents who made the decision to come to the U.S.

When recent immigrants first arrive, life can be difficult. Most recent immigrants have one <u>desire</u>. They want to settle down and start living a normal life. However, it may take a while for this to happen. New arrivals are being bombarded <u>constantly</u> by words and images that are not familiar to them. The new information around them is nonstop. Many are too <u>embarrassed</u> to admit that they don't know what is going on. They are too uneasy to let others know they are confused. They fear being <u>pitied</u>, and they don't want that kind of sympathy. For them, social <u>occasions</u> can seem like an important test or exam. They are afraid to go to parties or sporting events without knowing the right things to do and say.

That's why, if you have recent immigrants in your school, it's important to help them feel <u>included</u>. Look for ways in which you can help them feel they belong. Keep in mind that the last school they <u>attended</u>, or went to, may have been nothing at all like your school. They may be confused and might not know what is expected of them. You can help by being positive and friendly. Sometimes all it takes to make someone feel at home is a big smile and a warm welcome.

1. Underline the words that tell you what <u>recently</u> means. Write a sentence about something that happened to you *recently*.

2. Underline the sentence that tells what most immigrants <u>desire</u>. What is one thing you *desire*?

3. Circle the things that are <u>constantly</u> bombarding immigrants. Then, tell what *constantly* means.

4. Underline the word that means almost the same thing as <u>embarrassed</u>. What is one thing that could make someone feel *embarrassed*?

5. Circle the phrase that tells you what <u>pitied</u> means. How would you feel if you knew you were *pitied*?

6. Name two <u>occasions</u> described in the article. Describe an important *occasion* that you have enjoyed.

7. Underline the phrase that tells you what <u>included</u> means. Do you feel *included* at your school? Why or why not?

8. Circle the phrase that means the same thing as <u>attended</u>. Then, name the school you *attended* before your present one.

Name _____   Date _____

"Names/Nombres" by Julia Alvarez
Reading Warm-up B

Read the following passage. Pay special attention to the underlined words. Then, read it again, and complete the activities. Use a separate sheet of paper for your written answers.

When I first arrived here, I spent almost all my time feeling alone, confused, and completely <u>homesick</u>. I missed my old school and my old friends more than I could have imagined. Everything here seemed so <u>exotic</u>, so strange and unknowable.

I cried myself to sleep almost every night, muffling my tears in my pillow so that my mom wouldn't hear me. I didn't want to <u>reveal</u> to her how unhappy I was, how lonely I felt. I couldn't let her see that.

<u>Originally</u>, we had planned to stay for only a year, but it was <u>apparent</u> that my mom was really happy here. Anyone could see it. So I hid my unhappiness and encouraged her to rethink our plans and stay permanently.

I could never have <u>predicted</u>, though, how things would turn out. I guess it's not that easy to know the future. Who would have guessed that I would make a best friend and my life would change forever? And who would have thought that my mom would ever get married again—to the father of my best friend!

They met because of us, and now we're a funny, <u>complicated</u> sort of family. People who meet us don't find us easy to figure out. My best friend and I get along like sisters, but we're the same age, and we certainly don't look like twins. We make quite a <u>combination</u>—a fun, mixed-up pair of girls who found each other and made a family.

I can't imagine going back to my old home now! When I think about how I used to feel, it's like that was a different person. I guess that's how it should be, though—your home should be the place you love most in the world.

1. Underline two things the narrator misses because she is <u>homesick</u>. What does *homesick* mean?

2. Underline the words that tell what <u>exotic</u> means. Then, name a place you think is *exotic*.

3. What does the narrator not want to <u>reveal</u>? What's another word or phrase that means the same thing as *reveal*?

4. How long had the narrator and her mom planned to stay <u>originally</u>? Explain what *originally* means.

5. Underline the words that help you know what <u>apparent</u> means. What is *apparent* in the story?

6. Underline the words that help you know what <u>predicted</u> means. What could the narrator never have *predicted*?

7. Underline the words that help you know what <u>complicated</u> means. Are *complicated* problems easy to solve? Explain.

8. What <u>combination</u> is the narrator is talking about? How do you know?

Name _____ Date _____

"**Names/Nombres**" by Julia Alvarez
Writing About the Big Question

How do we decide what is true?

Big Question Vocabulary

confirm	decision	determine	evidence	fact
fantasy	fiction	investigate	opinion	prove
realistic	study	test	true	unbelievable

A. *Use one or more words from the list above to complete the following sentences.*

1. If a friend is being unfriendly, I find it _____ if that friend denies that he is angry at me.

2. If someone thinks I did something wrong when I didn't, I will make an effort to _____ that I am innocent.

3. In a friendship, people should make a _____ to be honest and open about their feelings.

B. *Respond to each item. Use at least one Big Question vocabulary word in each answer.*

1. Describe how you might confirm that a friend is not angry with you.

_____

_____

_____

2. When you find something that someone tells you is unbelievable, what do you do to get at the truth?

_____

_____

_____

C. *Complete the sentence below. Then, write a short paragraph connecting this situation to the Big Question.*

Sometimes it takes courage to show your true feelings because _____

_____

_____

_____

_____

_____

Name _____ Date _____

"Names/Nombres" by Julia Alvarez
Reading: Understand the Difference Between
Fact and Opinion; Use Resources to Check Facts

In order to evaluate a work of nonfiction, you must understand the difference between fact and opinion. A **fact,** unlike an opinion, can be proved. An **opinion** expresses a judgment that can be supported but not proved. For example, the statement "The Dominican Republic is in the Caribbean Sea" is a fact that can be proved by observation. All you need to do is look at a map. The statement "The climate in the Dominican Republic is perfect" is a judgment based on the weather.

You can **check facts by using resources** such as

- dictionaries
- encyclopedias
- reliable Web sites on the Internet
- maps

A. DIRECTIONS: *Identify the following passages from or about "Names/Nombres" as fact or opinion. Write* F *if the statement is a fact and* O *if it is an opinion.*

____ 1. "We had been born in New York City when our parents had first tried immigration."

____ 2. The Dominican Republic is south of Bermuda.

____ 3. "It was the ugliest name she had ever heard."

____ 4. "Tía Josefina . . . was not really an aunt but a much older cousin."

____ 5. "Our goodbyes went on too long."

B. DIRECTIONS: *Each statement below contains an error. Name the resource you would consult to check the statement. (If you would consult a Web site, write the name of the site.) Then, look up the statement in that resource, and rewrite it correctly.*

1. Julia Alvarez moved to the United States for good in 1962.

   Fact-checking resource: _____ **Correction:** _____

   _____

2. Julia Alvarez wrote a book called *How the Alvarez Girls Lost Their Accents.*

   Fact-checking resource: _____ **Correction:** _____

   _____

3. The Dominican Republic is on the same island as Cuba.

   Fact-checking resource: _____ **Correction:** _____

   _____

4. Bermuda is an island in the Caribbean Sea.

   Fact-checking resource: _____ **Correction:** _____

   _____

Name _____ Date _____

Literary Analysis: Tone

The **tone** of a literary work is the writer's attitude toward his or her audience and subject. The tone can often be described in one word, such as *playful, serious,* or *humorous.* Factors that contribute to the tone are word choice, sentence structure, and sentence length. Notice how the writer's word choice creates a friendly, informal tone:

By the time I was in high school, I was a popular kid, and it showed in my name.

Sometimes, as in "Names/Nombres," humorous ideas, exaggeration, and dialogue help create a casual, informal tone. Alvarez's use of contractions, such as *wouldn't* and *didn't,* also adds to the informal tone.

A. DIRECTIONS: *As you read "Names/Nombres," look for details that add to the essay's informal, humorous tone. On the spider diagram, write one example of each contributing factor.*

Informal word: _____

Mispronunciation of Spanish: _____

Untranslated Spanish word: _____

Exaggeration: _____

Humorous idea: _____

Sentence fragment: _____

Another informal word: _____

Contraction: _____

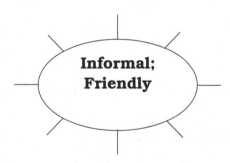

B. DIRECTIONS: *Read the following passage from "Names/Nombres." Underline three phrases or sentences that contribute to a relaxed, informal feeling. Then, rewrite the passage using a formal tone.*

At the hotel my mother was *Missus Alburest,* and I was little girl, as in, "Hey, *little girl,* stop riding the elevator up and down. It's *not* a toy."

Passage written in formal tone: _____

_____

_____

_____

Name _____ Date _____

"**Names/Nombres**" by Julia Alvarez
Vocabulary Builder

Word List

chaotic   inevitably   inscribed   mistook   pursue   transport

A. DIRECTIONS: *Write the letter of the word or phrase whose meaning is most nearly the same as the meaning of the Word List word.*

____ 1. inevitably
    A. finally
    B. unavoidably
    C. never
    D. invisibly

____ 2. chaotic
    A. confused
    B. noiseless
    C. tiny
    D. orderly

____ 3. transport
    A. bring in
    B. carry across
    C. send out
    D. extend

____ 4. inscribed
    A. remembered
    B. sewn
    C. scratched
    D. written on

____ 5. mistook
    A. became lost or stolen
    B. made a mistake
    C. provided help
    D. bragged

____ 6. pursue
    A. follow or go after
    B. forget
    C. dream or imagine
    D. wish or hope for

B. WORD STUDY: The Latin root *-scrib-* or *-scrip-* means "to write." Answer each question.

1. What message does a doctor write when he or she *prescribes* something?

    _____

2. A *scriptorium* is a special room in a monastery. What activity do the monks do in this room?

    _____

3. What *inscription* would you probably find on a birthday card?

    _____

Name _____ Date _____

"Names/Nombres" by Julia Alvarez
Enrichment: Your Own Name

What do you know about names? Choose a name you are interested in—the name of someone in history or someone in the news whom you admire. Find out as much as you can about that person's name: first, middle, and last. He or she may have other names, too, such as a nickname. What can you find out about where the names come from and what they mean?

A. DIRECTIONS: *Complete this chart by writing down what you already know about the names of the person you have chosen. Then, do some research in a library or on the Internet to see what else you can find out about this person's name. For example, for whom was he or she named, and who chose the name? Finally, look up the names in a book on names, or research the names on the Internet, and write down any additional information you discover.*

Full Name:			
Name	**What I Know About It**	**Whom Person Was Named For; Who Chose the Name and Why**	**Additional Information from Library or Internet Search**
First:			
Middle:			
Last:			
Other(s):			

B. DIRECTIONS: *In a short paragraph, describe your thoughts about names.*

_____

_____

_____

_____

_____

"Names/Nombres" by Julia Alvarez
Open-Book Test

Short Answer *Write your responses to the questions in this section on the lines provided.*

1. In "Names/Nombres," an immigration officer mispronounces the family's last name when they arrive in New York. Think about the narrator's reaction. How does she feel about her last name? Use details from the essay to support your answer.

    _____

    _____

    _____

2. In "Names/Nombres," Alvarez notes that during her first few years in America "ethnicity was not yet 'in.'" How might life in America have been different for her if it had been?

    _____

    _____

    _____

3. In "Names/Nombres," the narrator tells us that the Dominican Republic is in the Caribbean. How could you check this fact?

    _____

    _____

4. In "Names/Nombres," the author says her full name is "as chaotic with sounds as a Middle Eastern bazaar." In what way is the scene at Alvarez's graduation also chaotic?

    _____

    _____

    _____

    _____

5. How does the narrator of "Names/Nombres" feel about her large, extended family at graduation? Explain your answer.

    _____

    _____

    _____

    _____

    _____

6. A fact is information that can be proved. An opinion is a person's judgment or belief. In "Names/Nombres" the author writes, "1) Our goodbyes went on too long. 2) I heard my father's voice calling out across the parking lot. . . ." In the left column of the chart, write the number of the sentence that is a fact. Then, write an explanation of why it is a fact. In the right column, write the number of the sentence that is an opinion. Then, write an explanation of why it is an opinion.

Fact	Opinion
Sentence	
Explanation	

7. In "Names/Nombres," Julia's parents give her a typewriter for graduation. Explain why they choose this gift.

_____

_____

_____

8. Review Alvarez's word choice, sentence structure, and sentence length in "Names/ Nombres." What is the tone of this informal essay? Use an example from the essay to support your answer.

_____

_____

_____

9. How does humor contribute to the informal tone of "Names/Nombres"? Use examples from the essay to support your answer.

_____

_____

_____

_____

10. Explain how the Spanish words and phrases in "Names/Nombres" contribute to the tone.

_____

_____

_____

_____

Essay

Write an extended response to the question of your choice or to the question or questions your teacher assigns you.

11. In "Names/Nombres," Julia Alvarez tells her feelings about her name. In an essay, explain what those feelings are. Consider all the names she is called by different people. Use examples from the essay to support your ideas.

12. "Names/Nombres" is an informal essay. In an essay, discuss how Alvarez uses the characteristics of an informal essay to create an informal tone. Use specific examples from the text to support your ideas.

13. In "Names/Nombres," Julia Alvarez's mother quotes Shakespeare: "A rose by any other name would smell as sweet." In an essay, discuss the meaning of the quotation and how it applies to Julia. Use details from the essay to support your ideas.

14. **Thinking About the Big Question: How do we decide what is true?** In "Names/Nombres," Julia Alvarez hides some of her feelings from her new American friends. In an essay, discuss how Julia's friends decide what is true about her. Think about why they call her by Americanized names and why they single her out as a "foreigner." Also think about important things they never find out about her. Use details from the essay to support your ideas.

Oral Response

15. Go back to question 2, 5, 8, or 9 or to the question your teacher assigns to you. Take a few minutes to expand your answer and prepare an oral response. Find additional details in "Names/Nombres" that support your points. If necessary, make notes to guide your response.

Name _____ Date _____

"Names/Nombres" by Julia Alvarez
Selection Test A

Critical Reading *Identify the letter of the choice that best answers the question.*

_____ 1. Which set of characteristics best describes Julia Alvarez's family in "Names/Nombres"?
   A. small and argumentative
   B. small, distant, and cold
   C. large, distant, and cold
   D. large, close, and caring

_____ 2. According to "Names/Nombres," what does Alvarez think about her last name when she first arrives in New York from the Dominican Republic?
   A. It sounds foreign.
   B. It is too common.
   C. It has a beautiful sound.
   D. It is well known.

_____ 3. According to "Names/Nombres," what do Alvarez's nicknames *Jules* and *Hey Jude* show?
   A. Alvarez is sad and ashamed.
   B. Alvarez is proud and happy.
   C. Alvarez is popular and accepted.
   D. Alvarez is insulted and angry.

_____ 4. In "Names/Nombres," Julia Alvarez writes that the Dominican Republic is in the Caribbean. Which would be the best resource to check that fact?
   A. a friend who speaks Spanish
   B. a biography of Julia Alvarez
   C. a map
   D. a newspaper

_____ 5. In "Names/Nombres," why does Alvarez's full name interest her friends?
   A. It has been made to sound American.
   B. It does not translate into English.
   C. It has the sound of an orchestra.
   D. It is much longer than their names.

____ 6. Which statement about "Names/Nombres" is a fact?

A. Ana is one of the plainest names that anyone could have.

B. Shakespeare wrote, "A rose by any other name would smell as sweet."

C. Everyone knows that Mauran is the ugliest name a girl could have.

D. Names sound better when they are pronounced by a speaker of Spanish.

____ 7. In an informal essay, which factor is likely to contribute to the tone?

A. humor

B. scientific terms

C. complex sentences

D. lengthy sentences

____ 8. Imagine that Alvarez is advising you on how to write an informal essay. Which piece of advice is she most likely to give?

A. Be sure your sentences are grammatically correct.

B. Never use slang or informal language.

C. Make an outline, and follow it as you write.

D. Give your writing a friendly, conversational tone.

____ 9. In "Names/Nombres," why do Alvarez's family members sit in the first row at her graduation ceremony?

A. It is the only place where there are enough seats for them.

B. It is where all of the other immigrant families are seated.

C. They want to be sure to understand the fast-spoken English.

D. They are going to receive special recognition from the principal.

Vocabulary and Grammar

____ 10. In which sentence is *chaotic* used logically?

A. The *chaotic* waves were smooth as glass.

B. The town was *chaotic* after the tornado struck.

C. The baby's *chaotic* smiles were a delight.

D. An orderly person loves a *chaotic* room.

____ 11. Which sentence contains one or more personal pronouns?

A. My father had gotten into the habit of calling any famous author "my friend."

B. My older sister had the hardest time getting an American name for herself.

C. Introducing them to my friends was a further trial to me.

D. And her daughter, Aida Margarita, who was adopted, *una hija de crianza.*

____ **12.** How many possessive pronouns are in this passage?

> My mother blushed and admitted her baby's real name to the group. Her mother-in-law had recently died, she apologized, and her husband had insisted that the first daughter be named after his mother, *Mauran.*

 A. 1
 B. 3
 C. 5
 D. 7

Essay

13. According to "Names/Nombres," how does Julia Alvarez feel when she first comes to the United States and hears her name mispronounced? How does she feel when she is first called Judy or Judith? In an essay, describe Alvarez's thoughts about those experiences. Then, explain how her thoughts change as she grows up.

14. In an essay, describe the tone of "Names/Nombres," and name three factors that contribute to it.

15. **Thinking About the Big Question: How do we decide what is true?** In "Names/Nombres," Julia Alvarez tells about her relationship with her new American friends. Consider what feelings Julia hides from her friends. Then, in an essay, discuss how Julia's friends decide what is true about her. Think about important things they never find out about her. Use details from the essay to support your ideas.

Name _____ Date _____

"**Names/Nombres**" by Julia Alvarez
Selection Test B

Critical Reading *Identify the letter of the choice that best completes the statement or answers the question.*

____ 1. According to "Names/Nombres," what does Alvarez think about her "new names" after she has been in the United States for a while?
   A. She thinks that they are too long and sound too foreign.
   B. She is glad to have names that do not sound Spanish.
   C. She wonders whether she should correct her teachers and friends when they use them.
   D. She is sad because she believes she will never again be known by her Spanish names.

____ 2. According to "Names/Nombres," Alvarez's nicknames show that her classmates
   A. dislike her.
   B. are ignoring her.
   C. like and accept her.
   D. think she is a bad influence.

____ 3. Which statement is an opinion?
   A. Mauricia is a difficult name to have to transport across borders.
   B. Julia Alvarez immigrated from the Dominican Republic.
   C. *Hey Jude* and *Jules* were two of Alvarez's nicknames.
   D. Alvarez and her mother have the same first name.

____ 4. Which statement is a fact?
   A. Ana is one of the plainest names that anybody could have.
   B. Names sound more beautiful in Spanish than they do in English.
   C. We think life in New York is better than life in the Dominican Republic.
   D. For her graduation party, Alvarez had *sancocho* and a store-bought *pudín*.

____ 5. In "Names/Nombres," Alvarez writes that the Dominican Republic is south of Bermuda. The best resource to check that fact would be
   A. a Spanish textbook.
   B. an encyclopedia article.
   C. a map.
   D. an Internet site.

____ 6. Which statement is a fact that might be proved by checking a history book?
   A. At the hotel, Julia was told to stop riding the elevator as if it were a toy.
   B. In high school, Julia's friends called her *Jules, Hey Jude,* and *Alcatraz.*
   C. Julia's sister Ana was the most beautiful member of the Alvarez family.
   D. In the 1960s, American women wore hoop earrings and peasant blouses.

_____ 7. In "Names/Nombres," Alvarez's full name interests her friends because
  A. the final name is not Alvarez.
  B. they cannot pronounce it correctly.
  C. it sounds like a Middle Eastern name.
  D. it is longer than the names they know.

_____ 8. In "Names/Nombres," Alvarez mentions a change in attitude toward "ethnicity" in the United States during the 1960s. She suggests that the change made Americans more accepting of
  A. people with a dark complexion.
  B. girls who wore bobby socks.
  C. people from Bermuda.
  D. blond, blue-eyed Americans.

_____ 9. How does Julia Alvarez describe her extended family in "Names/Nombres"?
  A. Most of her relatives remained in the Dominican Republic.
  B. She has many relatives, and their relationships are complicated.
  C. She has few relatives, but they are close, warm, and loving.
  D. Her relatives got together only for big family events.

_____ 10. In "Names/Nombres," the graduation gift of a typewriter that Alvarez receives shows that
  A. her parents want her to have something useful.
  B. her parents know she will share it with her sisters.
  C. her parents hope she will get a job as a secretary.
  D. her parents are encouraging her interest in writing.

_____ 11. In "Names/Nombres," the writer chooses Julia Alvarez as the name she will "go by" as an adult because
  A. she wants to please her family.
  B. she is proud of her heritage.
  C. she dislikes her American names.
  D. she finds her full name impractical.

_____ 12. Alvarez most likely uses Spanish words and phrases in her essay because
  A. she believes they make her writing colorful and informal.
  B. she does not know the English translation of those words.
  C. she believes she will please her Spanish-speaking readers.
  D. she would like more of her readers to understand Spanish.

_____ 13. Which tip would Julia Alvarez most likely give to someone who wants to write an informal essay?
  A. Be sure the grammar and punctuation are correct.
  B. Be sure the work contains no sentence fragments.
  C. Include humorous anecdotes about your relatives.
  D. Use a friendly, conversational tone throughout.

____ 14. Which sentence does the most to create an informal tone?
   A. *Anita,* or as one goofy guy used to sing to her to the tune of the banana advertisement, *Anita Banana.*
   B. My initial desire to be known by my correct Dominican name faded.
   C. For if I specified, no one was quite sure on what continent our island was located.
   D. My Dominican heritage was never more apparent than when my extended family attended school occasions.

____ 15. In an informal essay, an author will most likely
   A. use difficult words and long sentences.
   B. focus on a tragic event from history.
   C. use humor to develop an idea.
   D. discuss his or her feelings about life.

Vocabulary and Grammar

____ 16. In which sentence is the word *chaotic* used logically?
   A. When the wind died, the ocean was as *chaotic* as plate glass.
   B. The *chaotic* state of the room made the detective suspicious.
   C. The mother's *chaotic* lullabies soothed the crying baby.
   D. The professional organizer left the room looking *chaotic.*

____ 17. Which sentence contains two possessive pronouns?
   A. I wondered if I shouldn't correct my teachers and new friends.
   B. By the time I was in high school, I was a popular kid, and it showed in my name.
   C. Who would ever trace her to me?
   D. Our goodbyes went on too long. I heard my father's voice calling out. . . .

Essay

18. In an essay, describe the characteristics of an informal essay. Explain how Julia Alvarez uses those characteristics to create an informal tone in "Names/Nombres."

19. According to "Names/Nombres," how does Julia Alvarez feel when she first comes to the United States and hears her name mispronounced? In an essay, describe Alvarez's changing thoughts about her name. How does she feel when she is first called Judy? How does she feel about her name when she graduates from high school? Finally, what does the name that appears below the title of this essay tell you about her feelings about her name as an adult?

20. **Thinking About the Big Question: How do we decide what is true?** In "Names/Nombres," Julia Alvarez hides some of her feelings from her new American friends. In an essay, discuss how Julia's friends decide what is true about her. Think about why they call her by Americanized names and why they single her out as a "foreigner." Also think about important things they never find out about her. Use details from the essay to support your ideas.

Vocabulary Warm-up Word Lists

Study these words from "The Lady and the Spider." Then, apply your knowledge to the activities that follow.

Word List A

clutches [KLUHCH ez] *v.* holds tightly, grabs at
As the bike begins to fall, she <u>clutches</u> at the handlebars to steady it.

disaster [di ZAS tuhr] *n.* a terrible event
The thunderstorm was a <u>disaster</u> for our picnic.

envy [EN vee] *v.* to want something someone else has; to be jealous
We all <u>envy</u> Marcia, because she gets such good grades without even studying.

fiber [FY buhr] *n.* a string-like thread of some material
The microscope made it easy to see each tiny <u>fiber</u> in the material.

flings [FLINGZ] *v.* throws, tosses
Tommy <u>flings</u> his coat onto the couch as soon as he steps in the house.

poisonous [POY zuhn us] *adj.* able to kill or harm a person or animal
A rattlesnake's bite contains <u>poisonous</u> venom that can kill.

terms [TERMZ] *n.* words, a way of saying something
When he put his idea in simple <u>terms</u>, it was easy to understand it.

torn [TAWRN] *v.* ripped
The dollar was <u>torn</u> in half when the two boys grabbed at it.

Word List B

favorable [FAY ver uh buhl] *adj.* approving or positive
Mia was happy when the coach made <u>favorable</u> comments about her after the game.

inhabited [in HA bi tid] *adj.* lived in
The house looks empty; I don't think that it's <u>inhabited</u>.

luggage [LUHG ij] *n.* bags or suitcases used to carry things
Five suitcases and four bags are too much <u>luggage</u> to fit in the car.

powerful [POW er fuhl] *adj.* very strong
A <u>powerful</u> wave knocked me down while I was swimming.

suburban [suh BERB in] *adj.* in an area that is near a city, but not in the country
We live in a <u>suburban</u> neighborhood, far from the farms, but not downtown.

survivors [ser VY verz] *n.* people or creatures that can live through terrible events
Amazingly, there were two <u>survivors</u> when the plane crashed.

tornado [tawr NAY doh] *n.* a dangerous, funnel-shaped column of whirling winds
The <u>tornado</u> ripped through the farming community, destroying everything in its path.

wherever [wair E ver] *n.* any place at all
I'm not picky; we can go <u>wherever</u> you like.

"The Lady and the Spider" by Robert Fulghum
Vocabulary Warm-up Exercises

Exercise A *Fill in each blank in the paragraph below with an appropriate word from Word List A. Use each word only once.*

I'll say this in simple [1] _____: My big brother and his dog drive me crazy. I can't stand it when Josh [2] _____ his stuff all over the house. In five minutes it looks like a [3] _____ struck the house. The little dog is even worse. Josh [4] _____ that monster in his arms all the time. The couch was [5] _____ up by that little mutt when he was just a puppy. You can still see [6] _____ sticking out of the ripped pillows. Not only that, but the dog's breath is so bad I'm sure that it is practically [7] _____. I can only say that I [8] _____ people whose brothers don't own dogs!

Exercise B *Decide whether each statement below is true or false. Then, circle T or F. Explain your answer.*

1. A *favorable* comment is often mean.
   T / F _____

2. "Go *wherever* you like" means be sure to choose one specific place.
   T / F _____

3. You can pack clothes for a trip in your *luggage*.
   T / F _____

4. *Survivors* are usually people with bad luck.
   T / F _____

5. Most *suburban* neighborhoods are far out in the country.
   T / F _____

6. A *tornado* always begins indoors.
   T / F _____

7. Zoos are *inhabited* mainly by animals.
   T / F _____

8. Only a *powerful* person could lift up a car.
   T / F _____

Name _____   Date _____

"The Lady and the Spider" by Robert Fulghum
Reading Warm-up A

Read the following passage. Pay special attention to the underlined words. Then, read it again, and complete the activities. Use a separate sheet of paper for your written answers.

It happens all the time. Someone feels a spider crawling in his or her hair. The person <u>clutches</u> at the spider, catches it, and <u>flings</u> it away as far as possible. Nothing gives people a scare like a spider does.

If you ask people what insects or animals they are afraid of, spiders are usually high on the list, along with sharks and snakes. Should people be scared of spiders? The answer is yes and no. When talking in <u>terms</u> of real danger, people shouldn't worry too much. Spiders don't usually attack people, and because most spiders are not <u>poisonous</u>, most spider bites are not harmful. Most of the time, a spider bite is not a <u>disaster</u>. It will only cause a small reaction. It may not cause anything at all.

That does not mean that *all* spider bites are harmless. Two common poisonous spiders in the United States are the black widow and the brown recluse. Both spiders live in attics, basements, and other dark and quiet places. Both spiders are equipped with venom, or poison. This venom can cause serious problems for the people they bite. A person bitten by one of these spiders should go to a hospital right away. Still, mosquitoes are probably more dangerous than spiders. Mosquitoes can carry many diseases, including the West Nile virus.

If people knew more about spiders they might <u>envy</u> them instead of being scared. After all, there's a lot to be jealous of. Spiders have eight of some things that people have only two of. Most spiders have eight legs and eight eyes.

So next time you walk into a spider web, don't get scared. You've <u>torn</u> apart the spider's hard work, a complicated web built <u>fiber</u> by <u>fiber</u>, but you probably haven't put yourself in danger.

1. Underline the words that tell what the person <u>clutches</u> at. Write a sentence that tells what *clutches* means.

2. Write a sentence explaining what the person who <u>flings</u> the spider is trying to do.

3. Circle the words that tell what kind of <u>terms</u> are being discussed. Then, tell what *terms* means.

4. Circle a phrase that is opposite of <u>poisonous</u>. Then, write a sentence using the word *poisonous*.

5. Circle the words that tell what is *not* a <u>disaster</u>. Write a sentence about something that *is*.

6. Underline the sentence explaining what spiders have that people might <u>envy</u>. Then, tell what *envy* means.

7. Underline the words that tell how you've <u>torn</u> apart a spider web. Then, tell what *torn* means.

8. Underline the words that tell what is made up of <u>fiber</u>. Then, tell what *fiber* means.

Name _____ Date _____

"**The Lady and the Spider**" by Robert Fulghum
Reading Warm-up B

Read the following passage. Pay special attention to the underlined words. Then, read it again, and complete the activities. Use a separate sheet of paper for your written answers.

My mother calls us <u>survivors</u>. That's because our family can live through almost anything, especially vacations. The place doesn't matter; <u>wherever</u> we go on vacation, something always goes wrong.

On our last vacation, we spent a week in the Oklahoma countryside. We were looking forward to getting away from our <u>suburban</u> neighborhood and engaging in outdoor activities, like hiking, fishing, and backpacking.

From the beginning, we had difficulties. On the plane flight to Tulsa, the airline misplaced every piece of our <u>luggage</u>. Since we are a family of survivors, we had no problem surviving one night without changing our clothes or brushing our teeth.

Our luggage arrived the next evening and we headed off to our isolated campsite. Sleeping out in tents was a phenomenal experience. That night, it seemed like we were alone in the wilderness. But by morning, we discovered that we weren't all alone. Our campground was <u>inhabited</u> by other creatures: hungry bears. They had broken into our cooler and eaten up our food. Fortunately, they hadn't decided to dine on us!

Now we had a stove, fuel, and utensils, but nothing to prepare for breakfast. Still, we attempted to look at things in a <u>favorable</u> way and maintain a positive attitude. This was an opportunity to sample the food at a local restaurant. We hopped into the car, but the skies began to look threatening. Pretty soon, a <u>powerful</u> storm arrived. Rain came pouring down, and branches and leaves went flying through the air. Then it appeared directly in front of us—a <u>tornado</u>! When my father saw that humongous funnel-shaped cloud, he put the car into reverse and headed straight back toward the airport.

Within hours, we were back in our suburban neighborhood. The vacation wasn't a success, but we had handled the difficulties. We are survivors, after all.

1. Underline the words that tell why the mother calls the family <u>survivors</u>. Then, write a sentence that gives the meaning of the word.

2. Circle the phrase that helps you figure out what <u>wherever</u> means. Then, write a sentence using the word.

3. Underline the activities that are not easy to do in a <u>suburban</u> neighborhood. Then, tell what *suburban* means.

4. Underline the words that tell what happened to the family's <u>luggage</u>. Then, tell what *luggage* means.

5. Circle the words that tell who else <u>inhabited</u> the campground. Then, tell what *inhabited* means.

6. Write a sentence telling how the family would have felt if they hadn't looked at things in a <u>favorable</u> way.

7. Circle the details that show that the storm is <u>powerful</u>. Then, tell what *powerful* means.

8. Explain why the father probably turned around as soon as he saw the <u>tornado</u>.

Name _____ Date _____

"The Lady and the Spider" by Robert Fulghum
Writing About the Big Question

How do we decide what is true?

Big Question Vocabulary

confirm	decision	determine	evidence	fact
fantasy	fiction	investigate	opinion	prove
realistic	study	test	true	unbelievable

A. *Use one or more words from the list above to complete the following sentences.*

1. Sometimes people think that their _____ are facts.

2. If someone is an expert on a subject, he or she has probably worked hard to _____ the facts.

3. To become an expert on something, you must _____ hard.

4. If you are a scientist with a new theory, you will have to _____ the theory in order to _____ it.

B. *Respond to each item. Use at least one Big Question vocabulary word in each answer.*

1. Tell how you distinguish between fact and fiction when you are reading something.

   _____

   _____

   _____

2. What words are a clue that you are reading or listening to an opinion as opposed to a fact?

   _____

   _____

   _____

C. *Complete the sentence below. Then, write a short paragraph connecting this situation to the Big Question.*

   An important truth about spiders is _____

   _____

   _____

   _____

   _____

   _____

Name _____ Date _____

"**The Lady and the Spider**" by Robert Fulghum
Reading: Understand the Difference Between Fact and Opinion; Use Resources to Check Facts

To evaluate a work of nonfiction, you must understand the difference between fact and opinion. A **fact,** unlike an opinion, can be proved. An **opinion** expresses a judgment that can be supported but not proved. For example, the statement "Spiders have eight legs" is a fact that can be proved by observation. All you need to do is look at a spider. The statement "Spiders are scary" is a judgment based on emotions.

You can **check facts by using resources** such as

- dictionaries
- encyclopedias
- reliable Web sites on the Internet
- maps

A. DIRECTIONS: *Identify the following passages from "The Lady and the Spider" as fact or opinion. Write F if the statement is a fact and O if it is an opinion.*

____ 1. This is my neighbor.

____ 2. Nice lady.

____ 3. Tries opening the front door without unlocking it.

____ 4. Spiders. Amazing creatures.

____ 5. Been around maybe 350 million years.

B. DIRECTIONS: *Each statement below contains an error. Name the resource you would consult to check the statement. (If you would consult a Web site, write the name of the site.) Then, look up the statement in that resource, and rewrite it correctly.*

1. A spider has six legs.

   Fact-checking resource: _____ **Correction:** _____

   _____

2. Spiders eat only gnats.

   Fact-checking resource: _____ **Correction:** _____

   _____

3. The scientific word describing the class that includes spiders is spelled *aracknid*.

   Fact-checking resource: _____ **Correction:** _____

   _____

4. In temperate climates, 20 species of spiders are dangerous to human beings.

   Fact-checking resource: _____ **Correction:** _____

   _____

"The Lady and the Spider" by Robert Fulghum
Literary Analysis: Tone

The **tone** of a literary work is the writer's attitude toward his or her audience and subject. The tone can often be described in one word, such as *playful, serious,* or *humorous.* Factors that contribute to the tone are word choice, sentence structure, and sentence length. Notice how the writer's sentence structure creates a playful tone:

> Spiders. Amazing creatures. Been around maybe 350 million years, so they can cope with about anything.

Sometimes, as in "The Lady and the Spider," exaggeration and surprising comparisons help create a casual, informal tone. Fulghum's use of contractions, such as *that's* and *what's,* also adds to the informal tone.

DIRECTIONS: *As you read "The Lady and the Spider," look for details that add to the essay's informal, playful tone. On the spider diagram, write one example of each contributing factor.*

1. **Informal word:** _____

2. **Sentence fragment:** _____

3. **Short sentence:** _____

4. **Exaggeration:** _____

5. **Surprising idea:** _____

6. **Humorous idea:** _____

7. **Joke word:** _____

8. **Contraction:** _____

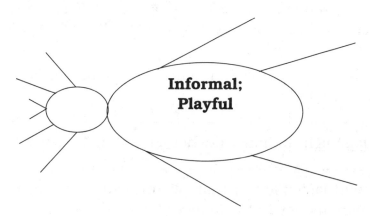

Informal;
Playful

"The Lady and the Spider" by Robert Fulghum
Vocabulary Builder

Word List

catastrophe   dimensions   equipped   frenzied   inhabited   mode

A. DIRECTIONS: *Write the letter of the word or phrase whose meaning is most nearly* the same as *the meaning of the Word List word.*

___ 1. inhabited
   A. dressed up   B. disowned   C. empty   D. lived in

___ 2. frenzied
   A. frantic   B. calm   C. angry   D. unhappy

___ 3. mode
   A. model   B. up-to-date   C. manner   D. dessert

___ 4. equipped
   A. provided with   B. missing or lacking   C. classified   D. joked

___ 5. dimensions
   A. problems   B. rewards   C. measurements   D. activities

___ 6. catastrophe
   A. celebration   B. disaster   C. illness   D. stage or phase

B. WORD STUDY: The Latin root *-met-* or *-mens-* means "to measure." Words containing this root include *thermometer* ("an instrument for measuring temperature"), *parking meter* ("a device for measuring the amount of time a car is parked in a given location") and *barometer* ("an instrument for measuring atmospheric pressure"). Each of the following sentences does not make sense. The underlined word is used incorrectly. Correct each sentence by replacing that word with *thermometer, parking meter,* or *barometer.*

1. When stormy weather is approaching, there is a reduction in air pressure. You can measure this with a <u>television</u>.

   _____

2. Brenda used a <u>flashlight</u> to find out whether she had a fever.

   _____

3. Mom's appointment lasted longer than she expected, so she had to dash out to the street and put more money in the <u>mailbox</u>.

   _____

"The Lady and the Spider" by Robert Fulghum
Enrichment: Songs

"The Lady and the Spider" is more than a humorous essay about spiders. Robert Fulghum relates his anecdote about a spider to the song "Eensy, Weensy Spider." He explains that the message of the song is important to all living things.

Many of the songs you learned when you were young have an important message. For example, "This Land Is Your Land" is about our relationship to our country. Other songs are about having adventures, doing a job, overcoming difficulties, enjoying the love of family—and many other subjects that people find meaningful.

A. DIRECTIONS: *Think about the songs you know. Choose one with such a special meaning that it is worth passing on to future generations. Answer the following questions about the song.*

1. What is the title? _____

2. Which lines of the song do you remember best? _____

_____

_____

_____

_____

_____

_____

3. What is the meaning, or message, of the song?

_____

_____

_____

B. DIRECTIONS: *Imagine that you are in charge of making a CD featuring the song you chose. You want the cover of the CD to show something about the song's special meaning or message. Describe the cover you would ask an artist to create. Would it be a drawing or a photograph? What scene would it show? What colors would it use?*

_____

_____

_____

_____

_____

_____

Name _____ Date _____

"The Lady and the Spider" by Robert Fulghum
"Names/Nombres" by Julia Alvarez
Integrated Language Skills: Grammar

Interrogative and Indefinite Pronouns

A **pronoun** is a word that takes the place of a noun or another pronoun.

- **Interrogative pronouns** are used in questions. Interrogative pronouns include *who, whom, whose, what,* and *which.*

- **Indefinite pronouns** can be singular or plural, depending on how they are used. Indefinite pronouns include *some, one, other,* and *none.*

A. DIRECTIONS: *In each of these sentences, underline the interrogative and indefinite pronouns. Above the interrogative pronouns, write* Inter, *and above the indefinite pronouns, write* Indef.

1. Who can remember some of the names Julia Alvarez gave herself?

2. From whose point of view do the spider and the lady see each other?

3. None of Julia's classmates seemed able to pronounce her name correctly.

4. Which essay do you prefer: the one by Alvarez or the one by Fulghum?

5. What do you think of some of the lady's and spider's reactions to each other?

6. What sort of name is Judy Alcatraz?

B. WRITING APPLICATION: *Write a brief paragraph about "The Lady and the Spider" or "Names/Nombres." Write at least four sentences, and use at least one interrogative pronoun and two indefinite pronouns. Then, underline those pronouns.*

_____

_____

_____

_____

Name _____ Date _____

Integrated Language Skills: Support for Writing
a Personal Anecdote

To prepare to write your anecdote, use this graphic organizer. First, name the experience you plan to write about. Then, in the left-hand column, write down the events that made up the experience. Write them in the order in which they happened. Finally, in the right-hand column, write your thoughts about each event.

The time when _____

Events	Thoughts About the Events
Key event in the beginning: 	
Key event in the middle: 	
Key event at most exciting moment: 	
Key event at end: 	

Now, use your notes to write your personal anecdote. Be sure to describe your thoughts about the experience.

Name _____ Date _____

"Names/Nombres" by Julia Alvarez
"The Lady and the Spider" by Robert Fulghum
Integrated Language Skills: Support for Extend Your Learning

Listening and Speaking
A. "Names/Nombres"
Answer the following questions to prepare your monologue presenting the thoughts of young Julia Alvarez when she first hears her name mispronounced. Imagine what you (Alvarez) might think.

- How do you feel the first time you hear your name mispronounced?

_____

_____

- What thoughts do you have the first time you hear your name mispronounced? (Describe at least three thoughts. Remember to use the first-person point of view and the pronoun *I*.)

1. _____

2. _____

3. _____

4. _____

5. _____

B. "The Lady and the Spider"
Answer the following questions to prepare your monologue presenting the thoughts of the woman or the spider in "The Lady and the Spider."

- Will my monologue present the thoughts of the woman or the spider? _____

- What situation or event will my character think about? _____

_____

- What thoughts will I include? (Describe at least three. Remember to use the first-person point of view and the pronoun *I*.)

1. _____

2. _____

3. _____

4. _____

5. _____

6. _____

Name _____ Date _____

"The Lady and the Spider" by Robert Fulghum
Open-Book Test

Short Answer *Write your responses to the questions in this section on the lines provided.*

1. The woman in "The Lady and the Spider" is frenzied. Who would more likely be frenzied—someone chased by bees or someone doing homework? Explain your answer.

   _____

   _____

   _____

2. In "The Lady and the Spider," the spider views the neighbor lady as "a huge piece of raw-but-painted meat." Explain why this is a fitting description.

   _____

   _____

   _____

   _____

3. Fulghum's neighbor in "The Lady and the Spider" fears she is inhabited. How will changing her outfit get rid of that fear?

   _____

   _____

   _____

4. The author of "The Lady and the Spider" says that spiders have been around for about 350 million years. Explain why this statement is a fact and where it could be checked.

   _____

   _____

   _____

5. An opinion expresses a judgment that can be supported but not proved. Explain why the following passage from "The Lady and the Spider" is an opinion.

   Cleaning up human-sized webs would be a mess, on the other hand.

   _____

   _____

   _____

6. When he talks about a children's song in "The Lady and the Spider," Fulghum asks, "What's the deal here?" Explain how this word choice contributes to the tone of the essay.

   _____

   _____

   _____

7. In "The Lady and the Spider," the author discusses the song "Eensy, Weensy Spider." Review how he describes the spider's adventure up the drainpipe. Then, explain what point Robert Fulghum is making about living things.

_____

_____

8. The author of "The Lady and the Spider" says that the neighbor lady will "be a little wiser coming out the door on her way to work." Explain in what way the woman might be wiser.

_____

_____

9. The tone is the writer's attitude toward his or her audience and subject. One word that describes the tone of "The Lady and the Spider" is *humorous*. In each of the blank ovals of the word web, write an example from the essay that contributes to the humorous tone. On the lines below, tell why the author chose to write in a humorous tone.

_____

_____

10. Explain how sentence structure and sentence length help contribute to the tone of "The Lady and the Spider."

_____

_____

_____

Essay

Write an extended response to the question of your choice or to the question or questions your teacher assigns you.

11. Fulghum describes both the lady and the spider in his essay. In an essay, discuss which one he seems to like more. In your answer, consider how the lady's actions and thoughts compare to those of the spider and how Fulghum seems to feel about spiders. Use details from the essay to support your answer.

Name _____ Date _____

12. "The Lady and the Spider" is an informal, friendly essay with some serious ideas. Suppose that the entire tone of this essay had been serious and formal. In an essay, describe two ways that a serious essay on the same subject would differ from "The Lady and the Spider." Then, tell which version you would prefer and why. Use details from the essay to support your ideas.

13. In "The Lady and the Spider," Fulghum makes two points about spiders: They are amazing, and they can teach us. In an essay, explain how Fulghum supports each point and how effective each method of support is. Use details from the essay to support your ideas.

14. **Thinking About the Big Question: How do we decide what is true?** The woman in "The Lady and the Spider" has one view of the spider and the author has another. In an essay, discuss each view and explain who has the truer view. Use specific examples from the essay to support your ideas.

Oral Response

15. Go back to question 6, 7, 8, or 10 or to the question your teacher assigns to you. Take a few minutes to expand your answer and prepare an oral response. Find additional details in "The Lady and the Spider" that support your points. If necessary, make notes to guide your response.

Name _____ Date _____

Critical Reading *Identify the letter of the choice that best answers the question.*

____ 1. When Fulghum's neighbor in "The Lady and the Spider" walks into the spider web, what does the spider think?

    A. A human being is trying to kill her.

    B. A haystack has blown apart.

    C. She is about to have a big meal.

    D. Something terrible is taking place.

____ 2. In "The Lady and the Spider," what does Fulghum's neighbor think of when she sees the spider?

    A. a piece of painted raw meat

    B. a dangerous escaped prisoner

    C. a creature with poisonous fangs

    D. an amazing million-year-old creature

____ 3. Which word best describes the tone of "The Lady and the Spider"?

    A. informal

    B. scary

    C. formal

    D. serious

____ 4. Which quotation from "The Lady and the Spider" contains a fact that can be proved by observation or by checking resources?

    A. "[It is a] medium gray . . . spider."

    B. "[She is] feeling good."

    C. "Spiders. Amazing creatures."

    D. "It boggles the mind."

____ 5. Which statement sums up one point that Robert Fulghum makes about spiders?

    A. They have a good sense of humor.

    B. They do not scare most human beings.

    C. Their webs are unique and amazing.

    D. Some of them are poisonous.

____ 6. Which statement is a fact that can be checked in an encyclopedia?

    A. Spiders have existed for about 350 million years.

    B. Most human beings fear spiders.

    C. Human beings and spiders are alike.

    D. Spiders are amazing creatures.

_____ 7. In "The Lady and the Spider," what point does Robert Fulghum make when he describes the song "Eensy, Weensy Spider"?

   A. It is important to teach songs to children.

   B. It is important to keep on going and not give up.

   C. People should be kind to all creatures, even spiders.

   D. Looking for adventure can be a dangerous undertaking.

_____ 8. According to the author of "The Lady and the Spider," how are all living things alike?

   A. They fear each other.

   B. They make mistakes.

   C. They sing in their own way.

   D. They are survivors.

_____ 9. Which is the best definition of the *tone* of "The Lady and the Spider"?

   A. The tone is Robert Fulghum's idea about life.

   B. The tone is the ancecdote at the beginning of the essay.

   C. The tone is Robert Fulghum's attitude toward his audience and subject.

   D. The tone is the combination of facts and opinions that Robert Fulghum presents.

_____ 10. Which characteristic describes the tone of "The Lady and the Spider"?

   A. It contains complex sentences.

   B. It contains many sentence fragments.

   C. It contains no contractions.

   D. It contains scientific vocabulary.

Vocabulary and Grammar

_____ 11. In which sentence is the vocabulary word *inhabited* used correctly?

   A. I *inhabited* money from my favorite aunt after she died.

   B. Sam *inhabited* nail biting even though he tried hard not to do it.

   C. So many children *inhabited* the tent that some had to sleep in bunk beds.

   D. One disaster after another *inhabited* the town until no one was left alive.

_____ 12. Which sentence contains a personal pronoun?

   A. "She's locking the door now."

   B. "Clutches at her face and hair."

   C. "Now a different view of this scene."

   D. "What's the deal here?"

Essay

13. "The Lady and the Spider" is a humorous essay that contains some serious ideas. How does Robert Fulghum make his essay funny? Explain your answer in an essay. Include two examples of humor from "The Lady and the Spider."

14. Robert Fulghum has written an informal, friendly essay that includes some serious ideas. Imagine that he had written a serious, formal essay instead. How would a serious essay on the same topic differ from "The Lady and the Spider"? In an essay, explain your answer. Name two ways in which the essays would be different. Would you prefer the serious, formal essay? Why or why not?

15. **Thinking About the Big Question: How do we decide what is true?** The woman in "The Lady and the Spider" has one view of the spider. The author has another view. In an essay, discuss each view and tell which view you think is truer. Use specific examples from the essay to support your ideas.

Name _____   Date _____

"The Lady and the Spider" by Robert Fulghum
Selection Test B

Critical Reading *Identify the letter of the choice that best completes the statement or answers the question.*

_____ 1. What does the following passage contribute to the tone of "The Lady and the Spider"?

> And goes "AAAAAAAAGGGGGGGGGGGHHHHHHHHHH!!!!" (That's a direct quote.)
> At about the level of a fire engine at full cry.

    A. It includes humor as well as an exaggerated comparison.
    B. It uses formal language and a complicated sentence structure.
    C. It includes humor, yet the language is formal and scientific.
    D. It uses an exaggerated comparison and formal language.

_____ 2. In "The Lady and the Spider," the author imagines the spider thinking that
    A. a human being is trying to kill her.
    B. a haystack has blown apart.
    C. a natural disaster is taking place.
    D. a delicious meal has landed in her web.

_____ 3. In "The Lady and the Spider," the woman thinks that the spider
    A. is a piece of raw, painted meat.
    B. is ready for action.
    C. has rubber lips and poisonous fangs.
    D. is an amazing creature.

_____ 4. In "The Lady and the Spider," Robert Fulghum's neighbor comes out her front door in the morning. He imagines that she ends up
    A. at her aerobics class.
    B. at her desk at work.
    C. in the shower.
    D. in the hospital.

_____ 5. Which sentence is an opinion?
    A. This is my neighbor.
    B. She has walked . . . into a spider web.
    C. Now a different view of this scene.
    D. The neighbor lady will probably strip to the skin.

_____ 6. Which statement is a fact that can be proved by observation?
    A. A woman walks out her front door and into a spider web.
    B. A scream can sound like the siren on a fire engine.
    C. There are 60,000 to 70,000 spiders per suburban acre.
    D. The woman does not care what her neighbor thinks about her.

____ 7. In "The Lady and the Spider," Fulghum's question "What's the deal here?" is an example of
   A. the essay's use of incorrect grammar.
   B. a question with many meanings.
   C. the essay's informal tone.
   D. language that is used in business.

____ 8. Which sentence contains a fact?
   A. [It is a] medium gray. . . lady spider.
   B. [She is] feeling good.
   C. Spiders. Amazing creatures.
   D. It's a little wiser now.

____ 9. Which two statements in "The Lady and the Spider" best reflect what the author thinks of spiders?
   I.   They have a good sense of humor.
   II. They do not scare most humans.
   III. Their webs are unique and amazing.
   IV. They can survive many disasters.
   A. I and II
   B. I and IV
   C. II and III
   D. III and IV

____ 10. In "The Lady and the Spider," Fulghum uses the song "Eensy, Weensy Spider" to make the point that
   A. spiders can survive rainstorms.
   B. spiders can teach us an important lesson.
   C. it is important to learn songs when we are young.
   D. it is important to be kind to all living creatures.

____ 11. Which statement is a fact that you can prove true or false by checking an encyclopedia?
   A. Women fear spiders, whereas men understand them.
   B. Spiders have been around for about 350 million years.
   C. Human beings and spiders are alike in some ways.
   D. Human beings have passed on a song about spiders.

____ 12. In "The Lady and the Spider," what does Fulghum say that living things have been doing for a long time?
   A. They have been surviving disasters, setbacks, and catastrophes.
   B. They have been fearing spiders and other kinds of insects.
   C. They have been singing songs about spiders and rainstorms.
   D. They have been teaching important lessons to their children.

____ 13. Which is the best definition of an essay's tone?
  A. It is the writer's central idea, or overall message, about life.
  B. It is the point of view from which the writer writes the essay.
  C. It is the writer's attitude toward his or her audience and subject.
  D. It is the audience's attitude toward the writer and his or her subject.

____ 14. The tone of "The Lady and the Spider" may best be described as
  A. scary and formal.
  B. humorous and informal.
  C. friendly and formal.
  D. serious and informal.

Vocabulary and Grammar

____ 15. In which sentence is *inhabited* used correctly?
  A. Your brother *inhabited* a large sum of money.
  B. Nail biting has *inhabited* you since you were a child.
  C. Too many people *inhabited* that small apartment.
  D. One disaster after another *inhabited* the town.

____ 16. Which sentence contains one or more personal pronouns?
  A. "She has walked full force into a spider web."
  B. "Now a different view of this scene. Here is the spider."
  C. "The web is torn loose and is wrapped around a frenzied moving haystack."
  D. "And if not, well, there are lots more spiders, and the word gets around."

____ 17. Which sentence contains one or more possessive pronouns?
  A. "It's too big to wrap up and eat later, and it's moving too much to hold down."
  B. "She's . . . thinking about the little gnats she'd like to have for breakfast."
  C. "And maybe spiders tell their kids about it too, in their spider sort of way."
  D. "Where is it going and what will it do when it gets there?"

Essay

18. In an essay, describe the tone of "The Lady and the Spider," and name three factors that contribute to it. Then, think of a very different tone, and imagine an essay on people and spiders written in that tone. How would it differ from Fulghum's essay? Explain your opinion in your essay, and explain which tone you would prefer.

19. In an essay, analyze two humorous characteristics of Robert Fulghum's writing. Explain what makes each one funny.

20. **Thinking About the Big Question: How do we decide what is true?** The woman in "The Lady and the Spider" has one view of the spider and the author has another. In an essay, discuss each view and explain who has the truer view. Use specific examples from the essay to support your ideas.

"**The Sound of Summer Running**" by Ray Bradbury
"**Eleven**" by Sandra Cisneros
Vocabulary Warm-up Word Lists

Study these words from the selections. Then, complete the activities.

Word List A

alleys [AL eez] *n.* narrow streets or passageways between buildings
 The city block was a maze of <u>alleys</u> sandwiched between the tall buildings.

clumsily [KLUHM zuh lee] *adv.* lacking skill or grace in movement
 Jessica <u>clumsily</u> tripped over her brother's toy car on the stairs.

downtown [DOWN TOWN] *n.* main business district
 Victor went shopping <u>downtown</u>, instead of at the mall near his house.

flex [FLEKS] *v.* bend or stretch something
 Tony liked to <u>flex</u> his muscles while he did his daily workout.

hushed [HUHSHT] *adj.* quiet
 The library had a <u>hushed</u> atmosphere because no one was talking.

possible [PAHS uh buhl] *adj.* could be done
 I stretched up as high as <u>possible</u>, but I still couldn't reach the shelf.

problem [PRAHB luhm] *n.* difficult situation that needs to be solved
 Laura's big <u>problem</u> was that she never paid attention in class.

tremendous [tri MEN dus] *adj.* astonishingly great or large
 Winning first place at the race was a <u>tremendous</u> achievement.

Word List B

absolutely [ab suh LOOT lee] *adv.* completely or totally
 The soldier was <u>absolutely</u> convinced that he saw an enemy tank.

arches [AHR chez] *n.* curved parts of the bony structure of the foot
 Good walking shoes provide support for the <u>arches</u> of your feet.

believes [buh LEEVZ] *v.* accepts as true
 Leigh <u>believes</u> her little brother's story, even though it's clear that he's pretending.

invisible [in VIZ uh buhl] *adv.* unable to be seen
 After everyone saw her fall, she wanted to become <u>invisible</u>.

painful [PAYN fuhl] *adj.* feeling or giving pain
 Falling on the sidewalk and landing on cement is <u>painful</u>.

soles [SOHLZ] *n.* the undersides of feet or of shoes
 Dress shoes usually have leather <u>soles</u>.

underneath [uhn der NEETH] *adv.* below or under
 The skier wore layers of clothes <u>underneath</u> his jacket to keep warm.

valuable [VAL yuh buhl] *adj.* of great use or service
 Anna found her sister's advice very <u>valuable</u>.

Name _____ Date _____

"The Sound of Summer Running" by Ray Bradbury
"Eleven" by Sandra Cisneros
Vocabulary Warm-up Exercises

Exercise A *Fill in each blank in the paragraph below with an appropriate word from Word List A. Use each word only once.*

Nick's favorite gym was located [1] _____ on Main Street. He

liked to work out there and [2] _____ his muscles as much as

[3] _____. Working out made him feel like he had

[4] _____ power. It also helped clear his mind. As he lifted weights, he

would think about a big [5] _____ he had and often solve it. Sometimes

he was awkward, lifting weights [6] _____, but other people rarely

noticed. They were busily working on their own exercise routines. After he left the gym,

Nick walked through the peaceful [7] _____ behind the buildings. They

had a [8] _____ feeling about them after the noise of the gym.

Exercise B *Revise each sentence so that the underlined vocabulary word is used in a logical way. Be sure to keep the vocabulary word in your revision.*

Example: Angel wanted to be <u>invisible</u> so everyone could see him.
Angel wanted to be <u>invisible</u> so no one could see him.

1. Carly always <u>believes</u> Lauren because she knows Lauren makes things up.

   _____

2. The ride looked a little scary so I felt <u>absolutely</u> safe going on it.

   _____

3. I reached up to grab the pencil that had rolled <u>underneath</u> my seat.

   _____

4. The <u>arches</u> of Jason's knees hurt after a long run.

   _____

5. Having a messy desk is a <u>valuable</u> way to stay organized.

   _____

6. The top of Jose's sneakers had rubber <u>soles</u>.

   _____

7. Douglas didn't think that breaking his arm was <u>painful</u>.

   _____

"The Sound of Summer Running" by Ray Bradbury
"Eleven" by Sandra Cisneros
Reading Warm-up A

Read the following passage. Pay special attention to the underlined words. Then, read it again, and complete the activities. Use a separate sheet of paper for your written answers.

Every morning, Alex would set out on a run. She would rise at 5:30, earlier than anyone else in her family. In the dawn, her house had a <u>hushed</u> feeling that Alex had grown to love. Only in the mornings did she feel that she could be truly alone.

As she ran, Alex would let her thoughts drift. She thought of her grandfather and how much she missed living with him in the country in the summers. The city was crowded by comparison, but at least she could still run here. Alex's grandfather had started her running. He would lecture her every day about running, saying it would help her keep in shape and build discipline.

Alex wasn't sure about that, but she loved to run anyway. In the darkness of the early morning, she would tip-toe about, trying not to wake her parents. Still sleepy, she would <u>clumsily</u> lace up her sneakers in the dark. Leaving her house, she would burst into the fresh morning air. How different the city seemed to her after a summer on the farm!

She ran to her usual destination: <u>downtown</u>. She darted through small, empty <u>alleys</u>, knowing they were the perfect shortcut. After she reached the main shopping street, she always stopped to peer into the plate-glass windows of the storefronts. At this hour of the morning, crowds weren't a <u>problem</u>. Alex had all the windows to herself.

After looking around for a while, Alex decided it was time to head home. It was during her journey home that Alex pushed her body the hardest. She always wanted to go as fast as <u>possible</u>, until she couldn't go any faster. She felt her muscles stretch and <u>flex</u> as she took on <u>tremendous</u> power of movement. Running in the mornings was how Alex found her strength in life.

1. Circle the words that hint at why the house had a <u>hushed</u> feeling. Write a sentence describing a house that has a *hushed* feeling.

2. Circle two phrases that tell you why Alex laced her sneakers <u>clumsily</u>. Write about something you have done *clumsily*.

3. Underline the words that tell you what is <u>downtown</u>. Write what you like to do when you go *downtown*.

4. Circle the words that let you know why Alex took the <u>alley</u>. Use your own words to define *alley*.

5. Underline the words that tell why crowds were not a <u>problem</u> as Alex looked in store windows.

6. Underline the phrase that tells you what <u>possible</u> means. Then describe a situation in which you might run as fast as *possible*.

7. Why did Alex <u>flex</u> her muscles? Describe a situation in which you might *flex* your muscles.

8. What does <u>tremendous</u> describe? Write a sentence about something you found *tremendous* this week.

"The Sound of Summer Running" by Ray Bradbury
"Eleven" by Sandra Cisneros
Reading Warm-up B

Read the following passage. Pay special attention to the underlined words. Then, read it again, and complete the activities. Use a separate sheet of paper for your written answers.

Americans love sneakers. We buy about three hundred and fifty million pairs of sneakers every year. That comes to 1.25 new pairs of sneakers a year for each person in the United States.

Sneakers were originally made out of canvas, with rubber <u>soles</u> on the bottom. That's because rubber soles were lightweight and lasted longer than leather ones. Today, however, many sneakers are made out of materials like nylon, with polyurethane and plastic <u>underneath</u>. Shoe engineers are always working to find better materials for making strong, lightweight sneakers.

Sneakers were invented in the United States in the 1800s. They did not become popular, however, until 1923. That's when a famous basketball player named Chuck Taylor started to wear sneakers on the basketball court. Soon, other athletes realized how <u>valuable</u> these lightweight shoes could be. The shoes really seemed to improve performance.

Today, there are many different kinds of sneakers on the market. The business of making sneakers is very high-tech. Engineers look at the way the bones and muscles of the foot and leg move when a person plays a sport, and design sneakers based on these observations. Many of their design features are <u>invisible</u> when you wear the sneakers. For example, sneakers are built with supports for the <u>arches</u> of a person's feet. These supports, which can't be seen when the shoe is on, provide balance for running.

These days, sneakers are designed for specific sports. Playing sports with the wrong shoes could be very <u>painful</u>, since they won't support the foot properly. So there are sneakers made especially for most types of sports.

Today, Americans spend around thirteen billion dollars on sneakers every year. Almost everyone <u>believes</u> that sneakers are the most comfortable shoes around, whether or not that's <u>absolutely</u> true. Many people now wear them every day. Do you?

1. Write one thing from the passage that tells you why rubber <u>soles</u> are good for shoes.

2. What goes <u>underneath</u> the tops of sneakers these days?

3. Circle the phrase that describes why sneakers are <u>valuable</u> to athletes. Do you find sneakers *valuable*? Why or why not?

4. Underline the phrase that tells you what <u>invisible</u> means. Name something that is *invisible*.

5. Write a sentence describing why engineers design supports for <u>arches</u> in sneakers.

6. Describe why the wrong shoes can be <u>painful</u> while playing sports.

7. Circle the phrase that helps you know what <u>believes</u> means. What is something you *believe*?

8. What might not be <u>absolutely</u> true? Describe something that you believe *absolutely*.

Name _____ Date _____

"The Sound of Summer Running" by Ray Bradbury
"Eleven" by Sandra Cisneros
Writing About the Big Question
How do we decide what is true?

Big Question Vocabulary

confirm	decision	determine	evidence	fact
fantasy	fiction	investigate	opinion	prove
realistic	study	test	true	unbelievable

A. *Use one or more words from the list above to complete the following sentences.*

1. To _____ the true meaning of a symbol, I would have to ask someone who understood its meaning.

2. The fact that a symbol stands for something it is not makes it a _____ that is accepted by a lot of people.

3. To _____ whether a symbol was widely known by a lot of people, I would have to talk to many people to see if they knew what it meant.

B. *Respond to each item. Use at least one Big Question vocabulary words in each answer.*

1. How do authors use symbols in works of fiction?

   _____

   _____

   _____

2. In your opinion, are symbols always clearly understood in works of fiction?

   _____

   _____

C. *Complete the sentence below. Then, write a short paragraph connecting this situation to the Big Question.*

If people relate happy or sad feelings or experiences to an object, it may become a symbol because _____

   _____

   _____

   _____

   _____

216

Name _____ Date _____

"The Sound of Summer Running" by Ray Bradbury
"Eleven" by Sandra Cisneros
Literary Analysis: Symbol

A **symbol** is a person, place, or thing that, in addition to its literal meaning, has other layers of meaning. In literature, symbols often stand for abstract ideas, such as love or hope. Writers often use symbols to reinforce the theme or message of a literary work. They might also use symbols to help express how a character feels. For example, a commonly recognized symbol is a flag that stands for a nation or a state.

DIRECTIONS: *Read the passages and answer the questions that follow.*

from "The Sound of Summer Running"

"Don't you see?" said Douglas. "I just *can't* use last year's pair."

For last year's pair were dead inside. They had been fine when he started them out, last year. But by the end of summer, every year, you always found out, you always knew, you couldn't really jump over rivers and trees and houses in them, and they were dead. But this was a new year, and he felt that this time, with this new pair of shoes, he could do anything, anything at all.

1. What time of year do last year's shoes symbolize for Douglas?

   _____

2. What feeling do last year's shoes symbolize for Douglas?

   _____

3. Underline the phrase that tells you how Douglas feels about new shoes. What feeling do the new shoes symbolize for Douglas?

   _____

from "Eleven"

"Rachel," Mrs. Price says. She says it like she's getting mad. "You put that sweater on right now and no more nonsense."

"But it's not . . ."

"Now!" Mrs. Price says.

This is when I wish I wasn't eleven, because all the years inside of me—ten, nine, eight, seven, six, five, four, three, two, and one—are all pushing at the back of my eyes when I put one arm through one sleeve of the sweater that smells like cottage cheese, and then the other arm through the other and stand there with my arms apart as if the sweater hurts me and it does, all itchy and full of germs that aren't even mine.

4. What object symbolizes Rachel's feelings about her birthday?

   _____

5. Underline two phrases that tell you how Rachel feels about the sweater. What feelings does the sweater symbolize?

   _____

Unit 1 Resources: Fiction and Nonfiction
217

Name _____ Date _____

"The Sound of Summer Running" by Ray Bradbury
"Eleven" by Sandra Cisneros
Vocabulary Builder

Word List

alley   invisible   raggedy   revelation   seized   suspended

A. DIRECTIONS: *In each sentence, a word from the Word List is used incorrectly. Revise each sentence to use the underlined vocabulary word correctly. The first one is done for you as an example.*

1. He rolled the trash bin to the <u>alley</u> above his house.

   He rolled the trash bin to the <u>alley</u> behind his house.

2. She <u>seized</u> the dog's leash as he sat quietly at her side.

   _____

3. The tennis match was <u>suspended</u> due to beautiful weather.

   _____

4. After a sudden <u>revelation</u>, the math problem confused Charles.

   _____

5. Words such as *dog* and *horse* name concepts that are <u>invisible</u>.

   _____

6. Because my coat was <u>raggedy</u>, it was thick and warm.

   _____

B. DIRECTIONS: *Use the Word List words in a sentence according to the instructions given.*

1. Use *seized* in a sentence about someone learning to skate.

   _____

2. Use *suspended* in a sentence about a track meet.

   _____

3. Use *revelation* in a sentence about a detective.

   _____

4. Use *alley* in a sentence about a traffic jam.

   _____

5. Use *raggedy* in a sentence that describes an old banner or flag.

   _____

6. Use *invisible* in a sentence that describes a hidden treasure.

   _____

Name _____ Date _____

Integrate Language Skills: Support for Writing a Paragraph

Before you draft your paragraph explaining how the symbols in these selections express feelings, complete the graphic organizers below. For each selection, write the main symbol the author uses, the feelings expressed by the symbol, and details from the story that help show those feelings.

The Sound of Summer Running
Main symbol:
Feelings expressed by symbol: Is the author expressing positive or negative feelings? _____
Details from the story that show these feelings:

Eleven
Main symbol:
Feelings expressed by symbol: Is the author expressing positive or negative feelings? _____
Details from the story that show these feelings:

Now use your notes to write a paragraph explaining how the authors of these selections use symbols to express positive or negative feelings.

Unit 1 Resources: Fiction and Nonfiction

"The Sound of Summer Running" by Ray Bradbury
"Eleven" by Sandra Cisneros
Open-Book Test

Short Answer *Write your responses to the questions in this section on the lines provided.*

1. When Douglas first spots the tennis shoes in "The Sound of Summer Running," he has an instant reaction. Describe how he feels. Use details from the selection.

   _____

   _____

2. In "The Sound of Summer Running," when Douglas talks excitedly about the sneakers, a change comes over Mr. Sanderson. What emotions do you think Mr. Sanderson might be feeling? On the word web, write an emotion in each empty oval. Then, on the lines, explain why Mr. Sanderson experiences these emotions.

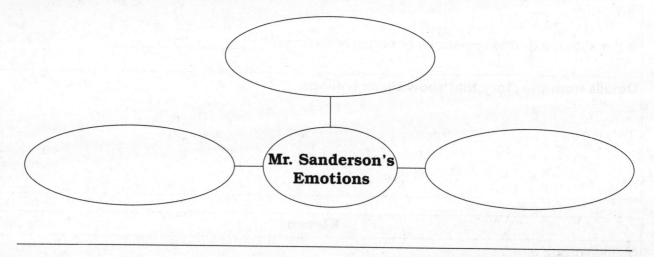

   _____

   _____

   _____

3. In "The Sound of Summer Running," Mr. Sanderson has a revelation after trying on the tennis shoes. Explain what happens and what the revelation is.

   _____

   _____

   _____

4. In "Eleven," Mrs. Price makes Rachel take the red sweater. Explain why this upsets Rachel so much.

   _____

   _____

   _____

5. In "Eleven," Rachel wants to toss the red sweater in the alley. Why does she think that would be a good place to get rid of it? Use the definition of *alley* in your answer.

_____

_____

6. At the end of "Eleven," Rachel says, "There'll be candles and presents and everybody will sing happy birthday, happy birthday to you, Rachel, only it's too late." Explain what she means by "it's too late."

_____

_____

_____

7. Consider how Douglas feels about the tennis shoes in "The Sound of Summer Running." Then, consider how Rachel feels about the red sweater in "Eleven." What do these symbols help you understand about the characters? Use details from the stories to support your answer.

_____

_____

_____

_____

8. Explain how the main symbols in "The Sound of Summer Running" and "Eleven" are alike.

_____

_____

_____

9. Explain how the main symbols in "The Sound of Summer Running" and "Eleven" are different.

_____

_____

_____

10. How does the main symbol in both "The Sound of Summer Running" and "Eleven" help move the action in each story? Explain your answer.

_____

_____

_____

_____

Essay

Write an extended response to the question of your choice or to the question or questions your teacher assigns you.

11. In "The Sound of Summer Running" and "Eleven," each main character puts on something for the first time. In a brief essay, describe what Douglas and Rachel put on and how each character feels at that moment. Then, explain how the situations are similar and how they are different.

12. In "The Sound of Summer Running," Mr. Sanderson asks Douglas if he would like a job as a shoe salesperson in five years. In a brief essay, describe the qualities he sees in Douglas that would make him a good salesperson. Then, explain how much you think Douglas would like this job.

13. Suppose that the main characters in "The Sound of Summer Running" and "Eleven" were switched. In an essay, explain how the stories would be different. Consider what Rachel would do to get the sneakers and whether she would succeed. Then consider what Douglas would do when Mrs. Price tries to make him take the red sweater and how he would feel.

14. **Thinking About the Big Question: How do we decide what is true?** In "Eleven," Rachel's teacher must decide what is true about the red sweater. View events from Mrs. Price's perspective. Consider why she finds it hard to believe Rachel when the girl protests. In an essay, explain how and why she comes to the conclusion that the sweater belongs to Rachel. Use examples from the selection.

Oral Response

15. Go back to question 4, 6, 7, or 10 or to the question your teacher assigns to you. Take a few minutes to expand your answer and prepare an oral response. Find additional details in "The Sound of Summer Running" or "Eleven" that support your points. If necessary, make notes to guide your oral response.

"The Sound of Summer Running" by Ray Bradbury
"Eleven" by Sandra Cisneros
Selection Test A

Critical Reading *Identify the letter of the choice that best answers the question.*

____ 1. During which month of the year does "The Sound of Summer Running" take place?
   A. June
   B. August
   C. September
   D. December

____ 2. In "The Sound of Summer Running," what catches Douglas's eye while he is walking home from a movie with his family?
   A. an ad showing a pair of sneakers
   B. a new pair of sneakers on a boy who passes by
   C. a pair of sneakers in a store window
   D. a help-wanted sign on a shoe store window

____ 3. Which phrase best describes Mr. Sanderson, the owner of the shoe store, at the end of "The Sound of Summer Running"?
   A. regretting his deal with Douglas
   B. unhappy about his business
   C. having dreamy memories
   D. happy with Douglas's offer to work

____ 4. Which of the following tells what the new sneakers are a symbol for in "The Sound of Summer Running"?
   A. Douglas's anger at his father
   B. last year's shoes
   C. the comforts of home
   D. summer freedom

____ 5. When Rachel is made to wear the red sweater in "Eleven," how does she feel?
   A. confused
   B. special
   C. important
   D. embarrassed

_____ 6. In "Eleven," what does Mrs. Price do when she learns that the sweater is not Rachel's?

A. She apologizes to Rachel.

B. She pretends that everything is okay.

C. She promises to get Rachel another sweater.

D. She ends class early.

_____ 7. What does Rachel mean by "it's too late" in this sentence from "Eleven"?

There'll be candles and presents and everybody will sing happy birthday, happy birthday to you, Rachel, only it's too late.

A. The party won't matter because her day has already been ruined.

B. Her birthday party will take place too late at night.

C. Her party won't be a surprise because she already knows about it.

D. She feels too sad to invite her classmates to the party.

_____ 8. In "Eleven," what does the red sweater symbolize?

A. Mrs. Price's classroom

B. Rachel's dishonesty

C. Rachel's unhappiness

D. a message of hope

_____ 9. At the end of "Eleven," why does Rachel wish she were one-hundred-and-two?

A. She wouldn't have to go to school.

B. She would be far from the embarrassments of childhood.

C. She would have her own red sweater.

D. She would have friends to stand up for her.

_____ 10. How are Douglas in "The Sound of Summer Running" and Rachel in "Eleven" different?

A. He knows exactly what to say, and she doesn't.

B. He enjoys summer, and she doesn't.

C. She knows exactly what to say, and he doesn't.

D. She enjoys summer, and he doesn't.

_____ 11. Why do the authors of "The Sound of Summer Running" and "Eleven" use symbols?

A. to persuade readers to buy new clothing

B. to help express the characters' feelings

C. to convey a message about old age

D. to inform readers about the seasons

    ___ **12.** How are the main symbols in "The Sound of Summer Running" and "Eleven" alike?

        A. They are both things you can wear.

        B. They are both times of the year.

        C. They both stand for good feelings.

        D. They both belong to the main characters.

Vocabulary

    ___ **13.** If a boy dashed down an *alley* in his new sneakers, where did he run?

        A. through tall grasses

        B. on a narrow street behind buildings

        C. down a hallway in a school

        D. on an athletic field

    ___ **14.** When Mr. Sanderson has a *revelation*, what has happened?

        A. He recognizes Douglas as the boy who looks into the shop window.

        B. He turns around several times.

        C. He has a new pair of shoes in his shop window.

        D. He has an understanding of how the new shoes make you feel.

Essay

15. In "The Sound of Summer Running" and "Eleven," there is a moment when the main character puts on something for the first time. In a short essay, tell what each character puts on and how the character feels at that moment. How are the experiences different for these characters? How are they similar?

16. Think about the words and actions of Douglas in "The Sound of Summer Running" and Rachel in "Eleven." In your opinion, which character seems to behave more like a real person? Write a short essay explaining why.

17. Thinking About the Big Question: How do we decide what is true? In "Eleven," Rachel's teacher must decide what is true about the red sweater. Mrs. Price does not believe Rachel when the girl says the sweater is not hers. In an essay, explain how and why Mrs. Price decides that the sweater belongs to Rachel. Use examples from the selection.

"The Sound of Summer Running" by Ray Bradbury
"Eleven" by Sandra Cisneros
Selection Test B

Critical Reading *Identify the letter of the choice that best completes the statement or answers the question.*

____ 1. In "The Sound of Summer Running" what does Douglas's father tell him when Douglas asks for new sneakers?
    A. They don't have enough money for new sneakers.
    B. He will buy Douglas the sneakers the next day.
    C. Douglas should save his own money for the sneakers.
    D. Douglas should forget about the new sneakers.

____ 2. Look at each group of words below. Which group contains items that all represent images and ideas presented in "The Sound of Summer Running"?
    A. tennis shoes, summer, youth
    B. fields of wheat, farmers, harvest
    C. Litefoot, low-cal soda, sugarless candy
    D. June, magic, socks

____ 3. In "The Sound of Summer Running," what is one thing that the new sneakers symbolize?
    A. freedom
    B. loss
    C. successful business
    D. resentment

____ 4. In "The Sound of Summer Running," what do last year's sneakers symbolize for Douglas?
    A. long, cold winters
    B. going barefoot
    C. the end of summer
    D. a job at the shoe store

____ 5. Around what symbol does the selection "Eleven" revolve?
    A. Rachel's desk
    B. Mrs. Price
    C. school
    D. the red sweater

____ 6. In "Eleven," what does Rachel mean when she says that
    . . .when you're eleven, you're also ten, and nine, and eight, and seven, and six, and five, and four, and three, and two, and one.
    A. She is really 55 years old.
    B. She will have lots of candles on her birthday cake.
    C. She is counting down the seconds until the end of school.
    D. She doesn't feel different on her birthday.

____ 7. How does Rachel feel as she puts her arms into the red sweater in "Eleven"?
   A. bored
   B. guilty
   C. miserable
   D. relieved

____ 8. In "Eleven," why doesn't Rachel want her classmates to think she owns the red sweater?
   A. It is ugly and smelly.
   B. It doesn't fit her properly.
   C. She doesn't like the color red.
   D. She wants a new sweater for her birthday.

____ 9. In "Eleven," why does Rachel wish she were one-hundred-and-two instead of eleven?
   A. If she were very old, she wouldn't have to go to school.
   B. She doesn't like being eleven.
   C. She wishes she could grow up faster.
   D. If she were older, she would know what to say to Mrs. Price.

____ 10. In "Eleven," what do Rachel's age and the red sweater have in common?
   A. Mrs. Price doesn't approve of either one.
   B. Both will be celebrated at the party.
   C. Neither one fits Rachel very well.
   D. Rachel loves one, but not the other.

____ 11. Which sentence best expresses how the authors use symbols in "The Sound of Summer Running" and "Eleven"?
   A. They use symbols to persuade the reader to buy new clothing.
   B. They use symbols to represent the characters' feelings.
   C. They use symbols to express messages about old age.
   D. They use symbols to stand for forces of nature.

____ 12. How are Rachel in "Eleven" and Douglas in "The Sound of Summer Running" alike?
   A. They both make a plan and follow through with it.
   B. They both have birthdays in the summer.
   C. They are both misunderstood by an adult.
   D. They both want to be older than they are.

____ 13. How are the main symbols in "The Sound of Summer Running" and "Eleven" alike?
   A. They are both items that you can wear.
   B. They are both times of the year.
   C. They are both attractive to the main characters.
   D. They both belong to the main characters.

____ **14.** What message about youth is conveyed in both "The Sound of Summer Running" and "Eleven"?
   A. Youth is a painful part of life.
   B. Shoes are important to eleven-year-olds.
   C. Some people spend their youth wishing they were older.
   D. Youth can be a time of very strong feelings.

____ **15.** What might Douglas in "The Sound of Summer Running" and Rachel in "Eleven" agree that they would like to do?
   A. go home
   B. speak up
   C. escape
   D. hide

Vocabulary

____ **16.** When Mr. Sanderson has a *revelation*, what does he do?
   A. He decides to retire and no longer sell Litefoot tennis shoes.
   B. He suspects that Douglas wants to buy the shoes on credit.
   C. He correctly guesses which shoes Douglas wants to buy.
   D. He suddenly understands how wonderful Litefoot tennis shoes are.

____ **17.** What is the best meaning of the word *suspended* in this sentence from "The Sound of Summer Running"?
   He glanced quickly away, but his ankles were seized, his feet <u>suspended</u>, then rushed.
   A. weakened
   B. hurried
   C. stopped
   D. cramped

Essay

18. A symbol is a person, place, or thing that stands for something else. For example, a heart shape is often used as a symbol of love. In an essay, identify the central symbol in "The Sound of Summer Running" and the central symbol in "Eleven." Explain what you think each symbol stands for. How are these two symbols alike? How are they different?

19. Think about the words and actions of Douglas in "The Sound of Summer Running" and Rachel in "Eleven." Write an essay that explains, in your opinion, which character seems more believable and which character seems less believable.

20. **Thinking About the Big Question: How do we decide what is true?** In "Eleven," Rachel's teacher must decide what is true about the red sweater. View events from Mrs. Price's perspective. Consider why she finds it hard to believe Rachel when the girl protests. In an essay, explain how and why she comes to the conclusion that the sweater belongs to Rachel. Use examples from the selection.

Name _____ Date _____

Narration: Autobiographical Narrative

Prewriting: Gathering Details

As you gather details to develop your story, list the events and supportive details in the correct order on the following timeline.

Event 1	Event 2	Event 3	Event 4	Event 5	Event 6

Drafting: Presenting Your Conflict

Use a conflict map like the one shown to record the events that take place in your story. Begin with events that build toward the climax, then follow with events that gradually reduce the tension until you come to the last scene.

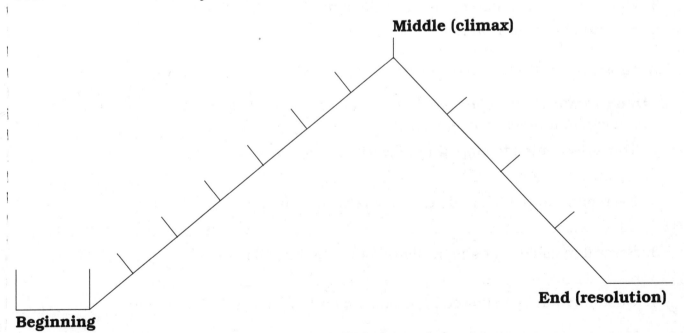

Middle (climax)

End (resolution)

Beginning

Writing Workshop—Unit 1, Part 2
Autobiographical Narrative: Integrating Grammar Skills

Revising for Pronoun/Antecedent Agreement

An antecedent is a noun to which a pronoun refers. The pronoun must agree in number with its antecedent. Use a singular pronoun with a singular antecedent. Use a plural pronoun with a plural antecedent. Follow the same rule when an indefinite pronoun is the antecedent for another pronoun.

Antecedent	Example	Rule	Example Sentence
singular noun	boy, girl, table	Use a singular pronoun.	The **boy** walked **his** dog.
plural noun	boys, girls, tables	Use a plural pronoun.	The **girls** rehearsed **their** speeches.
singular indefinite pronoun	anyone, everything, each, everyone, one, something, nothing	Use a singular pronoun.	**One** of my uncles said **he** would help.
plural indefinite pronoun	both, few, many, others, several	Use a plural pronoun.	**Both** of my sisters said **they** would help.

Using Pronoun/Antecedent Agreement

A. DIRECTIONS: *Circle the pronoun that correctly completes each sentence.*

1. The waitress took out (*their, her*) note pad to take our order.
2. Both boys wanted milk shakes with (*their, his*) sandwiches.
3. One of the boys ordered onions and mustard on (*their, his*) sandwich.
4. Several of the girls said (*she, they*) had to leave early.

Fixing Errors in Pronoun/Antecedent Agreement

B. DIRECTIONS: *On the lines provided, rewrite these sentences to correct errors in pronoun/antecedent agreement.*

1. The girls wanted to stop at her favorite ice cream shop.

_____

2. Everyone wanted to create their own special sundae.

_____

3. Several insisted that she be allowed to substitute flavors.

_____

4. Customers in line showed his dismay by rolling his eyes.

_____

Name _____ Date _____

Unit 1 Vocabulary Workshop—1
Using a Dictionary

A dictionary entry will tell you the meaning of a word and give you other information about the word. When a word has more than one meaning, the definitions are numbered.

> **de-scend** [di send´]. [**L** *descendere*, to climb down, fall < *de-*. down + *scandere*, to climb] **1** to come down from a higher to a lower place; go down **2** to come from an earlier to a later time **3** to go from greater to less, from general to particular, etc. **4** to slope or extend downward **5** to pass by inheritance; be handed down [the land descended to the son] **6** to lower oneself to a particular act; stoop **7** to make a sudden attack: *The wolves descended on the sheep.* **8** *Music* to move down the scale

DIRECTIONS: *Write five sentences with the above word, each using the word with a different one of its meanings. Write the meaning number from the dictionary entry in parentheses following each sentence.*

1. _____
   _____

2. _____
   _____

3. _____
   _____

4. _____
   _____

5. _____
   _____

Name _____   Date _____

Unit 1 Vocabulary Workshop—2
Using a Thesaurus

A thesaurus is useful if you are looking for a synonym or an antonym for a word. Be aware that synonyms contain shades of meaning that make different ones appropriate for different uses.

---

descend [v] *move down, lower*
Synonyms cascade, decline, dip, drop, fall, get down, go down, gravitate, ground, decline, lose balance, move down, sink, slip, pitch, plop, plummet, plunge, slant, slope, submerge, subside
Antonyms ascend, climb, increase, rise

DIRECTIONS: *Write six sentences, four using a synonym of and two using an antonym of* descend *from the thesaurus entry above. Pay attention to the shades of meaning of each synonym and antonym as you write your sentences.*

1. _____

   _____

2. _____

   _____

3. _____

   _____

4. _____

   _____

5. _____

   _____

6. _____

   _____

Name _____ Date _____

Following Oral Directions

Have your partner give you oral directions. Fill out the following chart to help you follow the directions.

Topic of directions: _____

What are the main ideas and details of the directions?
What are the key action words?
What transition words are used?
What words indicate time order?
What questions will you ask to clarify missing information?

Unit 1: Fiction and Nonfiction
Benchmark Test 2

MULTIPLE CHOICE

Reading Skill: Fact and Opinion

1. Which of these statements applies to all nonfiction?
   A. It usually focuses on the experiences of one person.
   B. It contains both facts and opinions.
   C. It contains some details that are real and some that are made up.
   D. It contains only facts, with no opinions.

2. What is a fact?
   A. A fact is something that can be proved.
   B. A fact is something that can be argued.
   C. A fact is something that has a value.
   D. A fact is a person's best judgment.

3. Which of these words or phrases most often signals an opinion?
   A. I believe
   B. I remember
   C. according to
   D. statistics show

4. Of these choices, which is the best source for checking facts?
   A. advertisements
   B. books of essays
   C. encyclopedias
   D. newspaper editorials

Reading Skill: Make and Support Assertions

Read the following list of details from an atlas entry on Guam. Then, answer the questions.

Guam

Guam, a territory of the United States, is an island in the Pacific Ocean. The economy of Guam depends on spending by the U.S. military, tourism, and the exports of fish and handicrafts. Tourism has grown rapidly over the past 20 years, with more than 1 million tourists visiting each year. Sometimes called "America in Asia," Guam boasts over 20 large hotels, 10 golf courses, superior entertainment, and American-style malls. Guam is a relatively short flight from Asia compared to tourist destinations like Hawaii. Ninety percent of Guam's tourists come from Japan. The economic revenue is divided as follows: agriculture: 7%; industry: 15%; services: 78%.

5. Which of the following assertions could you make about Guam based on the atlas entry?
   A. Guam is a rich country.
   B. Many people in Guam are fishers.
   C. People in Guam rely heavily on tourism.
   D. The country grows all of its own food.

6. Which sentence from the entry supports the assertion that most people living in Guam work in a service job?
   A. The economy of Guam depends on spending by the U.S. military, tourism, and the exports of fish and handicrafts.
   B. Tourism has grown rapidly over the past 20 years, with more than 1 million tourists visiting each year.
   C. Sometimes called "America in Asia," Guam boasts over 20 large hotels, 10 golf courses, superior entertainment, and American-style malls.
   D. The economic revenue is divided as follows: agriculture: 7%; industry: 15%; services: 78%.

7. Which of the following assertions about Japanese tourists in Guam is supported by the atlas entry?
   A. They do not spend a great deal of money on the island.
   B. They would rather travel to Hawaii, but it is too far away.
   C. They find Guam appealing because of its location and features.
   D. They do not care for the American-style malls, but they enjoy the entertainment.

Literary Analysis: Author's Perspective and Tone

8. What is an author's perspective?
   A. the viewpoint from which the author writes
   B. the background research an author does to check his or her facts
   C. the time and place in which the work happens
   D. the feeling or atmosphere that the work creates for the reader

9. Which of these most strongly affects the author's perspective?
   A. the pronouns that the author uses to identify characters
   B. the personalities of the different characters
   C. the background and beliefs of the author
   D. the background and beliefs of the reader

10. What does the tone of a literary work usually express?
    A. the attitude of the reader
    B. the attitude of the writer
    C. the mood of a character
    D. the loudness of a character's speech

11. Which phrase best describes the tone of these sentences?

Those Cruz brothers talk like jackhammers. I love those guys—don't get me wrong!—but when it comes to their chatter, I sure do wish they'd practice a little Cruz Control.

A. formal and serious
B. formal but lighthearted
C. informal but sad
D. informal and humorous

12. Which tone would be most suited to an obituary for someone who has died?
A. a happy, formal tone
B. a happy, informal tone
C. a sad and angry tone
D. a sad but admiring tone

Read the selection. Then, answer the questions that follow.

Greenlawn is a wonderful place to visit or live in. It's a small, kid-friendly city, with a brand new aquarium, a fine old zoo, and a first-class natural history museum. When the kids are busy playing in Prospect Park or swimming in its lifeguard-supervised pool, parents can lunch at some of the best restaurants in the state. As a lifelong resident, I've watched Greenlawn grow from a sleepy berg to a bustling small city. And as mayor, I promise you, this is one city that has never lost its small-town friendly ways.

13. What personal interest does the author of the selection seem to have in his or her subject?
A. As a lifelong resident of Greenlawn, he is interested in providing an accurate history.
B. As mayor of Greenlawn, he is interested in making the city look as good as possible.
C. As someone who loves science, he stresses the aquarium and natural history museum.
D. As someone who loves to eat, he gives a lot of information about Greenlawn's restaurants.

14. How would you describe the tone of this selection?
A. serious and formal
B. humorous and witty
C. angry and bitter
D. enthusiastic and admiring

Literary Analysis: Symbols

15. What is a symbol?
A. anything that represents something else
B. anything that expresses strong feelings
C. anything that makes a comparison
D. anything that cannot be proved

Read this selection. Then, answer the questions that follow.

At long last, the war was over. In front of row upon row of warriors, the two leaders met and shook hands. Suddenly, a dove flew overhead. Seeing the graceful white creature, the armies on both sides let out a loud cheer, and many threw down their swords.

16. What does the dove in the selection seem to be a symbol of?
    A. war
    B. peace
    C. grace
    D. nature

17. What do the swords in the selection seem be a symbol of?
    A. war
    B. peace
    C. fear
    D. technology

Vocabulary: Roots

18. Which language does the root of the word *pulsate* come from?
    A. Hebrew   C. Greek
    B. Arabic   D. Latin

19. Based on your understanding of the root *-sequ-*, which of these shows *sequential* order?
    A. 10, 8, 9, 7   C. 4, 5, 3, 2
    B. 5, 6, 7, 8   D. 2, 4, 16, 8

20. Based on your understanding of the root *-mens-*, which of these could be considered an *immense* body of water?
    A. a brook   C. an ocean
    B. a waterfall   D. a puddle

21. How does the meaning of the word *inscribe* reflect the meaning of the root *-scrib-*?
    A. To inscribe, you work with something valuable.
    B. To inscribe, you handle something with care.
    C. To inscribe, you write or engrave something.
    D. To inscribe, you must be skillful.

22. Based on your understanding of the root *-puls-*, which of these would *impulsive* buyers do?
    A. buy things for others but not themselves
    B. buy things they do not need
    C. return things that they have bought
    D. forget to buy the things they need

23. How does the meaning of the word *consecutive* reflect the meaning of the root *-sec-*?
    A. Consecutive items follow one right after the other.
    B. Consecutive items cannot be avoided.
    C. Consecutive items are very easy to recognize.
    D. Consecutive items go on without interruption.

Grammar

24. What is a pronoun?
    A. a word that describes or modifies a noun or another pronoun
    B. a word that takes the place of a noun or another pronoun
    C. a word that connects a noun to the rest of the sentence
    D. a word that shows the actions performed by a noun

25. What type of pronoun does this sentence contain?

    Who is donating blood today?

    A. interrogative
    B. indefinite
    C. personal
    D. possessive

26. Which pronoun correctly completes this sentence?

    Sally walked up to Joe and asked _____ the time.

    A. her
    B. him
    C. his
    D. them

27. What question do possessive pronouns answer?
    A. who?
    B. what?
    C. when?
    D. whose?

28. How many pronouns does this sentence contain?

    Geraldo stars in the play, and some of his classmates came to see him perform in it.

    A. one
    B. two
    C. three
    D. four

29. Which of these sentences uses pronouns correctly?
    A. Each of the boys had their own locker.
    B. Both of the boys had his own locker.
    C. Everyone had his own locker.
    D. All of the boys had his own locker.

Spelling

30. In which sentence is the italic word spelled correctly?
    A. I went *too* the library.
    B. I brought back *to* books.
    C. Sally was there *two*.
    D. I have *to* visit the library again.

31. In which sentence is the italic word spelled correctly?
    A. *Weather* or not I go depends on how much time I have.
    B. I also will probably cancel if the *whether* is bad.
    C. I believe the admission fee is only fifty *cents*.
    D. I hope you have enough *cents* to get out of the rain.

32. What should you do to spell the words in this sentence correctly?

    We've been waiting an our but are pictures are finally ready.

    A. Change *our* to *hour* and leave the rest as is.
    B. Change the first *are* to *our* and leave the rest as is.
    C. Change the second *are* to *our* and leave the rest as is.
    D. Change *our* to *hour* and the first *are* to *our*.

ESSAY

Writing

33. On your paper or a separate sheet, write a dramatic scene in which characters express both facts and opinions. For example, you might write a scene in which a character uses facts to convince another character or group of people to share his or her opinion.

34. Think of an interesting or humorous incident in someone else's life. It could be something you witnessed personally or something you heard or read about. Recount the incident in a personal anecdote.

35. Recall an incident in your life that you think others might be interested in reading about. Did you find the incident funny or sad? Did it make you angry? On your paper or a separate sheet, recount the incident in an autobiographical narrative. Try to capture the feelings you had about what happened.

Vocabulary in Context

Identify the answer choice that best completes the statement.

1. When the fire was reported, the fire department responded_____ .
   A. patiently
   B. rapidly
   C. completely
   D. according

2. The mother put the baby to bed and_____ him in.
   A. tangled
   B. examined
   C. tucked
   D. awakened

3. The children all went outside to run around and play a game of_____ .
   A. tag
   B. bike
   C. checkers
   D. television

4. Grandma had cake and ice cream for the children, and they_____ it down.
   A. coaxed
   B. licked
   C. gobbled
   D. dessert

5. Just before the curtains opened, the actors were jittery and_____ .
   A. excitedly
   B. anxious
   C. relief
   D. directed

6. As the sun rose on the cold day, it spread its_____over the land.
   A. looming
   B. streak
   C. twilight
   D. warmth

7. From where we stood, we could see up to the mountain's_____.
   A. peer
   B. tide
   C. quest
   D. peak

8. When you come in from the beach, please wipe your _____ feet.
   A. sweating
   B. migrating
   C. sandy
   D. stained

9. It is important in life to laugh a lot and to have a good sense of _____.
   A. humor
   B. patience
   C. majesty
   D. embarrassment

10. We did not fly on a jet plane, but rather on a smaller plane with _____.
    A. shafts
    B. thundering
    C. arrived
    D. propellers

11. Because it was hard for the little child to sit still for such a long time, she _____ in her chair.
    A. squirmed
    B. strolled
    C. sprawl
    D. spurred

12. You owe me the total _____ of ten dollars.
    A. plus
    B. sum
    C. undertake
    D. multiply

13. My dog is not thin at all—in fact, it is a little _____ .
    A. slight
    B. plump
    C. beastly
    D. gaining

14. On the bottom of my feet, I had two _____ , which made walking painful.
    A. warts
    B. numb
    C. shreds
    D. odor

15. I only want to know the ending of the book, so just tell me the _____ .
    A. resolved
    B. reference
    C. outcome
    D. theme

16. Apples dipped in a sweet red coating are called _____ apples.
    A. candied
    B. walnut
    C. crunch
    D. mint

17. I regularly ask Dad if we can have a dog, but he _____ refuses to let us have one.
    A. contrary
    B. equally
    C. frequent
    D. stubbornly

18. After he read the newspaper article, he frowned and angrily _____ the paper.
    A. crumpled
    B. memorized
    C. annoyed
    D. tormented

19. If you always try to stand up straight, you will have better _____ .
    A. ramparts
    B. posture
    C. tissue
    D. appointment

20. My desk at work is located in a small _____ .
    A. residence
    B. bookshelf
    C. assignment
    D. cubicle

Diagnostic Tests and Vocabulary in Context
Use and Interpretation

The Diagnostic Tests and Vocabulary in Context were developed to assist teachers in making the most appropriate assignment of *Prentice Hall Literature* program selections to students. The purpose of these assessments is to indicate the degree of difficulty that students are likely to have in reading/comprehending the selections presented in the *following* unit of instruction. Tests are provided at six separate times in each grade level—a *Diagnostic Test* (to be used prior to beginning the year's instruction) and a *Vocabulary in Context,* the final segment of the Benchmark Test appearing at the end of each of the first five units of instruction. Note that the tests are intended for use not as summative assessments for the prior unit, but as guidance for assigning literature selections in the upcoming unit of instruction.

The structure of all Diagnostic Tests and Vocabulary in Context in this series is the same. All test items are four-option, multiple-choice items. The format is established to assess a student's ability to construct sufficient meaning from the context sentence to choose the only provided word that fits both the semantics (meaning) and syntax (structure) of the context sentence. All words in the context sentences are chosen to be "below-level" words that students reading at this grade level should know. All answer choices fit *either* the meaning or structure of the context sentence, but only the correct choice fits *both* semantics and syntax. All answer choices—both correct answers and incorrect options—are key words chosen from specifically taught words that will occur in the subsequent unit of program instruction. This careful restriction of the assessed words permits a sound diagnosis of students' current reading achievement and prediction of the most appropriate level of readings to assign in the upcoming unit of instruction.

The assessment of vocabulary in context skill has consistently been shown in reading research studies to correlate very highly with "reading comprehension." This is not surprising as the format essentially assesses comprehension, albeit in sentence-length "chunks." Decades of research demonstrate that vocabulary assessment provides a strong, reliable prediction of comprehension achievement— the purpose of these tests. Further, because this format demands very little testing time, these diagnoses can be made efficiently, permitting teachers to move forward with critical instructional tasks rather than devoting excessive time to assessment.

It is important to stress that while the Diagnostic and Vocabulary in Context were carefully developed and will yield sound assignment decisions, they were designed to *reinforce*, not supplant, teacher judgment as to the most appropriate instructional placement for individual students. Teacher judgment should always prevail in making placement—or indeed other important instructional—decisions concerning students.

Name _____ Date _____

Diagnostic Tests and Vocabulary in Context
Branching Suggestions

These tests are designed to provide maximum flexibility for teachers. Your *Unit Resources* books contain the 40-question **Diagnostic Test** and 20-question **Vocabulary in Context** tests. At *PHLitOnline,* you can access the Diagnostic Test and complete 40-question Vocabulary in Context tests. Procedures for administering the tests are described below. Choose the procedure based on the time you wish to devote to the activity and your comfort with the assignment decisions relative to the individual students. Remember that your judgment of a student's reading level should always take precedence over the results of a single written test.

Feel free to use different procedures at different times of the year. For example, for early units, you may wish to be more confident in the assignments you make—thus, using the "two-stage" process below. Later, you may choose the quicker diagnosis, confirming the results with your observations of the students' performance built up throughout the year.

The **Diagnostic Test** is composed of a single 40-item assessment. Based on the results of this assessment, make the following assignment of students to the reading selections in Unit 1:

Diagnostic Test Score	Selection to Use
If the student's score is 0–25	more accessible
If the student's score is 26–40	more challenging

Outlined below are the three basic options for administering **Vocabulary in Context** and basing selection assignments on the results of these assessments.

1. For a one-stage, quicker diagnosis using the *20-item* test in the *Unit Resources:*

Vocabulary in Context Test Score	Selection to Use
If the student's score is 0–13	more accessible
If the student's score is 14–20	more challenging

2. If you wish to confirm your assignment decisions with a *two-stage* diagnosis:

Stage 1: Administer the 20-item test in the *Unit Resources*	
Vocabulary in Context Test Score	**Selection to Use**
If the student's score is 0–9	more accessible
If the student's score is 10–15	(Go to Stage 2.)
If the student's score is 16–20	more challenging

Stage 2: Administer items 21–40 from *PHLitOnline*	
Vocabulary in Context Test Score	**Selection to Use**
If the student's score is 0–12	more accessible
If the student's score is 13–20	more challenging

3. If you base your assignment decisions on the full 40-item **Vocabulary in Context** from *PHLitOnline:*

Vocabulary in Context Test Score	Selection to Use
If the student's score is 0–25	more accessible
If the student's score is 26–40	more challenging

Unit 1 Resources: Fiction and Nonfiction

Grade 6—Benchmark Test 1
Interpretation Guide

For remediation of specific skills, you may assign students the relevant Reading Kit Practice and Assess pages indicated in the far-right column of this chart. You will find rubrics for evaluating writing samples in the last section of your Professional Development Guidebook.

Skill Objective	Test Items	Number Correct	Reading Kit
Reading Skill			
Make Predictions	1, 2, 3, 4, 5		pp. 2, 3
Analyzing Structural Features	6, 7, 8		pp. 4, 5
Literary Analysis			
Plot	9, 10, 12, 13, 14		pp. 6, 7
Point of View	11, 15, 16		pp. 8, 9
Fiction and Nonfiction	17, 18		pp. 10, 11
Vocabulary			
Prefixes and Suffixes -ation, -able, pre-, be-	19, 20, 21, 22, 23, 24		pp. 12, 13
Grammar			
Common and Proper Nouns	25, 26, 27		pp. 14, 15
Singular and Plural Nouns	28, 29		pp. 16, 17
Errors with Possessive Nouns	30, 31		pp. 18, 19
Writing			
News Report	32	Use rubric	pp. 20, 21
Autobiographical Narrative	33	Use rubric	pp. 22, 23
Descriptive Essay	34	Use rubric	pp. 24, 25

Grade 6—Benchmark Test 2
Interpretation Guide

For remediation of specific skills, you may assign students the relevant Reading Kit Practice and Assess pages indicated in the far-right column of this chart. You will find rubrics for evaluating writing samples in the last section of your Professional Development Guidebook.

Skill Objective	Test Items	Number Correct	Reading Kit
Reading Skill			
Distinguish Between Fact and Opinion	1, 2, 3, 4		pp. 26, 27
Make and Support Assertions	5, 6, 7		pp. 28, 29
Literary Analysis			
Author's Perspective	8, 9, 13		pp. 30, 31
Tone	10, 11, 12, 14		pp. 32, 33
Symbolism	15, 16, 17		pp. 34, 35
Vocabulary			
Roots -*puls*-, -*sequ*-, -*mens*-, -*scrib*-	18, 19, 20, 21, 22, 23		pp. 36, 37
Grammar			
Pronouns (Personal, Possessive, Interrogative, and Indefinite)	24, 25, 26, 27, 28		pp. 38, 39 pp. 40, 41
Pronoun/Antecedent Agreement	29		pp. 42, 43
Spelling			
Easily Confused Words	30, 31, 32		pp. 44, 45
Writing			
Scene	33	See rubric	pp. 46, 47
Personal Anecdote	34	See rubric	pp. 48, 49
Autobiographical Narrative	35	See rubric	pp. 50, 51

ANSWERS

Big Question Vocabulary—1, p. 1

Sample Answers

1. Bill said, "Lacy, that story is complete *fantasy*. I find it *unbelievable* that you opened your door to a fairy tale character who granted you three wishes!"

2. Stuart said, "Everything Lacy said could have easily been *true*. It is *realistic* that her doorbell rang and an oddly dressed stranger was standing there. It could have been a long lost aunt."

3. Kim said, "Lacy, I believe you have the beginnings of a wonderful work of *fiction*."

Big Question Vocabulary—2, p. 2

Sample Answers

1. "It is your *opinion* that I need better grades. My grades are fine to get into college."

2. "Let's do a little research to *determine* what the *facts* are."

3. "Dad is trying to *prove* to me that I need better grades to get into college."

4. "I made a *decision* to study this afternoon so that I could get good grades."

Big Question Vocabulary—3, p. 3

Sample Answers

1. "I am the subject of a *study* to determine whether carrots improve eyesight. I am conducting a *test* to *investigate* whether Dr. Trooper's theory is true."

2. "We have gathered a lot of *evidence* that will *confirm* my theory!"

Diagnostic Test 1, p. 5

MULTIPLE CHOICE

1. ANS: A
2. ANS: D
3. ANS: A
4. ANS: C
5. ANS: B
6. ANS: B
7. ANS: B
8. ANS: B
9. ANS: B
10. ANS: C
11. ANS: A
12. ANS: C
13. ANS: A
14. ANS: C
15. ANS: D
16. ANS: C
17. ANS: B
18. ANS: D
19. ANS: A
20. ANS: D
21. ANS: C
22. ANS: B
23. ANS: D
24. ANS: A
25. ANS: D
26. ANS: C
27. ANS: A
28. ANS: D
29. ANS: B
30. ANS: C
31. ANS: C
32. ANS: B
33. ANS: D
34. ANS: A
35. ANS: B
36. ANS: C
37. ANS:C
38. ANS: B
39. ANS: A
40. ANS: A

"Greyling" and "My Heart Is in the Highlands"
by Jane Yolen

Vocabulary Warm-up Exercises, p. 14

A.
1. relatives
2. memories
3. childhood
4. mansions
5. stunned
6. mended
7. delicious
8. foam

B. Sample Answers
1. T; Cats are smooth and shiny animals.
2. T; You learn lots of new words by reading.
3. F; Driftwood is found on beaches, not mountains.
4. F; Rebuilding such a town would takes weeks, months, or years.
5. F; Most people like vacations, so vacations are not hard to put up with.
6. T; If the people and events don't exist in real life, it is fiction.
7. T; At a funeral, people are usually very sad.
8. F; When you dwell on something, you spend a long time thinking about it.

Reading Warm-up A, p. 15

Sample Answers

1. <u>completely unexpected</u>; I might be stunned if my mother said that we were moving.
2. <u>Auntie Jane and Uncle Reggie</u>. *Relatives* are people who are part of the same family.
3. Mollie's memories are probably foggy because it has been so long since her last trip to Scotland. *Memories* are "things that you remember from the past."
4. <u>six years old</u>;16
5. <u>extremely big houses</u>; Rich people might live in a *mansion*.
6. <u>waves gently breaking</u>; *Foam* might be found in a bubble bath.
7. Mollie found the meat pastries delicious; I find cupcakes delicious.
8. Mollie needs her shirt sleeve mended because it is torn.

Reading Warm-up B, p. 16

Sample Answers

1. <u>think about</u>
2. (fact)
3. *Rebuilding* at sea could be difficult because of a lack of tools, parts, or the motion of the sea.
4. Seals and sports cars are both sleek!
5. pounding by the waves; these boats break apart
6. The passage says that driftwood is found on an ocean beach.
7. <u>expert</u>
8. Such a family would be feeling terribly sad that the fisherman is lost at sea.

Jane Yolen

Listening and Viewing, p. 17

Sample answers and guidelines for evaluation:

Segment 1: Jane Yolen thinks that it is important to read the book because a movie can leave out important details such as special characters, emotional truth, and the point of a book. Students that choose the book may say that the movie is never as good as they imagined. Students that choose the movie may say that they enjoyed seeing onscreen what they had pictured while reading.

Segment 2: Jane Yolen takes a folk tale about selchies and makes it into a new story. The story is a combination of fiction and nonfiction because even though selchies do not exist, the story is based on folklore and its landscape is real.

Segment 3: Jane Yolen reads everything, watches movies, talks to people, and listens to song lyrics and gossip. Students may answer that they would gather information from their environment, read as much as possible, and listen to music and stories that their friends tell them.

Segment 4: The real reward for Jane Yolen is not money or awards, but the knowledge that she wrote a story that excites the reader and forever changes him or her.

Unit 1: Learning About Fiction and Nonfiction, p. 18

A.
1. fiction
2. nonfiction
3. nonfiction
4. fiction

B. Fiction. The paragraph is about an imaginary dog that can solve math problems.

"Greyling" by Jane Yolen

Model Selection: Fiction, p. 19

Sample Answers

Characters: a fisherman and his wife; a strange seal/human; *Plot:* The fisherman and his wife want a child. One day, the fisherman finds a seal pup and brings it home. It turns into a boy. The fisherman and his wife don't want the boy to go into the ocean, because he might turn back into a seal. Years later, there is a terrible storm. The fisherman is stranded and must be rescued. Greyling goes to save him. As he does, he turns back into a seal. He swims away, but returns once a year; *Narrator:* outside the story; third-person point of view; *Setting:* a hut by the side of the sea

"My Heart Is in the Highlands" by Jane Yolen

Model Selection: Nonfiction, p. 20

A.
1. the author and her husband
2. Scotland
3. She and her husband saw old, cozy stone cottages as they drove through rural Scotland. They learned that throughout history, new buildings were built on the sites with the materials of older buildings.
4. Sample answer: Homes and gardens are built on the sites of older buildings. The stones are reused. The walls are roughcast to make them strong.
5. Sample answer: Like the Scottish builders who reuse old materials, Yolen reshapes and reuses details from real people and real experiences when she writes fiction.

B. Guidelines for evaluation: Most students will probably say that Yolen's two purposes were to inform and to share an experience. She informs readers about the methods for reusing old building sites and materials; she also shares her experience and her thoughts about writing.

"Greyling" and "My Heart Is in the Highlands"
by Jane Yolen

Open-Book Test, p. 21
Short Answer

1. Her writing is nonfiction because she is writing about her true-life experiences.
   Difficulty: *Easy* **Objective:** *Literary Analysis*

2. The book is fiction because even though it is set in a real period of history and includes some historical figures, it contains a made-up character.
   Difficulty: *Average* **Objective:** *Literary Analysis*

3. An exciting nonfiction book on the same subject might tell true adventures of real-life astronauts or space missions.
   Difficulty: *Challenging* **Objective:** *Literary Analysis*

4. The story is set "by the side of the sea." The sea is where the fisherman works, where he finds the selchie baby, and where the selchie finally makes his home.
   Difficulty: *Easy* **Objective:** *Interpretation*

5. The fisherman's wife is afraid to let Greyling swim because she knows he is a selchie who will return to the sea forever. The fisherman goes along with her but feels "it was wrong."
   Difficulty: *Average* **Objective:** *Interpretation*

6. The word *cliffs* helps me understand that *sheared* means "cut off sharply." Cliffs drop straight down in a sharp drop.
   Difficulty: *Average* **Objective:** *Vocabulary*

7. Some students may say that the fisherman's wife would have stopped Greyling because he means so much to her. Others may suggest that love for her husband would have caused her to let Greyling dive into the sea to save him. She knows that the sea will kill her husband but not Greyling.
   Difficulty: *Challenging* **Objective:** *Interpretation*

8. Memory is something real that you remember. The word *re-memory* suggests that you are remembering again in a new way. Fiction writers often change the actual memory for their purposes.
   Difficulty: *Average* **Objective:** *Interpretation*

9. Sample answers: Details—real setting of Scotland; narrated from the author's perspective; explains her writing process. Importance—uses Scottish buildings to compare building and writing; gives insight into her works; main topic of the speech.
   Difficulty: *Average* **Objective:** *Literary Analysis*

10. The author uses people and experiences from her/his own past but then changes them in small and big ways to create a character.
    Difficulty: *Average* **Objective:** *Interpretation*

Essay

11. Students might indicate that Greyling's parents are relieved because they no longer have to worry about whether they are doing the right thing in keeping him from the sea. Students might note that like all parents, the couple knew they could not hold on to their son forever, even though they could not bring themselves to let him go. Because of the storm and the need for the rescue, Greyling's parents do not have to make the choice. He makes it for them.
    Difficulty: *Easy* **Objective:** *Essay*

12. Some students may suggest that the fisherman and his wife keep Greyling from the sea because they believe their love for him is the most important thing in his life. Others may find their actions selfish because they are denying their son's true identity.
    Difficulty: *Average* **Objective:** *Essay*

13. Students should indicate two ways in which Yolen might have used her own personal history to write "Greyling." In the introduction to the story, Yolen talks about the ballads she loved as a child. One of these gave her the setting for her story—the cold sea around Scotland. It also gave her the idea to use a selchie in her story. The introduction also tells about Yolen's first child. Yolen incorporated the love of a child in the story in the form of the love the fisherman and his wife have toward Greyling.
    Difficulty: *Challenging* **Objective:** *Essay*

14. Students should note that Greyling ignores the sign that he is always "looking and longing and grieving in his heart" for the sea. He also never questions why his parents do not allow him to go into the sea. Students might indicate he ignores the signs because he is a dutiful son who loves his parents. They might point out that he is happy when he discovers the truth because he finally assumes his true identity, but he also longs for his parents as evidenced by the fact that he keeps returning.
    Difficulty: *Average* **Objective:** *Essay*

Oral Response

15. Oral responses should be clear, well organized, and well supported by appropriate examples from the selection.
    Difficulty: *Average* **Objective:** *Oral Interpretation*

Selection Test A, p. 24
Learning About Fiction and Nonfiction

1.	ANS: A	DIF: Easy	OBJ: Literary Analysis
2.	ANS: D	DIF: Easy	OBJ: Literary Analysis
3.	ANS: C	DIF: Easy	OBJ: Literary Analysis
4.	ANS: B	DIF: Easy	OBJ: Literary Analysis
5.	ANS: C	DIF: Easy	OBJ: Literary Analysis

Critical Reading

6.	ANS: D	DIF: Easy	OBJ: Literary Analysis
7.	ANS: A	DIF: Easy	OBJ: Literary Analysis
8.	ANS: C	DIF: Easy	OBJ: Comprehension
9.	ANS: D	DIF: Easy	OBJ: Comprehension

10. ANS: A   DIF: Easy   OBJ: Interpretation
11. ANS: B   DIF: Easy   OBJ: Literary Analysis
12. ANS: C   DIF: Easy   OBJ: Comprehension
13. ANS: A   DIF: Easy   OBJ: Interpretation
14. ANS: D   DIF: Easy   OBJ: Interpretation
15. ANS: C   DIF: Easy   OBJ: Comprehension

Essay

16. Students should note that Greyling has gone back to the sea, where he belongs and where he will be happiest.
    Difficulty: *Easy*
    Objective: *Essay*

17. Students should include factual descriptions of real people or events, followed by details regarding the changes that the student writer would make.
    Difficulty: *Easy*
    Objective: *Essay*

18. Students should note one of these signs that Greyling ignores: he is always "looking and longing and grieving in his heart" for the sea; his parents do not allow him to go into the sea. Students might indicate he ignores the signs because he is a good son who loves his parents. He works hard to help them and make them happy.
    Difficulty: *Easy*
    Objective: *Essay*

Essay

19. Students should note that Greyling changes back into a seal and returns to the sea but returns to visit from time to time. They may or may not feel that he is happier, but they should support their views with reasons.
    Difficulty: *Average*
    Objective: *Essay*

20. Students may say that she based him on a young man who longed to be somewhere else. He solved that problem by moving away or going on a long journey. Probably his parents were sad to see him go, but they understood that he needed to be free and happy.
    Difficulty: *Challenging*
    Objective: *Essay*

21. Students should note that Greyling ignores the sign that he is always "looking and longing and grieving in his heart" for the sea. He also never questions why his parents do not allow him to go into the sea. Students might indicate he ignores the signs because he is a dutiful son who loves his parents. They might point out that he is happy when he discovers the truth because he finally assumes his true identity, but he also longs for his parents as evidenced by the fact that he keeps returning.
    Difficulty: *Average*
    Objective: *Essay*

Selection Test B, p. 27

Learning About Fiction and Nonfiction

1. ANS: D   DIF: Average   OBJ: Literary Analysis
2. ANS: B   DIF: Average   OBJ: Literary Analysis
3. ANS: C   DIF: Average   OBJ: Literary Analysis
4. ANS: A   DIF: Challenging   OBJ: Literary Analysis
5. ANS: C   DIF: Challenging   OBJ: Literary Analysis
6. ANS: A   DIF: Challenging   OBJ: Literary Analysis

Critical Reading

7. ANS: D   DIF: Average   OBJ: Literary Analysis
8. ANS: C   DIF: Challenging   OBJ: Comprehension
9. ANS: B   DIF: Challenging   OBJ: Interpretation
10. ANS: B   DIF: Challenging   OBJ: Interpretation
11. ANS: A   DIF: Challenging   OBJ: Interpretation
12. ANS: D   DIF: Average   OBJ: Comprehension
13. ANS: B   DIF: Challenging   OBJ: Interpretation
14. ANS: C   DIF: Challenging   OBJ: Interpretation
15. ANS: B   DIF: Average   OBJ: Comprehension
16. ANS: A   DIF: Challenging   OBJ: Interpretation
17. ANS: A   DIF: Average   OBJ: Comprehension
18. ANS: C   DIF: Challenging   OBJ: Comprehension

"Stray" by Cynthia Rylant

Vocabulary Warm-up Exercises, p. 31

A. 1. cough
2. sipped
3. warehouse
4. automobiles
5. abandoned
6. exhausted
7. mildly
8. ignore

B. Sample Answers
1. Biscuits are a type of bread people eat in the morning.
2. I would give away all my books, but I would only do so grudgingly.
3. I would probably speak timidly in front of a very large group of people.
4. Poverty might cause people to experience starvation.
5. The emergency workers trudged through the wreckage to reach the family.

6. When you make gingerbread men, <u>scraps</u> of dough are left over.

7. You would find <u>icicles</u> hanging from trees in winter.

8. If my pet fish died, I would feel <u>distress</u>.

Reading Warm-up A, p. 32

Sample Answers

1. <u>cold</u>; I might cough if I had the flu.

2. (just a few flakes); *Mildly* means "gently."

3. <u>driving</u>; My favorite kinds of *automobiles* are sports cars that go really fast.

4. (for storing salt); Food, cars, and packages might be kept in warehouses.

5. <u>pay attention</u>; I always *ignore* my little sister when she tries to bother me.

6. <u>along the sides of roadways</u>; People probably pick up their *abandoned* cars after the snow melts.

7. Hot chocolate is *sipped* because it is too hot to drink quickly without burning you.

8. <u>snow shoveling is hard work</u>; Playing basketball, lifting weights, and moving boxes will leave you *exhausted*.

Reading Warm-up B, p. 33

Sample Answers

1. <u>have difficulty finding food</u>; Animals at risk of *starvation* need food to eat.

2. Starving animals need more than small pieces of food; they need lots of food.

3. An old *biscuit* would probably feel hard, taste stale, and look moldy.

4. They would feed them *grudgingly* because it would create a nuisance problem to have a lot of strays hanging around.

5. (empty houses); (garbage dumps); *Trudged* means to walk slowly and with effort.

6. <u>hunger, illness</u>; Animals experience distress when they are sick or hungry.

7. <u>fear</u>

8. The weather would likely be freezing and snowy when *icicles* cover a cardboard box.

Writing About the Big Question, p. 34

A. 1. investigate

2. evidence

3. study

4. prove

B. Sample Answers

1. I have always had a dog. The dog I have now is named Gulliver. He is black and white with spotted paws, and he's my best friend.

2. Gulliver is a great companion. I tell him all my secrets, and he helps me make **decisions** and **determine** what I want to do about problems.

C. Sample Answer

Dog owners spend money on visits to the veterinarian, dog food, and dog toys.

"Stray" by Cynthia Rylant

Reading: Use Prior Knowledge to Make Predictions, p. 35

Sample Answers

Students should note their prior knowledge, details from the story, and predictions as indicated on the chart.

Sample Responses

1. About dogs: Prior knowledge—Some are good; others bite and bark. Story detail—This dog is good; it doesn't cry or howl. Prediction—Doris's parents will like the puppy because it is a good dog.

2. About children and adults in a family: Prior knowledge—Adults make the big decisions. Story detail—Doris tries to convince her parents that they should keep the dog. They ignore her. Prediction—Mr. Lacey is going to take the dog to the pound.

3. About families with little money: Prior knowledge—They may not be able to afford a pet. Story detail—Doris's father doesn't make much money. Prediction—The dog will be taken to the pound.

Literary Analysis: Plot, p. 36

A. Sample Answers

1. The Laceys have a small house.

2. A. Mr. Lacey agrees to let the dog sleep in the basement.

  B. Doris tries to talk her parents into letting her keep the puppy.

3. Mr. Lacey asks Doris if she is going to feed the dog.

Vocabulary Builder, p. 37

A. Sample Responses

1. moving cautiously. The puppy is fearful.

2. willingly. I would not resent helping someone I like.

3. angry. The coach wants the team to pay attention, not to behave as if the coach is not there.

4. No. Someone who trudged moved slowly.

5. You might go to sleep. If you are exhausted, you are very tired.

6. No. A bear would face starvation if it did not have enough to eat.

B. Sample Answers

1. Their separation might scare them both.

2. I like to have a conversation about my friends.

3. I feel admiration for a person who is honest and kind.

Enrichment, p. 38

A. Sample Answer

Accept any responses that include a sketch of an animal suitable for a pet and a title at the top (such as Unwanted! Can You Help?). On the lines following the heading **Information,** they should include the address of the local animal shelter or its phone number.

B. Sample Responses

1. 3 hours
2. Food: $3.00 a week

   Shots: $20.00 each year

   Toys: $5.00 a year

   License: $25.00

   (This will be blank if the pet is not a dog.)

   Checkups and medical care: $50 a year

   Cost for getting pet from shelter: $50

   Purchase price of pet from breeder $300
3. Advantage (of cat as pet): My cat keeps me company. She is always with me, even at night.

   Advantage (of dog as pet): We have fun together. She is a watchdog.
4. Disadvantage (of cat): Having to clean the litter box; fleas, clawing on furniture.

   Disadvantage (of dog): I have to take her on walks.

"Stray" by Cynthia Rylant

Open-Book Test, p. 39

Short Answer

1. Doris behaves timidly when she hugs the dog to her and says nothing.

   Difficulty: *Average*   **Objective:** *Vocabulary*
2. *Grudgingly* means "in an unwilling or resentful way." Mrs. Lacey unwillingly gives up food because she really does not want to keep or feed the dog.

   Difficulty: *Challenging*   **Objective:** *Vocabulary*
3. Children usually love their pets. This knowledge helps me predict that Doris will become fond of the dog.

   Difficulty: *Easy*   **Objective:** *Reading*
4. Doris's parents ignore her because they agree with her, but they still do not want to keep the dog. It is easier for them not to talk about it.

   Difficulty: *Average*   **Objective:** *Interpretation*
5. She wants Doris to stop crying and accept the fact that they cannot keep the dog.

   Difficulty: *Easy*   **Objective:** *Interpretation*
6. Rising Action: 1) Mrs. Lacey tells Doris to act more grown-up; 2) Doris hears her father drive away. From Mrs. Lacey's words, Doris knows she will not change her mind about the dog. When Doris hears her father drive away, she is sure the dog is going to the pound.

   Difficulty: *Average*   **Objective:** *Literary Analysis*

7. Doris and the reader predict the dog will go to the pound. Sample examples from story: "I know for sure where it's going."; "She knew her parents wouldn't let her keep it."; "You know we can't afford a dog, Doris."

   Difficulty: *Average*   **Objective:** *Reading*
8. In the falling action, Mr. Lacey shows he is a kind person who cannot leave the dog at the awful pound. The author waits to show this side of him in order to build tension in the plot.

   Difficulty: *Challenging*   **Objective:** *Literary Analysis*
9. Mrs. Lacey smiles and shakes her head because she is amused and surprised by her husband's softhearted action.

   Difficulty: *Challenging*   **Objective:** *Interpretation*
10. The resolution is a surprise because the story suggests that the dog will go to the pound. Doris's parents clearly state that they can't afford a pet. They ignore her when she praises the dog. Nothing points to the fact that Doris will be able to keep the dog.

    Difficulty: *Easy*   **Objective:** *Literary Analysis*

Essay

11. Students should conclude that there is love between Doris and her parents even though Mr. and Mrs. Lacey seem unfeeling at times. The Laceys are doing what they think is best. At the end of the story, they show that they are not as hard as they first appear and do care about Doris.

    Difficulty: *Easy*   **Objective:** *Essay*
12. Some students may indicate that Mr. and Mrs. Lacey learn that the sensible choice is not always the best one. Others may suggest that they learn how important their daughter's feelings are to them. They tell Doris that they cannot afford a dog and that the dog must go to the pound, despite Doris's pleas. Mr. Lacey uses the conditions at the pound as an excuse to give Doris what she wants.

    Difficulty: *Average*   **Objective:** *Essay*
13. Students should indicate that Doris's parents are not emotional people in the story. It seems fitting that they would give Doris the news in a quiet way. Students might also point out that Mr. Lacey is more softhearted than he cares to admit. Letting Doris find out about the dog in a roundabout way fits his character.

    Difficulty: *Challenging*   **Objective:** *Essay*
14. Students should include some of these observations: At the beginning, Doris's parents seem to be practical people. This leads Doris to believe that the stray dog will have to go because the family cannot afford a pet. Doris's conclusion turns out to be wrong because there are other factors involved. Her father is really a kind man who cannot stand the conditions in the pound. Both her parents love her and want her to be happy. These factors cause Mr. and Mrs. Lacey to be less practical and allow Doris to keep the dog.

    Difficulty: *Average*   **Objective:** *Essay*

15. Oral responses should be clear, well organized, and well supported by appropriate examples from the selections.

Difficulty: *Average*   **Objective:** *Oral Interpretation*

Selection Test A, p. 42

Critical Reading

1. ANS: B	DIF: Easy	OBJ: Reading
2. ANS: B	DIF: Easy	OBJ: Reading
3. ANS: D	DIF: Easy	OBJ: Comprehension
4. ANS: D	DIF: Easy	OBJ: Reading
5. ANS: B	DIF: Easy	OBJ: Literary Analysis
6. ANS: A	DIF: Easy	OBJ: Interpretation
7. ANS: C	DIF: Easy	OBJ: Comprehension
8. ANS: A	DIF: Easy	OBJ: Comprehension
9. ANS: D	DIF: Easy	OBJ: Literary Analysis
10. ANS: B	DIF: Easy	OBJ: Interpretation

Vocabulary and Grammar

11. ANS: B	DIF: Easy	OBJ: Vocabulary
12. ANS: B	DIF: Easy	OBJ: Grammar
13. ANS: D	DIF: Easy	OBJ: Grammar
14. ANS: D	DIF: Easy	OBJ: Vocabulary

Essay

15. A girl, Doris, sees a stray dog in the snow. She takes the dog in, but she encounters a conflict. Her parents don't want to keep the dog. In the rising action, Doris tries to talk to her parents about keeping the dog, but they ignore her. In the climax of the story, Doris's father takes the dog to the pound. The resolution is that he doesn't like the conditions at the pound, so he brings the dog back. Doris gets to keep the dog.

Difficulty: *Easy*

Objective: *Essay*

16. Doris's parents hoped to teach her to be like them, a sensible person who would not waste money or feelings on a dog. Students may say that Doris learned that people are not always what they seem, that they hide their true feelings. She learns that her father cares about her. She also learns that events that seem to be heading in a sad direction can take a surprising turn for the better.

Difficulty: *Easy*

Objective: *Essay*

17. Students should include some of these observations: Doris's conclusion turns out to be wrong because other things become more important than the money. Her father is horrified by the conditions at the pound. Both her parents love her and want her to be happy. These factors cause Mr. and Mrs. Lacey to be less practical and allow Doris to keep the dog.

Difficulty: *Easy*

Objective: *Essay*

Selection Test B, p. 45

Critical Reading

1. ANS: B	DIF: Average	OBJ: Reading
2. ANS: C	DIF: Challenging	OBJ: Literary Analysis
3. ANS: B	DIF: Average	OBJ: Literary Analysis
4. ANS: B	DIF: Average	OBJ: Reading
5. ANS: D	DIF: Average	OBJ: Comprehension
6. ANS: C	DIF: Challenging	OBJ: Interpretation
7. ANS: D	DIF: Average	OBJ: Literary Analysis
8. ANS: B	DIF: Average	OBJ: Interpretation
9. ANS: C	DIF: Challenging	OBJ: Interpretation
10. ANS: B	DIF: Challenging	OBJ: Interpretation
11. ANS: D	DIF: Average	OBJ: Reading
12. ANS: A	DIF: Average	OBJ: Interpretation
13. ANS: D	DIF: Challenging	OBJ: Comprehension

Vocabulary and Grammar

14. ANS: B	DIF: Average	OBJ: Vocabulary
15. ANS: D	DIF: Challenging	OBJ: Vocabulary
16. ANS: C	DIF: Average	OBJ: Vocabulary
17. ANS: D	DIF: Average	OBJ: Grammar
18. ANS: D	DIF: Average	OBJ: Grammar
19. ANS: B	DIF: Challenging	OBJ: Grammar

Essay

20. Doris learns that people are not always what they seem. She learns that her father loves her. As a result, Doris may become more optimistic in her future relationships with people. Some students may respond that remembering how her experience turned out happily in the end—despite her earlier despair—could make Doris a more optimistic person in general.

Difficulty: *Average*

Objective: *Essay*

21. The author delays the climax of the story to increase the tension. The reader is led to believe that when Doris wakes up, the dog will be gone. That is what Doris expected, and the details in the story lead the reader to expect it too. The story has a surprise ending, which makes it more enjoyable. In the resolution of the story, Mr. Lacey reveals that he does care about what happens to the puppy. He tells Doris that he couldn't leave the dog at the pound. It is smelly and crowded. Mr. Lacey also reveals, without saying so, that he wants to make Doris happy.

Difficulty: *Average*

Objective: *Essay*

22. Students should include some of these observations: At the beginning, Doris's parents seem to be practical people. This leads Doris to believe that the stray dog will have to go because the family cannot afford a pet.

Doris's conclusion turns out to be wrong because there are other factors involved. Her father is really a kind man who cannot stand the conditions in the pound. Both her parents love her and want her to be happy. These factors cause Mr. and Mrs. Lacey to be less practical and allow Doris to keep the dog.

Difficulty: *Average*

Objective: *Essay*

"The Homecoming" by Laurence Yep

Vocabulary Warm-up Exercises, p. 49

A. 1. odd
2. bulged
3. jabbed
4. advising
5. distracted
6. interesting
7. recipe
8. aroma

B. Sample Answers

1. I *don't want* to go to sleep since I have so much energy.
2. It is *hard* to find firewood in places were there aren't any trees.
3. A hatchet is a useful tool for cutting *wood*.
4. I was so involved in my book that I *didn't want to stop* reading it.
5. Harold was a big fan of games, so he *loved* playing chess.
6. In fall, the ground is covered with leaves because the area is *so* wooded.
7. Denise really *didn't* want Jackson to join us, so she began shooing him away.
8. We had been gone for almost five *years*, so people were excited about our homecoming.

Reading Warm-up A, p. 50

Sample Answers

1. strange; I would find it odd if my teacher stopped giving out homework.
2. He stuffed so many in his mouth; *Bulged* means "stuck out, or appeared swollen."
3. It probably explains how to make chocolate-chip cookies. A favorite *recipe* of mine is the one for "blonde brownies."
4. (smell); A papaya has an unusual *aroma*.
5. He poked his hand into the container with a quick motion.
6. Howard's chatter made her lose her concentration; A lot of people talking at once might make me feel *distracted*.
7. (boring); *Interesting* means "attracting your interest or curiosity."

8. Howard *advised* her to substitute margarine for butter.

Reading Warm-up B, p. 51

Sample Answers

1. games; To play *chess*, you need a lot of patience and the ability to concentrate.
2. Hiking and backpacking take *energy*; you need *energy* for playing basketball and dancing.
3. surrounded by trees; You might see chipmunks and woodpeckers in a *wooded* area.
4. *Firewood* comes from pieces of trees that grow in wooded areas.
5. chopping wood; an ax can also be used for chopping wood.
6. When you are *shooing* flies, you want flies to go away.
7. *Homecoming* is when you get back home after being away for a while.
8. (participating); I love the ocean and would like to get *involved* in surfing and sailing.

Writing About the Big Question, p. 52

A. 1. fiction
2. realistic
3. fantasy
4. unbelievable

B. Sample Answers

1. *My Side of the Mountain* is a realistic story. Its characters are like real people, and it is set in a real place, the Catskill Mountains.
2. *Cinderella* is a fantasy story. It is a fairy tale set in an imaginary kingdom, and it features a fairy godmother and magic.

C. Sample Answer

  If a woodcutter never cuts wood, he is not a **true** woodcutter. The **fact** that he doesn't cut wood is **evidence** that he isn't a real woodcutter, even if he calls himself one.

"The Homecoming" by Laurence Yep

Reading: Use Prior Knowledge to Make Predictions, p. 53

Sample Answers

Students should use their prior knowledge, details from the story, and predictions as indicated on the chart.

Sample Responses

1. About people who give unwanted advice: Prior knowledge—They bore their listeners. Story detail—The chess players ignore the woodcutter. Prediction—They will get angry with him.

2. About characters who look strange or magical: Prior knowledge—They are going to do something important, either good or evil. Story detail—They play a game of chess for seven days. Prediction—There is something magical about the two men.

3. About someone who is hungry: Prior knowledge—The person asks for some food. Story detail—The strange chess players throw away the peach stone. Prediction—The woodcutter will grab the peach stone and see if there is anything left on it.

Literary Analysis: Plot, p. 54

A. Sample Answers

1. The woodcutter is a busybody.
2. A. The woodcutter walks deep into the mountains.
   B. He meets two strange-looking men playing chess.
3. The schoolteacher finds the incident in the clan book.

Vocabulary Builder, p. 55

A. Sample Responses

1. not likely to accept that as a good reason. I should turn off the music if I am distracted by it and unable to concentrate with it on.
2. Your friend may not recognize you because he or she may need glasses.
3. The escorting boats might be honoring the ship.
4. No. If I am charitable, I am being generous and helpful.
5. No. If he murmured, he spoke in a low voice.
6. Yes. A fascinating show might be interesting.

B. Sample Answers

1. A likeable person would be nice, funny, and smart.
2. I might feel very full.
3. He might behave very sensibly.

Enrichment: Folk Tales, p. 56

A. Sample Answers

1. The woodcutter has a problem.
2. He is a busybody.
3. He leaves the village to cut firewood.
4. He meets two strange-looking men playing a game of chess.
5. The magic object is the peach or the peach stone.
6. The peach stone causes the woodcutter to be unaware that many, many years have passed. When he goes back to the village, he finds that several thousand years have gone by since he left the village.

B. Sample Response

Students should include all key elements of the folk tale: a character with a problem, the character's journey, a supernatural figure, a magical object, and an ending.

"Stray" by Cynthia Rylant
"The Homecoming" by Laurence Yep

Integrated Language Skills: Grammar, p. 57

Common and Proper Nouns; Possessives

A. Sample Responses

1. Cynthia Rylant-P, life's-C, story-C, children-C
2. Rylant-P, childhood-C, West Virginia's-P, hills-C
3. character-C, "Stray"-P, Rylant-P, animals-C
4. Laurence Yep-P, San Francisco-P, California-P
5. Yep-P, stories-C, high school-C

"The Homecoming" by Laurence Yep

Open-Book Test, p. 60

Short Answer

1. The woodcutter tries to give advice to a boy making a kite and to a man feeding his ducks. His actions help the reader predict that he will talk to the men playing chess.

   Difficulty: *Average*   **Objective:** *Reading*

2. Students who get distracted in class do not pay attention, so they do not learn the lesson.

   Difficulty: *Average*   **Objective:** *Vocabulary*

3. The woodcutter's wife warns her husband not to talk to anyone because she fears he will get distracted and forget his task.

   Difficulty: *Easy*   **Objective:** *Interpretation*

4. The woodcutter ignores his wife's advice and gets involved in the chess game. He stays longer and longer. The reader fears he will never get the firewood.

   Difficulty: *Easy*   **Objective:** *Literary Analysis*

5. Sample answers: Don't care for his advice; Don't want him to stay. The chess players view the woodcutter as unimportant, not worth their attention.

   Difficulty: *Average*   **Objective:** *Interpretation*

6. The climax of the story occurs shortly after the woodcutter sucks on the peach stone. The peach juices fill him with energy, and he doesn't realize so much time is passing. When the chess game ends, the men tell the woodcutter that he must go home quickly.

   Difficulty: *Average*   **Objective:** *Literary Analysis*

7. Prior knowledge of these folk tales would help the reader predict that the men playing chess are supernatural figures who will teach the busybody woodcutter a lesson.

   Difficulty: *Challenging*   **Objective:** *Reading*

8. It is too late for the woodcutter to go home. A great deal of time has passed without his realizing it, and there is nothing he can do to change what has happened.

   Difficulty: *Average*   **Objective:** *Interpretation*

9. The woodcutter would expect to recognize, or know, his wife and two children.

   Difficulty: *Easy*   **Objective:** *Vocabulary*

10. The resolution is the final outcome. At this point, it is too late for the woodcutter to take his wife's advice. Because he did not listen to her, he has lost everything.
   Difficulty: *Challenging*   **Objective:** *Literary Analysis*

Essay

11. Students' essays should include some of these observations: The story suggests that busybodies waste time and give unwanted advice. People do not like them and do not want them around. The woodcutter is easily distracted by minding other people's business. He neglects his work and does not make the money he needs to feed his family. The people in his village laugh at him because he thinks he knows everything. Because he is a busybody, the woodcutter stays to watch the saints play chess, causing him to lose everything.
   Difficulty: *Easy*   **Objective:** *Essay*

12. Some students might indicate that the woodcutter has learned not to be a busybody by the end of the story. On the way back to his village, he hurries home instead of giving a farmer advice on how to swing a hoe. When he reaches his village, he learns he has lost everything. From then on, he will probably stay out of other people's business. Other students may note that the woodcutter could not change so easily. On his way home, he is still tempted to give advice to a farmer. Although he loses everything at the end of the story, this might not be enough for him to change his character.
   Difficulty: *Average*   **Objective:** *Essay*

13. Students' essays should include some of these observations: The central character, a busybody, is laughed at by his fellow villagers. This suggests that the Chinese believe people should not interfere in the lives of others. The woodcutter is also scolded by his wife for not making money to take care of his family. This suggests that the Chinese traditionally believe a man should take care of the needs of his family. At the end of the story, the schoolteacher reads about the woodcutter in a clan book, suggesting that it was a tradition for the Chinese to record their local history.
   Difficulty: *Challenging*   **Objective:** *Essay*

14. Students should note that the woodcutter sees things through a slanted view. He thinks he knows "a little of everything," but he really knows "most of nothing." At the chess game, he waits and waits for the players to take his valuable advice. He does not realize that it is unusual for people to play chess night and day for seven days. The players eat nothing but a shared peach, and the woodcutter only sucks the peach stone. The woodcutter fails to realize that this is not enough food. He never questions how a peach stone could give him so much energy.
   Difficulty: *Average*   **Objective:** *Essay*

Oral Response

15. Oral responses should be clear, well organized, and well supported by appropriate examples from the selection.
   Difficulty: *Average*   **Objective:** *Oral Interpretation*

"The Homecoming" by Laurence Yep

Selection Test A, p. 63

Critical Reading

1. ANS: D	DIF: Easy	OBJ: Comprehension
2. ANS: C	DIF: Easy	OBJ: Reading
3. ANS: B	DIF: Easy	OBJ: Comprehension
4. ANS: D	DIF: Easy	OBJ: Interpretation
5. ANS: A	DIF: Easy	OBJ: Literary Analysis
6. ANS: C	DIF: Easy	OBJ: Interpretation
7. ANS: D	DIF: Easy	OBJ: Interpretation
8. ANS: A	DIF: Easy	OBJ: Comprehension
9. ANS: A	DIF: Easy	OBJ: Literary Analysis
10. ANS: B	DIF: Easy	OBJ: Reading

Vocabulary and Grammar

11. ANS: C	DIF: Easy	OBJ: Vocabulary
12. ANS: D	DIF: Easy	OBJ: Vocabulary
13. ANS: C	DIF: Easy	OBJ: Grammar
14. ANS: A	DIF: Easy	OBJ: Grammar

Essay

15. The climax of the story occurs shortly after the woodcutter sucks on the peach stone. The peach juices fill him with energy, so he doesn't realize all the time that has passed. When the chess game ends, the two men tell the woodcutter that he must go home quickly. In the resolution of the story, the woodcutter returns to his village and finds that it has changed quite a bit. He discovers that thousands of years have passed since he left the village. He realizes that he should have listened to his wife's warning, but it is too late now.
   Difficulty: *Easy*
   Objective: *Essay*

16. Students should choose one lesson from the story and identify it clearly as the one they consider most important. They may, for instance, choose the lesson that people should not hang around those who ignore them. They would then explain that the two strangers ignored the woodcutter. He should have gone on looking for wood. By staying with the strangers and trying to give them advice, he was giving in to his old bad habit. The woodcutter had responsibilities back at the village. The

strangers were never going to accept any advice from him, and he should have realized that. Students may say that self-respect is very important. Hanging around people who ignore you shows lack of respect for yourself.

Difficulty: *Easy*

Objective: *Essay*

17. Students should note that the villagers say the wood-cutter "knew a little of everything and most of nothing." He is sure that he knows the best way to do anything. At the chess game, he waits and waits for the players to take his advice. He does not realize that it is unusual for people to play chess night and day for seven days. The players eat nothing but a shared peach, and the wood-cutter only sucks the peach stone. Because he is so sure he is important, he ignores the clues and is gone for thousands of years.

Difficulty: *Easy*

Objective: *Essay*

Selection Test B, p. 66

Critical Reading

1. ANS: D	DIF: Average	OBJ: Comprehension
2. ANS: D	DIF: Challenging	OBJ: Interpretation
3. ANS: B	DIF: Average	OBJ: Interpretation
4. ANS: A	DIF: Challenging	OBJ: Reading
5. ANS: B	DIF: Average	OBJ: Comprehension
6. ANS: C	DIF: Average	OBJ: Reading
7. ANS: D	DIF: Average	OBJ: Interpretation
8. ANS: B	DIF: Average	OBJ: Literary Analysis
9. ANS: B	DIF: Average	OBJ: Interpretation
10. ANS: B	DIF: Average	OBJ: Reading
11. ANS: C	DIF: Average	OBJ: Literary Analysis
12. ANS: A	DIF: Challenging	OBJ: Literary Analysis
13. ANS: C	DIF: Average	OBJ: Comprehension
14. ANS: A	DIF: Average	OBJ: Comprehension

Vocabulary and Grammar

15. ANS: C	DIF: Challenging	OBJ: Vocabulary
16. ANS: B	DIF: Average	OBJ: Vocabulary
17. ANS: C	DIF: Average	OBJ: Vocabulary
18. ANS: A	DIF: Average	OBJ: Grammar
19. ANS: C	DIF: Challenging	OBJ: Grammar

Essay

20. Students should explain that the main elements of a plot are the exposition (an introduction to setting, characters, and situation); a conflict or problem that is central to the story; a series of events called the rising action, in which someone tries to solve the problem; a climax or turning point; the events called the falling action following the climax; and a resolution, or conclusion. To support their explanations, students might say: In the exposition we learn about a woodcutter who doesn't mind his own business; the climax of the story occurs when the woodcutter sucks on the peach stone; in the resolution of the story, the woodcutter finds out that thousands of years have passed.

Difficulty: *Average*

Objective: *Essay*

21. The lesson in the story is that people should mind their own business. The woodcutter learned this lesson when he stopped to give advice to the strange men he met on his journey. He tried to interfere with their chess game and did not take the hint when they ignored him. When they became hungry, they shared a magic peach, which gave them energy to keep playing. When the woodcutter sucked on the peach stone, he gained new energy, and became unaware of how much time had passed. Most students will say that there are times when it's a good idea to give advice or mind someone else's business and times when it is not. If the strangers had been ordinary men, not immortals, they might have welcomed the woodcutter's advice or help if they had been in trouble.

Difficulty: *Average*

Objective: *Essay*

22. Students should note that the woodcutter sees things through a slanted view. He thinks he knows "a little of everything," but he really knows "most of nothing." At the chess game, he waits and waits for the players to take his valuable advice. He does not realize that it is unusual for people to play chess night and day for seven days. The players eat nothing but a shared peach, and the woodcutter only sucks the peach stone. The wood-cutter fails to realize that this is not enough food. He never questions how a peach stone could give him so much energy.

Difficulty: *Average*

Objective: *Essay*

"The Drive-In Movies" by Gary Soto

Vocabulary Warm-up Exercises, p. 70

A. 1. nightfall
2. snails
3. migrated
4. evident
5. remedy
6. plucked
7. brew
8. disgusting

B. Sample Answers
1. F; <u>Waxing</u> helps to keep a car clean.
2. T; <u>Glinting</u> involves the sun reflecting off of something.
3. T; Putting shampoo on your hair cleans it.
4. F; People <u>dedicated</u> to their jobs care a lot about them.

5. F; A person minding his or her own business wouldn't get mixed up in an argument.

6. F; <u>Chrome</u> is a metal that is used on cars.

7. T; Doing something with a lot of effort and energy makes you tired.

8. F; <u>Buffing</u> means using a dry cloth with no grease.

Reading Warm-up A, p. 71

Sample Answers

1. (cure); An illness or a problem needs a *remedy.*

2. <u>we got to stay up later</u>, <u>it got dark</u>; We usually eat dinner after *nightfall.*

3. <u>moving as slowly as</u>; Long, boring summer days move as slowly as *snails.*

4. (obvious); It is *evident* to me that drive-in movies are a lot of fun.

5. <u>several things he had mixed together, lemonade, fruit punch, and root beer</u>; A *brew* is a liquid mixture of things.

6. (horrible); I think sticky floors in movie theaters are *disgusting.*

7. (with my fingers); Popcorn or candy might get *plucked* out of a bag at the movies.

8. <u>from the top of the bag to the bottom</u>; All the black jelly beans seem to have *migrated* to the top of the box.

Reading Warm-up B, p. 72

Sample Answers

1. First, get out the wax and dab it onto your car; once you've applied the wax, rub it vigorously all over.

2. <u>dab it on</u>; <u>put on</u>; A bandage or antibiotic ointment could be applied to a cut.

3. (gently); I like to run vigorously every morning.

4. You would find *chrome* on the hubcaps, fenders and on the door handles.

5. Shoes and furniture can both be *buffed.*

6. Joe picked up a penny from the ground after he saw it *glinting* in the sunlight.

7. If you're *dedicated* to keeping the car looking nice, you have to wax it once a week or twice a month.

8. I enjoy being *involved* in sports and chorus.

Writing About the Big Question, p. 73

A. 1. determine

2. unbelievable

3. prove; fiction

4. test

B. Sample Answers

1. When my friend Rikki took my homework and copied it, my **opinion** of her went way down. It was **unbelievable** that she could do that to me.

2. Rikki apologized. She said she would never do it again, and her actions proved that in time. I made the **decision** to be her friend and give her another

chance. Now, my **opinion** of her is that she is a good person.

C. Sample Answer

someone who learns from his or her mistakes.

Everyone has a good side and a bad side. There is no such thing as a perfect person who never does anything wrong. A truly good person will try to do his or her best to do the right thing, but everyone is human, has weaknesses, and makes mistakes.

"The Drive-In Movies" by Gary Soto

Reading: Read Ahead to Verify Predictions, p. 74

Sample Answers

1. *Will Rick help?* 2. He watched Gary from the window and pointed at part of the lawn that Gary had missed when Gary was mowing it. 3. Children in a family usually do help each other with chores. 4. Prediction: Rick will help. **C** or correct.

2. *Will a good job be done on the car?* 2. The boys run out of wax. 3. The car is not going to look good if it's only half waxed. 4. Prediction: The car is going to look worse than it looked before. **C** or correct.

3. *How will Mom react to the way the car looks?* 2. Gary and Rick expect that Mom will be very upset and may hit them for what they did to her car. 3. Mom might appreciate how hard they worked. 4. Prediction: Mom will not be angry with the boys. **C** or correct.

4. *Will Gary enjoy the movies?* 2. He tries to stay awake. 3. He worked so hard that he might fall asleep. 4. Prediction: He will fall asleep. **C** or correct.

Literary Analysis: Narrator and Point of View, p. 75

A. 1. FP; 2. TP; 3. TP; 4. FP

B. Sample Response

I went out and looked at my car. My first reaction was, "Oh, no!" I could see that the boys had put too much wax on one side because it was foggy white. The other side had no wax at all. I realized that the kids had put a lot of work into the car. I had to give them credit for trying. I know I made them feel good when I said, "You boys worked so hard." I turned on the hose and washed off the extra soap. That didn't take much time at all. Even though I was tired from working all week, I took the kids to the drive-in. Gary especially deserved a treat. He had worked the whole day and he'd been extra good, doing his best to help me out.

Vocabulary Builder, p. 76

A. Sample Answers

1. No. It is beginning because a *prelude* is a beginning or introduction.

2. The wild geese will probably migrate again when the season changes. The sentence suggests that they are there "for the winter."

3. No, Dad's collar was probably too tight. *Winced* means that Dad drew back as if he were pinched.

4. Yes, the police will know who robbed the bank. *Evident* means "clear or obvious."

5. The heart is always pulsating, or beating.

6. Yes, John would walk vigorously, using energy and force to move rapidly.

B. Sample Responses

1. Before I wore my new jeans, I washed them to *preshrink* the fabric.

2. The United States Constitution begins with a *preamble.*

3. Correct.

Enrichment: Comic Movies, p. 77

Sample Answer

1. *Shrek*; the funniest part shows what happens when a number of fairy-tale creatures take over Shrek's swamp. This animated movie contains both physical and verbal comedy. The Donkey character's lines are especially good verbal comedy.

"The Drive-In Movies" by Gary Soto

Open-Book Test, p. 78

Short Answer

1. The narrator expects to go to the movies. Watching cartoons on the small TV screen is an introduction to watching a movie on the big screen.
   Difficulty: *Average*   **Objective:** *Vocabulary*

2. Because the narrator has started the day doing something extra for his mother, he will probably continue to do extra work all day so she will take him to the movies.
   Difficulty: *Average*   **Objective:** *Reading*

3. He sees his mother just as the bee stings him. He doesn't want to do anything that might bother her and make her decide to stay home.
   Difficulty: *Challenging*   **Objective:** *Interpretation*

4. *Winced* means "cringed." Since the mother cringed, she must have seen something wrong with the grille.
   Difficulty: *Easy*   **Objective:** *Vocabulary*

5. The reader most likely predicts that the boys will get in trouble and will not get to go to the movies.
   Difficulty: *Easy*   **Objective:** *Reading*

6. Sample answers for the web: Gary works hard to please his mother; Rick comes out to help Gary; Debra gives the boys ice cubes; Mom praises her sons even for bad wax job. The family members are close and love one another.
   Difficulty: *Average*   **Objective:** *Interpretation*

7. The narrator seems to lead a simple life and comes from a family without much money. There is no father mentioned, and the mother has an unskilled job candling eggs. Going to the movies with his family is probably a luxury for the narrator.
   Difficulty: *Average*   **Objective:** *Interpretation*

8. Students should provide one of the narrator's statements from the story that uses the pronoun *I.*
   Difficulty: *Easy*   **Objective:** *Literary Analysis*

9. A third-person narrator could reveal how the other family members feel and think. For example, a third-person narrator could reveal exactly what the mother feels as she steps out of the house.
   Difficulty: *Average*   **Objective:** *Literary Analysis*

10. Some students might say the narrator will think his hard work was worth it. He pleased his mother and got the reward he wanted. Others may feel that he will not think his hard work was worth it because he did not get to fully enjoy the reward.
    Difficulty: *Challenging*   **Objective:** *Literary Analysis*

Essay

11. Students should make some of the following observations: Gary Soto came from a poor family consisting of his mother, brother, and sister. His mother had a tiring job candling eggs. The family did not seem to have many luxuries, but they enjoyed simple things like going to the movies together. They also seemed to care about each other. Gary liked doing things to please his mother and spending time with his family.
    Difficulty: *Easy*   **Objective:** *Essay*

12. Students should make some of the following observations: Gary works hard in order to persuade his mother to take him to the drive-in movies. He also works hard just to please her. She praises his work, so he gains her appreciation. He gets to go to the movie, but he learns a lesson from the experience: it doesn't pay to overdo. He also learns that doing a job well is its own reward.
    Difficulty: *Average*   **Objective:** *Essay*

13. Students should note that if the story were written by a neighbor, the reader would not know what Gary was thinking and feeling. For example, readers would know he was frantically working, but they would not know why. The neighbor's version would be more objective. Readers would know that Gary did certain tasks, but they wouldn't know how he felt about them. Most students should say that they prefer Gary's version because it allows more insight into the character.
    Difficulty: *Challenging*   **Objective:** *Essay*

14. Students might note that the narrator believes his mother will take him to the movies if she is in a good mood. He bases his belief on her past behavior and works hard to please her. He is correct because she does take him to the drive-in. He also believes that if his work does not please her, he will not go to the movies and

might even be punished. When he can't clean off the car, he fears the worst. However, he does not consider how much his mother loves him. Instead of punishing him, she appreciates his hard work and takes him to the movies.

Difficulty: *Average*   **Objective:** *Essay*

Oral Response

15. Oral responses should be clear, well organized, and well supported by appropriate examples from the selection.

    Difficulty: *Average*   **Objective:** *Oral Interpretation*

Selection Test A, p. 81

Critical Reading

1. ANS: B	DIF: Easy	OBJ: Literary Analysis
2. ANS: A	DIF: Easy	OBJ: Comprehension
3. ANS: D	DIF: Easy	OBJ: Comprehension
4. ANS: A	DIF: Easy	OBJ: Comprehension
5. ANS: B	DIF: Easy	OBJ: Literary Analysis
6. ANS: B	DIF: Easy	OBJ: Interpretation
7. ANS: B	DIF: Easy	OBJ: Reading
8. ANS: C	DIF: Easy	OBJ: Comprehension
9. ANS: B	DIF: Easy	OBJ: Literary Analysis
10. ANS: D	DIF: Easy	OBJ: Interpretation
11. ANS: B	DIF: Easy	OBJ: Reading
12. ANS: B	DIF: Easy	OBJ: Interpretation

Vocabulary and Grammar

13. ANS: C	DIF: Easy	OBJ: Vocabulary
14. ANS: A	DIF: Easy	OBJ: Grammar

Essay

15. Students may say they were surprised at how much work the boy did. They may say it was unfair that he worked so hard, or they may say that the hard work was good for him. They may have been surprised that the car wax job turned out badly and that the mother did not seem to mind. Students might say they were happy that the mother seemed to appreciate the work that the narrator did, even though the job didn't turn out well. They might say they were surprised that the family ended up at the movies and that the narrator fell asleep because he was tired from working. They might express various feelings about the surprises in the story, but most will say they liked the way the story ended.

    Difficulty: *Easy*

    Objective: *Essay*

16. Students may describe the child Gary Soto as determined, hardworking, and strong. He is determined or stubbornly devoted to reaching a goal. In the story, he makes a decision to be extra good and sticks to it all day. His hardworking nature is shown by the long list of

chores he does to put his mother in a good mood. Even though he works so hard in the hot sun that he gets sweaty, he keeps on working. Students may say that he must be a strong boy to be able to work so hard. Other qualities students may mention are good role model, sympathetic, and kind. He is a good example for his brother and sister; he seems to have a great deal of sympathy for his mother; and he plays with the dog and pulls ticks from its nose.

Difficulty: *Easy*

Objective: *Essay*

17. Students might note that the narrator bases his belief on his mother's past behavior. He is correct because she does take him to the drive-in as a reward for his hard work. When he can't clean off the car, he fears the worst. He has probably been punished before. However, he does not consider how much his mother loves him. She looks past the mistake and focuses on the hard work.

Difficulty: *Easy*

Objective: *Essay*

Selection Test B, p. 84

Critical Reading

1. ANS: A	DIF: Average	OBJ: Comprehension
2. ANS: C	DIF: Average	OBJ: Reading
3. ANS: C	DIF: Challenging	OBJ: Interpretation
4. ANS: B	DIF: Average	OBJ: Literary Analysis
5. ANS: C	DIF: Challenging	OBJ: Literary Analysis
6. ANS: D	DIF: Challenging	OBJ: Interpretation
7. ANS: A	DIF: Average	OBJ: Interpretation
8. ANS: B	DIF: Challenging	OBJ: Interpretation
9. ANS: A	DIF: Average	OBJ: Literary Analysis
10. ANS: A	DIF: Average	OBJ: Comprehension
11. ANS: D	DIF: Challenging	OBJ: Comprehension
12. ANS: D	DIF: Average	OBJ: Reading
13. ANS: A	DIF: Challenging	OBJ: Reading
14. ANS: C	DIF: Challenging	OBJ: Comprehension

Vocabulary and Grammar

15. ANS: C	DIF: Average	OBJ: Vocabulary
16. ANS: C	DIF: Average	OBJ: Vocabulary
17. ANS: D	DIF: Average	OBJ: Grammar

Essay

18. The narrator is determined, hardworking, and energetic (or strong). Some students may say he is also single-minded. He makes a decision to be extra good, and he sticks to it all day. He describes in detail an exhausting list of chores he did to put his mother in a good mood. Even though he works hard enough to get sweaty and he is stung by a bee, he keeps right on working. He

must be a strong boy with a great deal of energy to work so hard in the hot sun. His single-mindedness is shown by his concentration. He ignores his brother's attempt to annoy him and keeps focusing on mowing the grass. He and his brother concentrate so much on polishing the car that the paint begins to come off. Students may also point out that he is a good example to his brother and sister. He doesn't argue with them and force them to work with him. He blames his brother only when it looks as if the boys have damaged the car.

Difficulty: *Average*

Objective: *Essay*

19. Some students may like the way the story ends. They may point out that Mom understood that it was important to reward the boys for their efforts. Other students might say that the ending is not realistic because a mother probably would not reward her children for making a mess of a wax job and creating more work for her. They may say that a more interesting ending would have Mom punish the children, have them help wash the car, and then surprise them by taking them to the movies.

Difficulty: *Average*

Objective: *Essay*

20. Students might note that the narrator believes his mother will take him to the movies if she is in a good mood. He bases his belief on her past behavior and works hard to please her. He is correct because she does take him to the drive-in. He also believes that if his work does not please her, he will not go to the movies and might even be punished. When he can't clean off the car, he fears the worst. However, he does not consider how much his mother loves him. Instead of punishing him, she appreciates his hard work and takes him to the movies.

Difficulty: *Average*

Objective: *Essay*

"The Market Square Dog" by James Herriot

Vocabulary Warm-up Exercises, p. 88

A. 1. surgery
2. stitched
3. bruised
4. healed
5. meantime
6. various
7. appealing
8. injured

B. Sample Answers
1. No, I think fringed items are not attractive, because they look too stringy.
2. If a man ate his food that quickly, he might be really hungry or not have enough time to eat.
3. Yes, it's probably wise to pause and think before deciding something big.

4. If someone labeled me as boring, I would be upset and determined to prove the person wrong.
5. If I saw an ownerless animal on the street, I would call the animal shelter.

Reading Warm-up A, p. 89

Sample Answers
1. (hurt); A kid might get *injured* trying to jump too high.
2. turns dark purple; The baby got *bruised* when a box fell on her.
3. (sewn together); Someone might have to get *stitched* if he or she cut themselves cooking.
4. (when an operation is involved); Yes, it would be scary to be cut open.
5. Kids could get bruised or cut or break a bone.
6. recovered; If you're not completely healed, you could injure yourself again.
7. Getting back in the game; *Appealing* means attractive, or looking like something kids want to do.
8. In the meantime, people should practice prevention.

Reading Warm-up B, p. 90

Sample Answers
1. The cat was squatting on the steps of a building. It was probably crouching down with its knees bent low.
2. didn't look owned; You might find a stray in the street.
3. (ugly); I think cats and hamsters are attractive.
4. Fringed paws probably have tufts of hair coming out over the claws.
5. The cat paused and then ate it up. That's not surprising, as cats are naturally wary.
6. after a few seconds; Cats are naturally wary, and the cat wanted to make sure it was okay to eat.
7. (eaten); *Devoured* means to have *eaten* faster and more hungrily.
8. She wasn't sure exactly how she felt; I would have *classified* her feelings as love.

Writing About the Big Question, p. 91

A. 1. determine; confirm
2. decision; proven/true
3. true; confirmed/proven
4. opinions; realistic

B. Sample Answers
1. Everyone said that a girl in my class named Darla was mean. In **fact**, she was a nice girl, and what they said was not **true**.
2. I became Darla's best friend. After I shared my **opinion** of her with my friends, they realized that what others said was **unbelievable**.

C. Sample Answer

friendly.

The people who refused to adopt a mixed breed believed a fiction. It was not true that only a purebred dog can be a good pet. A better way to decide would have been to get to know the dog and study its habits to see if it is a good pet.

"The Market Square Dog" by James Herriot

Reading: Reading Ahead to Verify Predictions, p. 92

Sample Answers

1. *Will the dog be caught?* 2. He's friendly but he's also afraid. 3. Cute dogs find people willing to adopt them. 4. Prediction: The dog will be caught. **W** or wrong because he is hit by a car.

2. *Will the dog survive the accident?* 2. He has some injuries that look serious; he might lose his sight in one eye. 3. Stories like this usually end happily. 4. Prediction: The dog will survive. **C** or correct.

3. *Will the dog's owners claim him at the kennels?* 2. After a few days, the dog's owners have not come to claim him. 3. If the dog's owners were interested in him, they would have been looking for him. 4. Prediction: The dog will not end up with his former owners. **C** or correct.

4. *Will the dog find a good home?* 2. The vet says the dog would make a perfect pet for anyone. 3. Stories like this usually have a happy ending. 4. Prediction: The dog will find a good home. **C** or correct.

Literary Analysis: Narrator and Point of View, p. 93

A. 1. FP; 2. TP; 3. FP; 4. TP; 5. FP

B. Sample Response

It was hard for me not to laugh when I told the vet I'd arrested the dog he had operated on. He looked astounded! The vet asked me if he could see the dog, so I took him down the road to my cottage. We went inside, and there were my dear little daughters stroking the dog in his big new doggy bed. They looked pretty as a picture. I laughed and laughed at the expression on the vet's face. I told him this was my house, and these were my daughters. They had wanted a dog for some time, and I thought this one would be just right for them.

Vocabulary Builder, p. 94

Sample Answers

A. 1. The children will not catch up with the girl because she is on a skateboard, which moves more quickly than trotting children; *trotted* implies a graceful, light movement, not necessarily swift.

2. The family is worried about where the storm will strike. The word *anxiously* means "nervously or worriedly."

3. We will feel that the car is safer when the thief is in *custody*. The police will be guarding the law-breaker.

4. The horse seemed hungry before he ate the oats. *Devoured* suggests that the horse ate quickly or greedily.

5. The children will not be able to solve it quickly. *Bewildered* means "puzzled or confused."

6. No, Ms. Snow's action did not indicate her judgment of the book's worth. She merely identified it as nonfiction. *Classified* means "to sort according to type."

B. 1. Please clean the floor because it is *besmeared* with mud.

2. Correct.

3. On that rainy, cloudy day, the island was totally *befogged*.

Enrichment: Veterinarians, p. 95

A. 1. C; 2. C; 3. D

B. Sample Questions

1. What made you decide to become a veterinarian?

2. What kinds of courses have you taken in school?

3. What experience do you have in working with animals?

"The Drive-In Movies" by Gary Soto
"The Market Square Dog" by James Herriot

Integrated Language Skills: Grammar, p. 96

1. foxes; 2. dishes; 3. crosses; 4. marks; 5. keys; 6. lakes; 7. couches; 8. Saturdays; 9. pets; 10. strays; 11. hippopotamuses; 12. sandwiches; 13. classes; 14. waxes

"The Market Square Dog" by James Herriot

Open-Book Test, p. 99

Short Answer

1. The story is told in first person. Herriot uses the pronoun "I" when talking about himself.
   Difficulty: *Easy*   **Objective:** *Literary Analysis*

2. The reader knows only what the narrator, the veterinarian, knows. Since the veterinarian does not know where the dog goes, neither does the reader.
   Difficulty: *Average*   **Objective:** *Literary Analysis*

3. The veterinarian and the policeman share an interest in dogs and sympathy for them. They are first brought together when they both notice the stray dog in the market square.
   Difficulty: *Average*   **Objective:** *Interpretation*

4. Because the story is told in first person by Herriot, the reader gets to learn exactly what Herriot thinks and feels about every event. Students should give an example that specifically shows Herriot's thoughts or feelings.
   Difficulty: *Challenging*   **Objective:** *Literary Analysis*

5. The dog is seriously injured by a car. It seems as though he might not survive long enough to find a home.

Difficulty: *Easy*   **Objective:** *Reading*

6. The tail wag not only shows that the dog is still alive, but it also shows that he still has some spirit. This suggests he might be able to recover.

Difficulty: *Challenging*   **Objective:** *Interpretation*

7. *Anxiously* means "in a worried or uneasy way." The word shows that the couple is concerned about the dog, which suggests they are fond of him.

Difficulty: *Easy*   **Objective:** *Vocabulary*

8. Answers for the boxes: runs from people [at the market]; is friendly [at the kennels]. Because of the gentle care given him by Herriot and the policeman, the dog has learned to trust people.

Difficulty: *Average*   **Objective:** *Interpretation*

9. When Herriot sees the dog curled up in his new doggy bed at the policeman's house, the reader knows the dog has found a good home.

Difficulty: *Average*   **Objective:** *Reading*

10. The veterinarian feels that the dog has found a good home because the policeman is kind. He takes an interest in the dog from the beginning and saves his life after the accident. He also treats the dog with kindness in the kennels and seems to be doing so at his house.

Difficulty: *Average*   **Objective:** *Interpretation*

Essay

11. Students should note that the dog is clever, friendly, and lively. However, the dog was also most likely abused in the past, which is why he was wary of people. Students might say that the dog needs a loving, patient home, with people who appreciate his cleverness. They might also mention that a lively dog would like to play with children. The policeman's home seems perfect for the dog. The policeman is a kind, good-natured man with children.

Difficulty: *Easy*   **Objective:** *Essay*

12. Students' essays should include some of these observations: James Herriot seems to be well suited to his job. He genuinely likes and understands animals. He feels a great deal of compassion for the market square dog. He understands immediately that the dog is friendly but also afraid. When the dog is injured, Herriot gives up his plans in order to help the dog. He is obviously a good veterinarian because the dog recovers completely after the operation.

Difficulty: *Average*   **Objective:** *Essay*

13. Students may note that Herriot makes the point that people should not abandon or mistreat their pets. He makes his point by presenting the troubles of an appealing stray dog, abandoned and forced to beg for his food. Another main point is that pets add love to our lives. Both Herriot and the policeman are drawn to the little dog, who repays them with attention and love. At the end of the story, the stray dog enriches the lives of the policeman and his family.

Difficulty: *Challenging*   **Objective:** *Essay*

14. Students' essays may include some of these observations: The narrator decides the dog is friendly but also afraid. Later, he correctly predicts that the dog will make a perfect pet for someone. He also has good feelings about the policeman. He feels that the policeman is kind and will make a good owner. His conclusions are good because he is experienced with both animals and people. Being a veterinarian, he knows animal behavior. He also has seen how people treat animals, so he can recognize an animal lover when he sees one.

Difficulty: *Average*   **Objective:** *Essay*

Oral Response

15. Oral responses should be clear, well organized, and well supported by appropriate examples from the selection.

Difficulty: *Average*   **Objective:** *Oral Interpretation*

"The Market Square Dog" by James Herriot

Selection Test A, p. 102

Critical Reading

1. ANS: C	DIF: Easy	OBJ: Literary Analysis
2. ANS: B	DIF: Easy	OBJ: Comprehension
3. ANS: A	DIF: Easy	OBJ: Comprehension
4. ANS: A	DIF: Easy	OBJ: Comprehension
5. ANS: B	DIF: Easy	OBJ: Reading
6. ANS: A	DIF: Easy	OBJ: Comprehension
7. ANS: C	DIF: Easy	OBJ: Interpretation
8. ANS: B	DIF: Easy	OBJ: Interpretation
9. ANS: D	DIF: Easy	OBJ: Comprehension
10. ANS: D	DIF: Easy	OBJ: Reading
11. ANS: A	DIF: Easy	OBJ: Literary Analysis

Vocabulary and Grammar

12. ANS: D	DIF: Easy	OBJ: Vocabulary
13. ANS: B	DIF: Easy	OBJ: Vocabulary
14. ANS: C	DIF: Easy	OBJ: Grammar
15. ANS: A	DIF: Easy	OBJ: Grammar

Essay

16. Students may say that a country vet works hard. He has to be available at all times to help sick and injured animals. He works with both large animals, such as cows, and small animals, such as dogs. He operates on animals that have been hurt. He seems to know many of the farmers and townspeople, and he likes to talk to them. He doesn't have much time for himself. Students may say that they would like being able to help animals.

They might dislike having to operate on animals, or they might dislike having to live in the country. They might also say that they would prefer a job with regular hours.

Difficulty: *Easy*

Objective: *Essay*

17. Students might say that everyone in town may already have a dog, or that people prefer a big dog, a working dog, or a purebred dog. They may also say that although this dog seems friendly at a distance, he is difficult to get close to. He is a clever dog, if not a beautiful dog. He knows how to beg for food. In the kennel, he "smiles" and wags his tail to call attention to himself. Students might say that the best home is a loving, patient home, with people who appreciate the cleverness of the dog and who will accept the dog's independence and perhaps a bit of mischievousness.

Difficulty: *Easy*

Objective: *Essay*

18. Students' essays may include some of these observations: The narrator decides the dog is friendly but also afraid. He correctly predicts that the dog will make a perfect pet for someone. He feels that the policeman is kind and will make a good owner. He comes to these conclusions through his observations. Because he has spent years working with animals and people, he can recognize the truth about both.

Difficulty: *Easy*

Objective: *Essay*

Selection Test B, p. 105

Critical Reading

1. ANS: C	DIF: Average	OBJ: Literary Analysis
2. ANS: B	DIF: Average	OBJ: Comprehension
3. ANS: A	DIF: Average	OBJ: Literary Analysis
4. ANS: A	DIF: Average	OBJ: Comprehension
5. ANS: D	DIF: Challenging	OBJ: Literary Analysis
6. ANS: B	DIF: Challenging	OBJ: Reading
7. ANS: D	DIF: Average	OBJ: Reading
8. ANS: B	DIF: Challenging	OBJ: Interpretation
9. ANS: A	DIF: Average	OBJ: Comprehension
10. ANS: D	DIF: Average	OBJ: Interpretation
11. ANS: B	DIF: Average	OBJ: Interpretation
12. ANS: C	DIF: Average	OBJ: Reading
13. ANS: B	DIF: Average	OBJ: Comprehension
14. ANS: C	DIF: Challenging	OBJ: Interpretation

Vocabulary and Grammar

15. ANS: B	DIF: Average	OBJ: Vocabulary
16. ANS: B	DIF: Challenging	OBJ: Grammar

17. ANS: B	DIF: Average	OBJ: Vocabulary
18. ANS: C	DIF: Average	OBJ: Grammar
19. ANS: D	DIF: Average	OBJ: Vocabulary

Essay

20. The country vet seems to be well suited to his job. He seems to genuinely like and understand animals. He feels a great deal of compassion for the market square dog, which seems lost and was probably mistreated. He understands immediately that the dog is friendly but also afraid. When the dog is injured, the vet gives up his plans for an outing with his wife and tries to help the dog. He is obviously a good vet because the dog manages to recover completely as a result of the medical care the vet gives him. The vet seems to like people. He has made an effort to get to know the farmers. He walks across the square to meet the farmers and listen to the problems they are having with their animals. He seems to be well respected in the community. The policeman brings the injured dog to him, knowing that the vet will give the dog the help it needs.

Difficulty: *Average*

Objective: *Essay*

21. Students may say that at the beginning of the story, they could predict that the stray dog would find a home. The dog is attractive and has learned to beg from strangers in an appealing way. When the dog is struck by a car, students might change their original prediction. They might know from their experience that an injured dog may die or may be unadoptable. When the dog is taken to the kennels, they may predict that the owner will come to claim him. The owner does not visit the kennels, and no one else seems to want the dog, so once again students will change their predictions. They might predict that the vet will take the dog home, because Helen seems to be a good-hearted person and seems to like the dog. When the policeman tells the vet that the dog has been arrested, students will be surprised, but their original prediction that the dog would be adopted will be confirmed.

Difficulty: *Average*

Objective: *Essay*

22. Students' essays may include some of these observations: The narrator decides the dog is friendly but also afraid. Later, he correctly predicts that the dog will make a perfect pet for someone. He also has good feelings about the policeman. He feels that the policeman is kind and will make a good owner. His conclusions are good because he is experienced with both animals and people. Being a veterinarian, he knows animal behavior. He also has seen how people treat animals, so he can recognize an animal lover when he sees one.

Difficulty: *Average*

Objective: *Essay*

"Why Monkeys Live in Trees" by Julius Lester
"The Case of the Monkeys That Fell From the Trees" by Susan E. Quinlan

Vocabulary Warm-up Exercises, p. 109

A. 1. incidents
2. involved
3. evidence
4. determine
5. behavior
6. suspiciously
7. individual
8. bellowed

B. Sample Answers
1. People who research animal behavior might study how they eat and socialize.
2. You wouldn't expect to see it often, because uncommon means unusual.
3. I would love to have an unlimited amount of books because I love to read.
4. I would eat different things every day because to vary is to change things.
5. I just can't tolerate it when people scream at each other. It gives me a headache and I think it's mean.
6. No, I would expect him or her to feel terrible because toxic things are poisonous.

Reading Warm-up A, p. 110

Sample Answers
1. strange occurrences; Last week, a stranger smiled at me and someone gave me a free T-shirt.
2. had a part in; I am very *involved* in student government.
3. (acting); The narrator is both curious and upset.
4. was any person who lived here acting more strangely than usual; I avoided the *individual* because he was acting *suspiciously* outside the building.
5. figure it out; The narrator wants to *determine* who is behind the incidents.
6. carefully writing down each clue I discovered; She uses the *evidence* to create a profile.
7. A little monkey climbed in through the window and grabbed some bananas off the kitchen table. I might *bellow* if someone stole something from me.

Reading Warm-up B, p. 111

Sample Answers
1. (studying) (curious); A *researcher* studies something in depth.
2. (poisonous); The *toxic* berries made her feel sick.
3. (simple); Something is *complicated* if it is difficult or has a lot of steps.

4. The passage claims there is an almost *unlimited* number of foods to choose from.
5. If people couldn't *tolerate* a food, they stopped eating it.
6. An *uncommon* food is probably untested and might make you sick.
7. In spite of that, humans around the world still managed to eat a wide range of foods. *Nonetheless* means "in spite of."
8. eating a wide variety of foods; That's the only way to make sure we get the right nutrients.

Writing About the Big Question, p. 112

A. 1. fantasy; realistic
2. true
3. determine
4. evidence

B. Sample Answers
1. I read a book that took place during the Civil War, and it contained many **facts** about what life was like at that time for African Americans. Although it was **fiction**, it included much historical **fact**.
2. You can use nonfiction sources to **investigate** and **study** your topic.

C. Sample Answer

have some characteristics of real monkeys. For example, the monkeys may really behave the way they do in the story, or they may eat the foods described. The way to confirm this would be to look up monkeys' habits in a nonfiction source.

Literary Analysis: Fiction and Nonfiction, p. 113

1. fiction; leopards don't talk or take interest in beauty contests
2. nonfiction; it contains facts about howling monkeys that exist in the real world
3. fiction; animals can't draw numbers or be disappointed by the number another animal draws
4. nonfiction; it contains facts about the feeding habits of howling monkeys

Vocabulary Builder, p. 114

A. Sample Answers
1. It began to rain so abruptly that we all got soaked.
2. She felt great distress when she heard that her best friend was moving.
3. In the mirror, I saw the reflection of a sleepy girl.
4. The three burglaries seemed to be related incidents.
5. "Rover!" he bellowed. "Where are you?"
6. "Welcome to our festival," King Henry announced regally.

B. 1. D; 2. B; 3. A; 4. C

"Why Monkeys Live in Trees"
by Julius Lester
"The Case of the Monkeys That Fell From the Trees" by Susan E. Quinlan

Open-Book Test, p. 116

Short Answer

1. Since *reflection* means "image," Leopard likes to look at himself. This suggests that he is vain.
   Difficulty: *Challenging* **Objective:** *Vocabulary*

2. The dust is pepper. None of the animals learn from the experiences of those who went before them. They see that the dust cannot be eaten at one time, but they continue to try to do so.
   Difficulty: *Challenging* **Objective:** *Interpretation*

3. Monkeys are quick, clever, and mischievous. They are the best animals to plan and pull off such a stunt.
   Difficulty: *Easy* **Objective:** *Interpretation*

4. *Distress* means "serious pain." A poisoned animal might fall, cry out in pain, or hold itself in a way that indicates pain.
   Difficulty: *Average* **Objective:** *Vocabulary*

5. The tropical forest that the monkeys call home is filled with a mixture of foods and poisons. Sometimes the monkeys select poisonous leaves for medicinal purposes. By observing these monkeys, scientists might discover plants that can be used to make medicines for humans.
   Difficulty: *Average* **Objective:** *Interpretation*

6. Students should name a quality that can be supported by the selection. For example, the Glanders spent much time observing and collecting data. This shows that scientists must have patience.
   Difficulty: *Average* **Objective:** *Interpretation*

7. Diagram: left circle, "gorilla as king"; right circle, "scientists"; middle section, "trees." A gorilla can't really be king so "Why Monkeys Live in Trees" is fiction.
   Difficulty: *Average* **Objective:** *Literary Analysis*

8. Leopard's children talk. Since young animals can't talk in real life, this is a made-up element, indicating a work of fiction. The young monkey clings to its mother, which real animals do.
   Difficulty: *Easy* **Objective:** *Literary Analysis*

9. For "Why Monkeys Live in Trees" students can provide any sentence indicating a made-up element; for example, "Leopard laughed." For "The Case of the Monkeys That Fell From the Trees," students can provide any sentence indicating a true element; for example, "All told, the monkeys had eaten from only 331 of the 1,699 trees in the area."
   Difficulty: *Average* **Objective:** *Literary Analysis*

10. Sample answer: The author of "The Case of the Monkeys That Fell From the Trees" wrote to share interesting facts about monkeys. Nonfiction is writing that tells about real things. Quinlan wanted to present true information about real monkeys.
    Difficulty: *Challenging* **Objective:** *Literary Analysis*

Essay

11. Students should make some of these observations: "The Case of the Monkeys That Fell From the Trees" tells about real people, animals, and events. Everything in the essay is true. The monkeys look and act like real monkeys. The scientists are actual people who made a study of the howler monkeys. Everything in the essay is factual and can be proved. Also, the scientists in the essay use facts and research to back up all of their logical conclusions about the monkeys.
    Difficulty: *Easy* **Objective:** *Essay*

12. Students may observe that the monkeys in "Why Monkeys Live in Trees" are typical because they live in the jungle, live in groups, and are good climbers. They are unusual because they speak and play a deliberate trick. Students may observe that the monkeys in "The Case of the Monkeys . . ." are typical because they live in the jungle, live in groups, are good climbers, nibble on their food, and tend to their young. They are unusual because they fall mysteriously from trees.
    Difficulty: *Average* **Objective:** *Essay*

13. Students should make some of these observations: Leopard and the scientists both have mysteries to solve involving monkeys. They both observe the monkeys to solve the mystery. However, Leopard will probably not make a good scientist. He is not objective and has little patience.
    Difficulty: *Challenging* **Objective:** *Essay*

14. Students should indicate that the animals have a hard time deciding what is true because what they see seems to be logically impossible. On one hand, they see the dust disappearing. On the other hand, they can't believe that Monkey could succeed where all the other animals failed. Only Leopard is able to find out the truth because he observes what is actually happening. This reveals that Leopard is curious and questions the truth about events.

    Students should note that the Glanders use a scientific method to find out why the monkeys are falling from trees. For a year they observe the monkeys, take careful notes on their observations, record data, and check ideas and data of other scientists. This reveals that they take the study very seriously and are careful in their work. Their conclusions are trustworthy because of the logic they use and the solid data that forms the basis of their conclusions.
    Difficulty: *Average* **Objective:** *Essay*

Oral Response

15. Oral responses should be clear, well organized, and well supported by appropriate examples from the selections.
    Difficulty: *Average* **Objective:** *Oral Interpretation*

Selection Test A, p. 119

Critical Reading

1. ANS: D   DIF: Easy   OBJ: Comprehension
2. ANS: A   DIF: Easy   OBJ: Comprehension
3. ANS: B   DIF: Easy   OBJ: Interpretation
4. ANS: C   DIF: Easy   OBJ: Literary Analysis
5. ANS: A   DIF: Easy   OBJ: Comprehension
6. ANS: A   DIF: Easy   OBJ: Comprehension
7. ANS: B   DIF: Easy   OBJ: Interpretation
8. ANS: D   DIF: Easy   OBJ: Literary Analysis
9. ANS: C   DIF: Easy   OBJ: Comprehension
10. ANS: A   DIF: Easy   OBJ: Interpretation
11. ANS: D   DIF: Easy   OBJ: Literary Analysis
12. ANS: D   DIF: Easy   OBJ: Interpretation
13. ANS: B   DIF: Easy   OBJ: Literary Analysis

Vocabulary

14. ANS: A   DIF: Easy   OBJ: Vocabulary
15. ANS: C   DIF: Easy   OBJ: Vocabulary

Essay

16. Students should identify "Why Monkeys Live in Trees" as fiction. Clues that show the work is fictional include speaking animals, animals entering a contest, and animals having human emotions.

    Difficulty: *Easy*
    Objective: *Essay*

17. Students may note that the monkeys live in a jungle or forest, live in groups, and are skilled climbers. Monkeys also nibble their food, tend to their young, and are usually clever about the food that they eat.

    Difficulty: *Easy*
    Objective: *Essay*

18. • Students should indicate that the animals are willing to accept the truth based on what they see in front of them. They see the dust disappearing. Leopard is able to find out the truth because he looks beyond what is in front of him to find out what is actually happening. This reveals that Leopard is curious and questions the truth about events.
    • Students should note that the Glanders use a scientific method to find out why the monkeys are falling from trees. For a year they observe the monkeys, take careful notes, record data, and check with other scientists. This reveals that they take the study very seriously and are careful in their work. Their conclusions are trustworthy because they are based on scientific evidence and research.

    Difficulty: *Easy*
    Objective: *Essay*

Selection Test B, p. 122

Critical Reading

1. ANS: D   DIF: Average   OBJ: Comprehension
2. ANS: A   DIF: Average   OBJ: Comprehension
3. ANS: B   DIF: Average   OBJ: Interpretation
4. ANS: A   DIF: Challenging   OBJ: Interpretation
5. ANS: D   DIF: Average   OBJ: Comprehension
6. ANS: C   DIF: Challenging   OBJ: Literary Analysis
7. ANS: D   DIF: Average   OBJ: Comprehension
8. ANS: C   DIF: Average   OBJ: Comprehension
9. ANS: B   DIF: Challenging   OBJ: Interpretation
10. ANS: C   DIF: Average   OBJ: Literary Analysis
11. ANS: D   DIF: Average   OBJ: Comprehension
12. ANS: A   DIF: Average   OBJ: Interpretation
13. ANS: B   DIF: Average   OBJ: Literary Analysis
14. ANS: C   DIF: Challenging   OBJ: Comprehension
15. ANS: C   DIF: Average   OBJ: Literary Analysis
16. ANS: B   DIF: Average   OBJ: Literary Analysis

Vocabulary

17. ANS: A   DIF: Average   OBJ: Vocabulary
18. ANS: B   DIF: Average   OBJ: Vocabulary
19. ANS: B   DIF: Challenging   OBJ: Vocabulary

Essay

20. Students should identify "Why Monkeys Live in Trees" as the fictional work. Clues that tell the reader the story is a work of fiction include animals that speak, participate in a contest, and feel emotions such as greed and dismay.

    Difficulty: *Average*
    Objective: *Essay*

21. Students may observe that the monkeys in "Why Monkeys Live in Trees" are typical because they live in the jungle, live in groups, and are agile climbers. They are unusual because they speak and play a deliberate trick on other animals. Students may observe that the monkeys in "The Case of the Monkeys . . ." are typical because they live in the jungle, live in groups, are agile climbers, nibble on their food, and tend to their young. They are unusual because they fall mysteriously from trees.

    Difficulty: *Average*
    Objective: *Essay*

22. • Students should indicate that the animals have a hard time deciding what is true because what they see seems to be logically impossible. On one hand, they see the dust disappearing. On the other hand, they can't believe that Monkey could succeed where all the other animals failed. Only Leopard is able to find out the

truth because he observes what is actually happening. This reveals that Leopard is curious and questions the truth about events.

- Students should note that the Glanders use a scientific method to find out why the monkeys are falling from trees. For a year they observe the monkeys, take careful notes on their observations, record data, and check ideas and data of other scientists. This reveals that they take the study very seriously and are careful in their work. Their conclusions are trustworthy because of the logic they use and the solid data that form the basis of their conclusions.

Difficulty: *Average*

Objective: *Essay*

Writing Workshop—Unit 1

Descriptive Essay: Integrating Grammar Skills, p. 126

A. 1. Wes's; 2. water's; 3. wood ducks'; 4. geese's

B. 1. Men's shouts came from across the lake.

2. Charley's dad and his friends were trying to get our attention.

3. They wanted us to canoe across to see several birds' nests.

4. The water level was too high after the three days' rain.

5. Just then I saw a bass's sleek body near the water's surface.

Benchmark Test 1, p. 127

MULTIPLE CHOICE

1. ANS: D
2. ANS: A
3. ANS: C
4. ANS: A
5. ANS: B
6. ANS: C
7. ANS: D
8. ANS: B
9. ANS: A
10. ANS: D
11. ANS: B
12. ANS: A
13. ANS: A
14. ANS: C
15. ANS: D
16. ANS: B
17. ANS: B
18. ANS: D
19. ANS: B
20. ANS: A
21. ANS: B
22. ANS: D
23. ANS: A
24. ANS: B
25. ANS: A
26. ANS: C
27. ANS: A
28. ANS: B
29. ANS: D
30. ANS: C
31. ANS: A

ESSAY

32. Students should provide accurate details from the book or story. They should use short, clear sentences that sum up the basic events, characters, and setting. Good reports may open with a catchy element, such as a quotation or a particularly interesting detail.

33. Students should focus on a single event or experience. They should make clear the basic facts—where it happened, when it happened, and so on. In addition to the facts, they should include details about why the event or experience was so important to them.

34. Students should make clear their main impression of the place, whether positive or negative. They should support that impression with specific details about the place and language that helps convey the impression. Students should use vivid language and comparisons and details that appeal to one or more of the five senses.

"My Papa, Mark Twain" by Susy Clemens

Vocabulary Warm-up Exercises, p. 135

A. 1. rudely
2. charming
3. seldom
4. snatched
5. style
6. fled
7. humor
8. desperate

B. Sample Answers

1. A pop star can gain <u>recognition</u> by making a hit record.

2. You might make a new <u>acquaintance</u> on the first day of school.

3. You could find a <u>biography</u> in a library.

4. A microwave oven would <u>enable</u> you to cook a hot dog.

5. You can <u>reveal</u> the secret identity of a superhero by taking off his mask.

6. You can find a <u>variety</u> of things to buy at a mall or department store.

7. My teacher is not <u>sympathetic</u> if I turn in my home-work late.

8. An <u>author</u> might find ideas for a book by thinking about his own life.

Reading Warm-up A, p. 136

Sample Answers

1. <u>Everyone wants to be in the same room with him</u>; It's important to be *charming* when you are trying to impress someone.

2. <u>rarely</u>; I *seldom* go skiing.

3. (tough guy); My favorite movie star has a romantic *style*.

4. (laughed hysterically); I find *humor* in a really funny movie.

5. <u>run away</u>; People have *fled* from burning buildings.

6. People might feel *desperate* when they lose their wallets.

7. Will took his lunch out of his backpack *very quickly*.

8. Jake was acting *rudely* when he made fun of Will's father. The opposite of behaving *rudely* is behaving politely.

Reading Warm-up B, p. 137

Sample Answers

1. <u>fame</u>; My principal earned statewide *recognition* for the good grades at our school.

2. <u>easy for people to understand and relate to</u>; I feel *sympathetic* toward the migrant boy in "The Circuit."

3. No, a *biography* is not fictional; it contains facts about someone's life.

4. <u>writer</u>; This sentence tells about the *author* Samuel Clemens.

5. It will *allow you to* gain a greater appreciation for his work.

6. It will *reveal* how his experiences in the place where he grew up appear in his work.

7. Clemens held a *variety* of jobs, including riverboat pilot, miner, and reporter.

8. A friend would be sadder because an *acquaintance* probably wouldn't know Clemens as well.

Writing About the Big Question, p. 138

A. 1. opinion; true

2. realistic

3. decision

4. evidence

B. Sample Answers

1. Somebody could **determine** that I was unfriendly because I am shy.

2. It would be **true** that I am not very friendly at first, but the reason is that I am shy and not that I want to be unfriendly.

C. Sample Answer

wait to make a decision until you get to know the person. Often somebody will seem a certain way because you see only one side of him or her. But if you get to know him or her, you will find out the truth about his or her person-ality and often you will find that your first impression was wrong.

"My Papa, Mark Twain" by Susy Clemens

Reading: Recognize Clues That Indicate Fact or Opinion, p. 139

Sample Answers

2. Underlined: <u>unquestionably the best book he has ever written</u>. Fact: One of papa's latest books is *The Prince and the Pauper.*

3. Underlined: <u>kind sympathetic nature, and *The Prince and the Pauper* partly does it</u>. Fact: I have wanted papa to write a book that would tell something about the kind of person he is.

4. Underlined: <u>full of lovely charming ideas, and oh the language! It is perfect</u>. Fact: The book contains many ideas.

5. Underlined: <u>so much variety, touching places, always a streak of humor</u>. Fact: *The Prince and the Pauper* con-tains scenes that appeal to the reader's feelings.

Literary Analysis: Author's Perspective, p. 140

A. Sample Answers

1. Papa refuses to attend school.

2. The author feels that her father's dislike of school is understandable; she sympathizes with him.

3. Underlined details: <u>how readily, pretend to be dying, gradually picked up enough education to enable him to do about as well as those who were more studious in early life</u>.

B. Sample Answer

Dear Livy,

I don't know what I'm going to do with my naughty boy. I worry that he's going to turn out to be a rascal, a crim-inal, or worse. He just won't go to school. I have cried and cried over this, but he pays no attention to me.

Vocabulary Builder, p. 141

Sample Answers

A. 1. Absent-minded Jean forgot her math textbook at school; consequently, she was not able to study for the math test.

2. The brilliant fireworks were striking against the night sky, and their loud explosions rang out incessantly.

3. As I stood in line, I grew impatient because I knew that this delay would cause me to be late to the movies.

4. His chicken costume was really peculiar. It had green feathers and a huge purple beak.

B. 1. February, March, May, September

2. A 16-year-old. A secondary school would follow an elementary school and a middle school.

3. The person would tend to be a follower. *Sequacious* contains the root *-sequ-*, which means "follow."

Enrichment: Expressing Facts and Opinions, p. 142

Sample Answers

A. 1. My mother

2. My mother is a wonderful mother, a generous and kind friend, and a hard worker.

3. My mother has three children, two girls and a boy, who are all doing well in school. She does volunteer work at the children's hospital. She did not graduate from high school, but she took classes to get her GED so she could become a secretary. Sometimes she works two jobs to help support our family.

4. brown eyes; about 5 feet 4 inches; green eyes; short, curly brown hair; lives in Chicago

B. 1. My mother is a short, thin woman with brown eyes and curly, brown hair. She has lived in Chicago all of her life. She works as a secretary. She is the mother of three children, two girls and a boy.

2. My mother is a great mother and a hard worker. Physically, my mother is short with an even shorter hairdo that is as tightly curled as she is tightly wired. In addition to keeping her three children on the straight and narrow, she also works two jobs and finds time and energy to volunteer at the children's hospital. She's always been determined. When her high-school education was interrupted, she completed school by getting a GED. Since then she has had a career as the world's most efficient secretary.

"My Papa, Mark Twain" by Susy Clemens

Open-Book Test, p. 143

Short Answer

1. Someone absentminded, or forgetful, would forget to take the umbrella.

Difficulty: *Average*   **Objective:** *Vocabulary*

2. The statement is a fact that can be proved by observing that the alarm is not working properly.

Difficulty: *Easy*   **Objective:** *Reading*

3. Sample answers: Twain is very fond of cats; consequently, he owns many cats. Twain cannot bear to hear anyone talk but himself; consequently, he does not like to go to church.

Difficulty: *Challenging*   **Objective:** *Vocabulary*

4. Susy wants to reveal that Twain does not have a logical mind. He has a "writer's mind."

Difficulty: *Easy*   **Objective:** *Interpretation*

5. Susy wants to show how much her father loves animals, suggesting he has a "kind, sympathetic nature."

Difficulty: *Average*   **Objective:** *Interpretation*

6. This statement tells what Susy Clemens believes. The phrase "I think" indicates an opinion, and the phrase "most touching" indicates a personal judgment.

Difficulty: *Average*   **Objective:** *Reading*

7. Sample details: "The book is full of lovely charming ideas, and oh the language!" "There is always a streak of humor in them somewhere."

Author's perspective: Twain is a talented writer who successfully mixes sentiment with humor.

Difficulty: *Average*   **Objective:** *Literary Analysis*

8. People read articles about Mark Twain written by strangers. Susy probably wanted to give a daughter's view of a father. She especially wanted to counter negative reports about his appearance and the narrow-minded view that he was just a humorist.

Difficulty: *Challenging*   **Objective:** *Interpretation*

9. Susy Clemens knows personal details about Mark Twain and his family that another author couldn't know. For example, only someone in Twain's family would be able to tell the story about the burglar alarm.

Difficulty: *Easy*   **Objective:** *Literary Analysis*

10. The description in "My Papa, Mark Twain" is given through the eyes of a loving daughter. A biography written by someone not related to Twain would probably not reveal such a loving attitude toward Twain.

Difficulty: *Average*   **Objective:** *Literary Analysis*

Essay

11. Most students will probably say that Mark Twain seems to be a loving father. His daughter describes him as "the loveliest man" and talks about his kindness. She says he has a temper but is quick to explain that everyone in the family has one. She also talks about his "kind, sympathetic nature." From her descriptions, it is obvious that she loves him very much. A few students might use his temper, smoking, and use of strong language to indicate that he is not a very good father.

Difficulty: *Easy*   **Objective:** *Essay*

12. Students should note that Susy Clemens views her father as attractive and intelligent. She suggests that he is the center of the family and everyone caters to him. She tells the reader that he is fond of animals, that he has a kind, sympathetic nature, and that he is humorous. The faults she describes are his excessive billiard playing, smoking, talking, strong language, absent-mindedness, and lack of logic.

Difficulty: *Average*   **Objective:** *Essay*

13. Students' essays should include some of these observations: Twain's version would differ because it would be

written from a different perspective. Twain might choose to emphasize his good points and make little of his faults. He might not even see himself as having the faults mentioned by his daughter. Twain might write about the same topics, but he would have more of a sense of humor about it. He would also present events through his eyes. For example, he would probably defend his position when telling about the burglar alarm.

Difficulty: *Challenging*   **Objective:** *Essay*

14. Some students may suggest that Susy Clemens goes overboard in praising her father. Such phrases as "love-liest man" would support this assumption. Susy might also be hesitant to describe the extent of his faults. However, there are things readers can believe. They can believe in his wonderful writing ability because of his success as a writer. They can also believe in his fond-ness for animals since Susy supports this statement with facts about the pet cats. Readers might also believe that Twain played hooky from school since it can be ver-ified with Grandma.

Difficulty: *Average*   **Objective:** *Essay*

Oral Response

15. Oral responses should be clear, well organized, and well supported by appropriate examples from the selection.

Difficulty: *Average*   **Objective:** *Oral Interpretation*

"My Papa, Mark Twain" by Susy Clemens

Selection Test A, p. 146

Critical Reading

1. ANS: D	DIF: Easy	OBJ: Literary Analysis
2. ANS: A	DIF: Easy	OBJ: Comprehension
3. ANS: D	DIF: Easy	OBJ: Comprehension
4. ANS: D	DIF: Easy	OBJ: Interpretation
5. ANS: B	DIF: Easy	OBJ: Reading
6. ANS: D	DIF: Easy	OBJ: Reading
7. ANS: B	DIF: Easy	OBJ: Interpretation
8. ANS: A	DIF: Easy	OBJ: Reading
9. ANS: B	DIF: Easy	OBJ: Literary Analysis

Vocabulary and Grammar

10. ANS: B	DIF: Easy	OBJ: Vocabulary
11. ANS: B	DIF: Easy	OBJ: Grammar
12. ANS: A	DIF: Easy	OBJ: Grammar

Essay

13. Students might say that they like that Mark Twain seems to be a loving father and that he is famous and wealthy. They might say they would dislike the lack of privacy from being in the public eye. They also might

not like that people attacked Mark Twain's writing or his looks. Students may say that a famous father might have to travel a great deal. They might say they like—or dislike—the idea of having a father who works at home as a writer.

Difficulty: *Easy*
Objective: *Essay*

14. Susy Clemens describes Mark Twain as a loving, hand-some, charming, humorous, and good man. She also says he is forgetful and short-tempered. She says he cannot understand mechanical things, such as how a burglar alarm works, and he tends to get impatient when his wife tries to explain what he does wrong. Susy admits that her father talks too much, smokes too much, does not go to church, and uses bad language. She also feels that he is a wonderful writer and has a kind and sympathetic nature.

Difficulty: *Easy*
Objective: *Essay*

15. Some students may suggest that Susy Clemens goes overboard in praising her father with phrases like "love-liest man." Susy might also be less than truthful about her father's faults. However, there are things readers can believe. They can believe he has wonderful writing ability because he is a successful writer. They can also believe he likes animals because Susy supports this statement with facts about the pet cats. Readers might also believe that Twain played hooky from school since it can be verified with Grandma.

Difficulty: *Easy*
Objective: *Essay*

Selection Test B, p. 149

Critical Reading

1. ANS: A	DIF: Average	OBJ: Literary Analysis
2. ANS: C	DIF: Average	OBJ: Comprehension
3. ANS: C	DIF: Average	OBJ: Interpretation
4. ANS: D	DIF: Average	OBJ: Literary Analysis
5. ANS: D	DIF: Average	OBJ: Interpretation
6. ANS: C	DIF: Challenging	OBJ: Reading
7. ANS: B	DIF: Average	OBJ: Interpretation
8. ANS: B	DIF: Average	OBJ: Reading
9. ANS: A	DIF: Average	OBJ: Comprehension
10. ANS: C	DIF: Average	OBJ: Comprehension
11. ANS: B	DIF: Average	OBJ: Reading
12. ANS: D	DIF: Average	OBJ: Literary Analysis

Vocabulary and Grammar

13. ANS: D	DIF: Average	OBJ: Vocabulary
14. ANS: C	DIF: Average	OBJ: Grammar
15. ANS: B	DIF: Average	OBJ: Grammar
16. ANS: B	DIF: Average	OBJ: Vocabulary

Essay

17. In Susy Clemens's opinion, Mark Twain is attractive and intelligent. She suggests that he is the center of the family and that everyone, especially her mother, caters to him. She tells the reader that he is fond of animals, that he has a kind, sympathetic nature, and that he is humorous. The faults she describes are his excessive billiard playing, smoking, talking, strong language, absentmindedness, and lack of mechanical ability.

Difficulty: *Average*

Objective: *Essay*

18. Susy Clemens's description of her father shows that she loves him. It is her opinion that he is very handsome and a good person. She admires his writing and believes that the public does not appreciate him or know his writing as well as she does. She is aware of some of his shortcomings, such as his fondness for wanting to talk more than to listen. Susy speaks of her father's shortcomings with fondness.

Difficulty: *Average*

Objective: *Essay*

19. Some students may suggest that Susy Clemens goes overboard in praising her father. Such phrases as "loveliest man" would support this assumption. Susy might also be hesitant to describe the extent of his faults. However, there are things readers can believe. They can believe in his wonderful writing ability because of his success as a writer. They can also believe in his fondness for animals since Susy supports this statement with facts about the pet cats. Readers might also believe that Twain played hooky from school since it can be verified with Grandma.

Difficulty: *Average*

Objective: *Essay*

Unit 1, Part 2, Answers

"Stage Fright" by Mark Twain

Vocabulary Warm-up Exercises, p. 153

A. 1. speech
2. audience
3. auditorium
4. horrible
5. awed
6. memory
7. kindness
8. appreciation

B. Sample Answers

1. I don't like watching movies on TV; I prefer the *big* screen of a theater.
2. Tim didn't want to go to the lecture because he hates listening for long periods.
3. The novel is still a manuscript; it *hasn't been* printed.

4. This candy is so good that I'm saving it for a special occasion.
5. Marvin did so *poorly* in the race that he needed some sympathy.
6. The performance was so *good* that the singer received lots of applause.
7. The pain medicine made the agony of my twisted ankle *go away*.

Reading Warm-up A, p. 154

Sample Answers

1. something to be read aloud; Politicians have to give lots of *speeches*.
2. would do anything to help a student learn; *Kindness* is helpful or friendly behavior.
3. (amazed); Amazing animal acts always leave me feeling *awed*.
4. a large hall that was perfect for putting on plays and concerts; The last time I was in an *auditorium* was for a wonderful dance recital.
5. going to be huge; An *audience* is a group of people gathered together to see something.
6. The speechwriter wants to show *appreciation* for being taught by Ms. Hagerty.
7. The speechwriter reached back into *memory* to recall all the things Ms. Hagerty had done for her/him.
8. the microphone; When my baby sister cries, she makes a *horrible* sound.

Reading Warm-up B, p. 155

Sample Answers

1. on a boat; If you feel *seasick*, you would probably take medicine and avoid boats.
2. (the pain of having stage fright); *Agony* is severe pain.
3. Singers, actors, and dancers might perform in a *theater*.
4. (performers who fail); *Applause* means clapping to show you like something.
5. They can't understand a performer's troubles; *Sympathy* is "feelings of understanding for another person."
6. Writers often read from an unpublished *manuscript* before an audience; A *manuscript* is a written text that hasn't been printed yet.
7. (subject he knows very well); I'd like to attend a *lecture* about the history of film.
8. stage fright shows up; An *occasion* is a particular time when something happens.

Writing About the Big Question, p. 156

A. 1. true
2. realistic
3. unbelievable
4. fiction/fantasy

B. Sample Answers

1. You can be kind to your friend and offer to listen. If your friend doesn't want to share her true feelings, you can respect that.

2. If someone gave me a present I did not like, I might not let them know that I was disaappointed.

C. Sample Answer

I might help them if it wouldn't hurt anyone.

If people hide their true feelings it is difficult to determine what is true. People close to you can pretend to be happy and you would not know that inside, they are really sad. On the other hand, usually when you know people well, you can tell if they are sad even when they are trying to hide it.

"Stage Fright" by Mark Twain

Reading: Recognize Clues That Indicate Fact or Opinion, p. 157

Sample Answers

A. 2. Underlined: lonely. Fact: It was dark behind the scenes in that theater.

3. Underlined: a gem. Fact: In the speech, I had included a joke that I considered my best.

4. Underlined: moving, pathetic part, get at the hearts and souls of my hearers. Fact: I expected that the audience would respond to that part of my speech.

5. Underlined: agonizing. Facts: After the first five minutes, my stage fright disappeared.

Literary Analysis: Author's Perspective, p. 158

A. Sample Answers

1. Twain describes a part of his speech to which the audience did not respond. The audience sat there silently, without laughing.

2. Twain probably felt that the middle part of his speech was the best, the funniest part.

3. Because the audience sat silently, Twain describes the middle of his speech as "moving and pathetic," even though he may have hoped that the audience would find it humorous. He felt that the middle part of his speech had failed.

4. The audience may have been disinterested, sleepy, or bored.

5. Underlined details: a gem, moving, pathetic part which was to get at the hearts and souls of my hearers, they did just what I hoped and expected. They sat silent and awed. I had touched them.

B. Sample Answer

Dear Richard,

Last night, I went to a wonderful lecture given by Mark Twain. Some friends told me that this was the first time he has ever given a humorous lecture. He is a very funny man, and I think he is going to be successful at whatever he does. Everybody in the audience was laughing so hard we could hardly hear the next joke. The best thing about Twain's comedy is the way he makes fun of himself.

Vocabulary Builder, p. 159

A. Sample Answers

1. Her compulsion to rock climb has forced her, against her common sense, to attempt the dangerous peaks.

2. We could not distract the cat as he watched the mouse intently for more than two minutes.

3. After my bike accident, a classmate, who had also broken her leg, expressed her sympathy for my misfortune.

4. The sight of the oncoming tornado awed us into silence for a few seconds; then, we overcame our fear and ran for shelter.

5. I was so nervous that standing up in front of the whole school to deliver a speech became a totally agonizing experience.

6. Everyone in my family has the hereditary trait of brown eyes.

B. 1. A child might *repulse* neighbors with impolite behavior.

2. The strong wind hit us in the face and *propelled* us backward.

Enrichment: Being a Reporter, p. 160

A. Sample Answers

1. Interest in a wide range of topics can help a reporter write about many different subjects. Read a wide variety of magazines and newspapers.

2. Ability to see humor in everyday events can help a reporter keep a sense of balance about life. Readers are often interested in humorous articles. One way to develop this skill is to read humorous articles and listen to people who are skillful at writing and performing comedy.

3. Ability to write well can help a reporter grab and hold readers' attention. Keep a journal; volunteer for the school newspaper; create e-mail and a Web site for friends and relatives to read.

4. Ability to talk to other people and put them at ease can help a reporter gather information. Become active in community volunteer work; volunteer for a political campaign.

B. Students should briefly describe an experience that they have had or imagined and explain why it would provide material for an interesting newspaper story. News stories should answer the journalistic questions of *who, what, when, where, why,* and *how.*

"Stage Fright" by Mark Twain
"My Papa, Mark Twain" by Susy Clemens

Integrated Language Skills: Grammar, p. 161

Possessive Personal Pronouns

A. 1. our
2. his
3. her; her
4. my

B. Sample Answers

2. Her home is on Grant Street. The home on Grant Street is hers.
3. My speech will be brief. Mine will be brief.
4. You heard our cheers. The cheers you heard were ours.

"Stage Fright" by Mark Twain

Open-Book Test, p. 164

Short Answer

1. The phrase "an awful, horrible malady" is an opinion because it indicates the author's personal judgment.
Difficulty: *Average* **Objective:** *Reading*

2. The opinion is "I'm older than I look." This statement gives Twain's personal belief about how old he looks. The fact is "It was on a little ship on which there were two hundred other passengers." This is information that can be proved.
Difficulty: *Average* **Objective:** *Reading*

3. *Intently* means "purposefully, earnestly." If the dog watches its owner intently, it is very interested in learning the trick.
Difficulty: *Easy* **Objective:** *Vocabulary*

4. Twain is nervous and wants to arrive early to make sure he has plenty of time to prepare.
Difficulty: *Easy* **Objective:** *Interpretation*

5. The height and size of a towering mountain could fill someone with feelings of fear and wonder.
Difficulty: *Average* **Objective:** *Vocabulary*

6. Twain accidentally looks up at the governor's wife. She laughs because he told her to laugh whenever he looked up at her.
Difficulty: *Average* **Objective:** *Interpretation*

7. The friends give Twain the courage he needs to get through the speech. He knows before he starts that at least part of the audience will be friendly to him.
Difficulty: *Challenging* **Objective:** *Interpretation*

8. The statement reveals just how nervous Twain was about giving his first big lecture.
Difficulty: *Easy* **Objective:** *Literary Analysis*

9. Twain feels that the middle of his speech is especially effective. He writes, "Right in the middle of the speech I had placed a gem."
Difficulty: *Average* **Objective:** *Literary Analysis*

10. Twain makes fun of himself throughout the speech and never takes himself seriously. This perspective is supported by such statements as "I was young in those days and needed the exercise."
Difficulty: *Challenging* **Objective:** *Literary Analysis*

Essay

11. Students should note that Twain's perspective is that although the stage fright was terrifying, it never returned and has made him stronger. He also knows that nothing will ever be as terrifying as that first appearance. His knowledge of stage fright makes him sympathetic toward others making a first appearance.
Difficulty: *Easy* **Objective:** *Essay*

12. Students' essays should include some of these observations: Twain fears he will be a failure because he has never given a speech in front of an audience. Even though his speech is written out, he is so nervous that he feels sick. He has packed the audience with friends who will laugh at his jokes. One of these is the governor's wife, who is to laugh on cue. At a touching part of the speech, Twain accidentally looks at her, causing her to laugh. Twain then loses his fear because it seems nothing worse can happen. His stage fright leaves, never to return. Twain goes on to have a successful career as a lecturer and writer.
Difficulty: *Average* **Objective:** *Essay*

13. Students' essays should include some of these observations: Twain talks about stage fright at the recital to show sympathy for what his daughter has just gone through and to inform the audience how difficult it is to perform for the first time. He might also want to send his daughter the message that the experience will make her stronger. He probably does it after the recital so as not to take the spotlight off of his daughter before her performance.
Difficulty: *Challenging* **Objective:** *Essay*

14. Some students may suggest that the audience is not aware of just how nervous Twain is because he remembers his speech without having to look at the written copy. Other students may suggest that the audience does know how frightened he is. The audience might use clues to help them. Being nervous, Twain probably moves around more than is necessary. The audience might also notice some of the friends planted among them to encourage laughter. After the governor's wife laughs at the wrong moment, Twain's stage fright leaves him. The audience might notice that he is more confident and relaxed at this point.
Difficulty: *Average* **Objective:** *Essay*

Oral Response

15. Oral responses should be clear, well organized, and well supported by appropriate examples from the selection.
    Difficulty: *Average*   **Objective:** *Oral Interpretation*

Selection Test A, p. 167

Critical Reading

1. ANS: C	DIF: Easy	OBJ: Comprehension
2. ANS: B	DIF: Easy	OBJ: Comprehension
3. ANS: A	DIF: Easy	OBJ: Interpretation
4. ANS: A	DIF: Easy	OBJ: Reading
5. ANS: D	DIF: Easy	OBJ: Literary Analysis
6. ANS: A	DIF: Easy	OBJ: Interpretation
7. ANS: B	DIF: Easy	OBJ: Reading
8. ANS: D	DIF: Easy	OBJ: Literary Analysis
9. ANS: B	DIF: Easy	OBJ: Interpretation

Vocabulary and Grammar

10. ANS: C	DIF: Easy	OBJ: Vocabulary
11. ANS: D	DIF: Easy	OBJ: Grammar
12. ANS: B	DIF: Easy	OBJ: Vocabulary

Essay

13. Twain's perspective is that although the stage fright was terrifying and actually made him ill at the time, it never returned. He also knows that nothing will ever be as terrifying as that first stage appearance. His knowledge of stage fright makes him sympathetic toward others making a first appearance.
    Difficulty: *Easy*
    Objective: *Essay*

14. Mark Twain lost his fear because it looked as if nothing worse could happen. His stage fright left him forever, and Twain went on to have a successful career both as a lecturer and a writer. The event also left him with a good story to entertain listeners with years later, and it made him sympathetic toward anyone making a first appearance.
    Difficulty: *Easy*
    Objective: *Essay*

15. Some students may suggest that the audience does not recognize how nervous Twain is and simply enjoys his speech. He remembers his speech without having to look at the written copy. The audience is "touched" by his speech. Other students may suggest that the audience does see how nervous he is. He walks up and down the stage a great deal. He has friends planted among them to encourage laughter. He probably reacts when the governor's wife laughs at the wrong moment.
    Difficulty: *Easy*
    Objective: *Essay*

Selection Test B, p. 170

Critical Reading

1. ANS: C	DIF: Average	OBJ: Comprehension
2. ANS: B	DIF: Average	OBJ: Comprehension
3. ANS: A	DIF: Average	OBJ: Interpretation
4. ANS: A	DIF: Average	OBJ: Reading
5. ANS: B	DIF: Challenging	OBJ: Reading
6. ANS: A	DIF: Average	OBJ: Literary Analysis
7. ANS: A	DIF: Average	OBJ: Interpretation
8. ANS: C	DIF: Challenging	OBJ: Literary Analysis
9. ANS: B	DIF: Average	OBJ: Reading
10. ANS: C	DIF: Challenging	OBJ: Literary Analysis
11. ANS: A	DIF: Average	OBJ: Literary Analysis
12. ANS: B	DIF: Average	OBJ: Interpretation
13. ANS: B	DIF: Average	OBJ: Comprehension

Vocabulary and Grammar

14. ANS: A	DIF: Average	OBJ: Vocabulary
15. ANS: C	DIF: Average	OBJ: Vocabulary
16. ANS: A	DIF: Average	OBJ: Grammar
17. ANS: C	DIF: Average	OBJ: Grammar

Essay

18. Mark Twain experienced stage fright when he made his first public appearance forty years prior to the speech recorded in "Stage Fright." He was actually ill with fright and feeling very alone in the theater prior to his appearance. He tried to ensure his success by having friends in the audience react appropriately. Five minutes into his appearance, his stage fright disappeared, never to return. He learned that he can get through anything and that he has sympathy for others making a first appearance.
    Difficulty: *Average*
    Objective: *Essay*

19. Twain fears he will be a failure because he has never given a speech in front of an audience. He is nervous even though he has his speech written out, and he gets to the theater early. He has packed the audience with friends who will laugh at his jokes. He feels overcome by stage fright, with his knees shaking so much that he says he feels seasick. When the governor's wife laughs at the wrong time in his speech, Twain loses his fear because it seems that nothing worse can happen. His stage fright leaves him, never to return, and Twain goes on to have a successful career as a humorous lecturer and writer.
    Difficulty: *Average*
    Objective: *Essay*

20. Some students may suggest that the audience is not aware of just how nervous Twain is because he remembers his speech without having to look at the written

copy. Other students may suggest that the audience does know how frightened he is. The audience might use clues to help them. Being nervous, Twain probably moves around more than is necessary. The audience might also notice some of the friends planted among them to encourage laughter. After the governor's wife laughs at the wrong moment, Twain's stage fright leaves him. The audience might notice that he is more confident and relaxed at this point.

Difficulty: *Average*

Objective: *Essay*

"Names/Nombres" by Julia Alvarez

Vocabulary Warm-up Exercises, p. 174

A. 1. constantly
2. embarrassed
3. pitied
4. Recently
5. desire
6. attended
7. occasions
8. included

B. Sample Answers

1. He could not believe that he had correctly predicted his *future*.
2. Everyone thought the game was easy to play because it was *not very* complicated.
3. *During* Josh's vacation to exotic places, he felt really homesick.
4. Jen originally wanted to be Persephone, *before* she changed her mind.
5. It was apparent that Malik was unhappy, so *everyone* could tell.
6. I ordered a combination, since I wanted *pepperoni and veggies* on my pizza.

Reading Warm-up A, p. 175

Sample Answers

1. in the past couple of decades; *Recently* I made the school soccer team.
2. They want to settle down and start living a normal life; I *desire* a room of my own.
3. (words), (images); *Constantly* means "all the time or without stopping."
4. uneasy; Saying the wrong thing could make someone *embarrassed*.
5. (kind of sympathy); I would feel bad if I knew that people *pitied* me.
6. parties, sporting events; I went to my sister's wedding last year.
7. feel that they belong; I do feel *included* at my school because I have lots of friends.

8. (went to); I *attended* John Sehorn School before this school.

Reading Warm-up B, p. 176

Sample Answers

1. my old school and my old friends; To be *homesick* means to miss your home or your old life.
2. strange, unknowable; Mongolia seems really *exotic* to me.
3. She doesn't want to *reveal* how unhappy she is; A word that means the same thing as *reveal* is "show."
4. Originally they had planned to stay a year.; *Originally* means "at first."
5. anyone could see it; It is *apparent* that the narrator's mom is really happy in the new place.
6. know the future; guessed; She could never have guessed that she would find a best friend and her mother would marry the best friend's father.
7. don't find us easy to figure out. No, *complicated* problems usually have a lot of parts and are hard to solve, not easy to solve.
8. The combination is the narrator and her best friend. I know because after the word *combination*, she describes the two of them.

Writing About the Big Question, p. 177

A. 1. unbelievable
2. confirm
3. decision

B. Sample Answers

1. I would ask my friend for the **truth** and let her know that it is okay for her to be honest with me.
2. I **investigate** for myself to find out the **facts**.

C. Sample Answer

when you show your true feelings, people may laugh at you.

It is useful to tell your true feelings to family and friends because then, in the future, they will know how to act not to hurt your feelings. In this way, you build a better relationship. If you do not tell the truth, you will continue to feel bad.

"Names/Nombres" by Julia Alvarez

Reading: Understand the Difference Between Fact and Opinion; Use Resources to Check Facts, p. 178

A. 1. F; 2. F; 3. O; 4. F; 5. O

B. Sample Answers

1. reliable Web site; Julia Alvarez moved to the United States for good in 1960.
2. reliable Web site; Julia Alvarez wrote a book called *How the García Girls Lost Their Accents.*

3. encyclopedia, reliable Web site, or map; The Dominican Republic is on the same island as Haiti.

4. encyclopedia, reliable Web site, or map; Bermuda is an island in the Atlantic Ocean.

Literary Analysis: Tone, p. 179

Sample Answers

A. Informal word: "ya"

Mispronunciation of Spanish: *"Missus Alburest"*

Untranslated Spanish word: *"sancocho"*

Exaggeration: "old world folk whom I would just as soon go back to where they came from"

Humorous idea: "as in, 'Hey, *little girl*, stop riding the elevator up and down'"

Sentence fragment: "South of Bermuda."

Another informal word: "super"

Contraction: "Why'd"

B. *"Missus Alburest,"* "as in 'Hey, *little girl*'" "'It's *not* a toy.'" Passage written in formal tone: At the hotel my mother's name was mispronounced. I, on the other hand, was called "little girl" and scolded for treating the elevator as though it were a plaything.

Vocabulary Builder p. 180

A. 1. B; 2. A; 3. B; 4. D; 5. B; 6. A

B. Sample Answers

1. The message tells the pharmacist what medicine to give to the doctor's patient.

2. The monks write in a scriptorium.

3. Happy birthday!

Enrichment: Your Own Name, p. 181

A. Students' success in completing the charts will depend on the amount of information available on the person whose name they choose to research and on their own research skills.

B. Students' statements might reflect their thoughts about Alvarez's essay, the research they conducted for this activity, or their feelings about their own names.

"Names/Nombres" by Julia Alvarez

Open-Book Test, p. 182

Short Answer

1. She thinks her last name has a beautiful sound. She doesn't understand how anyone could "get *Elbures* out of that orchestra of sound."

   Difficulty: *Average*   **Objective:** *Interpretation*

2. The change in attitude toward "ethnicity" might have made Americans more accepting of people of other cultures. As a result, Alvarez would have had an easier time fitting in with her American friends.

   Difficulty: *Challenging*   **Objective:** *Interpretation*

3. I could look in an encyclopedia or on a map.

   Difficulty: *Easy*   **Objective:** *Reading*

4. *Chaotic* means "completely confused." There is confusion when her big family is talking in Spanish in the front row at her graduation and when she introduces them to her friends.

   Difficulty: *Average*   **Objective:** *Vocabulary*

5. The fact that she has so many relatives coming to her graduation, while her American friends do not, makes her feel different. Though her relatives' constant chattering in Spanish embarrasses her, she appreciates their love, support, and many gifts.

   Difficulty: *Average*   **Objective:** *Interpretation*

6. Sentence 2 is a fact. It can be proved because many people observed the event. Sentence 1 is the opinion. It is Alvarez's belief ("too long") and cannot be proved.

   Difficulty: *Average*   **Objective:** *Reading*

7. They know she has an interest in writing and they want to encourage her interest.

   Difficulty: *Easy*   **Objective:** *Interpretation*

8. The essay has a friendly, conversational tone. For example, Alvarez writes, "*Anita*, or as one goofy guy used to sing to her to the tune of the banana advertisement, *Anita Banana*."

   Difficulty: *Easy*   **Objective:** *Literary Analysis*

9. Humor takes the edge off of some serious situations and feelings, making the essay more casual. For example, the humorous mispronunciations of Alvarez's name add a light touch to an emotional situation.

   Difficulty: *Average*   **Objective:** *Literary Analysis*

10. They make the writing colorful and informal. Alvarez does not define the Spanish words, further making the point that she is part of two cultures without making a formal statement.

    Difficulty: *Challenging*   **Objective:** *Literary Analysis*

Essay

11. Students should recognize that Alvarez is proud of her name. She dislikes hearing her name mispronounced and dislikes her American names. When she is in high school, she likes her nicknames because they show that she is popular, but she never gives up her real name.

    Difficulty: *Easy*   **Objective:** *Essay*

12. Students should note that the characteristics of an informal essay are casual word choice, humor, and simple sentence structure. Students might point to Alvarez's use of slang, informal language, and contractions. They might point to the humor in her essay. They might further note examples of short sentences and simple sentence construction.

    Difficulty: *Average*   **Objective:** *Essay*

13. Students should indicate that the quality of something or someone remains the same no matter what the name. At first, Julia's name is mispronounced and changed to be more American, making her uncomfortable. She is equally uncomfortable when her friends make a big deal about her Spanish name and single her out as a foreigner. However, throughout all of this, she is the same

person with the same qualities. As with the rose, it makes no difference by which name she is called. Alvarez seems to realize this at the end of the essay when she wonders which name she would use when she becomes a well-known writer.

Difficulty: *Challenging*   **Objective:** *Essay*

14. Students should make some of these observations: Julia's friends decide what is true about her through very American eyes. They call her by Americanized names because it's easier for them. They do not try to make Julia feel like a "foreigner," but their lack of sensitivity achieves the same effect. Because they never go beneath the surface to find out what Julia is really like, they never learn her true feelings about her Dominican culture and about trying to fit into a new culture.

Difficulty: *Average*   **Objective:** *Essay*

Oral Response

15. Oral responses should be clear, well organized, and well supported by appropriate examples from the selection.

Difficulty: *Average*   **Objective:** *Oral Interpretation*

"Names/Nombres" by Julia Alvarez

Selection Test A, p. 185

Critical Reading

1. ANS: D	DIF: Easy	OBJ: Interpretation
2. ANS: C	DIF: Easy	OBJ: Interpretation
3. ANS: C	DIF: Easy	OBJ: Comprehension
4. ANS: C	DIF: Easy	OBJ: Reading
5. ANS: D	DIF: Easy	OBJ: Interpretation
6. ANS: B	DIF: Easy	OBJ: Reading
7. ANS: A	DIF: Easy	OBJ: Literary Analysis
8. ANS: D	DIF: Easy	OBJ: Literary Analysis
9. ANS: C	DIF: Easy	OBJ: Comprehension

Vocabulary and Grammar

10. ANS: B	DIF: Easy	OBJ: Vocabulary
11. ANS: C	DIF: Easy	OBJ: Grammar
12. ANS: C	DIF: Easy	OBJ: Grammar

Essay

13. Students should recognize that at first Alvarez dislikes hearing her name mispronounced and dislikes the American names she is called by. Later, however, she gets used to them, and when she is in high school she likes her nicknames because they show that she is popular. Still, she is uncomfortable when her friends show curiosity about her long full name. At the end of the essay, she wonders what name she will use if she becomes a well-known writer.

Difficulty: *Easy*

Objective: *Essay*

14. Students should recognize that "Names/Nombres" is largely informal, friendly, and humorous. As evidence, they might point to exaggeration (as in the initial explanation of the orchestral sound of the proper pronunciation of *Alvarez*), slang and informal language, and humor (as in the various mispronunciations of the Spanish names).

Difficulty: *Easy*

Objective: *Essay*

15. Students should make some of these observations: Julia's friends decide what is true about her through very American eyes. They call her by Americanized names because it's easier for them. They do not try to make Julia feel like a "foreigner," but that is the end result of their attention. Because she does not reveal her feelings to them, they never go beneath the surface to find out what is true about Julia's life and culture.

Difficulty: *Easy*

Objective: *Essay*

Selection Test B, p. 188

Critical Reading

1. ANS: C	DIF: Average	OBJ: Comprehension
2. ANS: C	DIF: Average	OBJ: Comprehension
3. ANS: A	DIF: Average	OBJ: Reading
4. ANS: D	DIF: Average	OBJ: Reading
5. ANS: C	DIF: Challenging	OBJ: Reading
6. ANS: D	DIF: Challenging	OBJ: Reading
7. ANS: D	DIF: Average	OBJ: Interpretation
8. ANS: A	DIF: Challenging	OBJ: Interpretation
9. ANS: B	DIF: Average	OBJ: Comprehension
10. ANS: D	DIF: Average	OBJ: Interpretation
11. ANS: B	DIF: Average	OBJ: Interpretation
12. ANS: A	DIF: Challenging	OBJ: Literary Analysis
13. ANS: D	DIF: Average	OBJ: Literary Analysis
14. ANS: A	DIF: Challenging	OBJ: Literary Analysis
15. ANS: C	DIF: Challenging	OBJ: Literary Analysis

Vocabulary and Grammar

16. ANS: B	DIF: Average	OBJ: Vocabulary
17. ANS: D	DIF: Average	OBJ: Grammar

Essay

18. Students should describe an informal essay as one with a friendly or casual tone. They should recognize that word choice, sentence structure, and sentence length contribute to tone, and that humor and exaggeration may help to create an informal tone. Students might point to the humor in Alvarez's essay (the mispronunciation of her name, the names her friends give her, her friends' lack of knowledge about the Caribbean), the use of Spanish words to add color and interest, and the use

of slang, informal language, short sentences, contractions, and humorous quotations.

Difficulty: *Average*

Objective: *Essay*

19. Students should recognize that at first Alvarez dislikes hearing her family name mispronounced and is uncomfortable when she is called Judy or Judith. In high school, she accepts her nicknames, believing they demonstrate her popularity, and she is uncomfortable when friends treat her name (and her) as if she were exotic. When she graduates from high school, she wonders what name she will use as an adult. The fact that she has chosen Julia Alvarez suggests her allegiance to her Dominican heritage.

Difficulty: *Average*

Objective: *Essay*

20. Students should make some of these observations: Julia's friends decide what is true about her through very American eyes. They call her by Americanized names because it's easier for them. They do not try to make Julia feel like a "foreigner," but their lack of sensitivity achieves the same effect. Because they never go beneath the surface to find out what Julia is really like, they never learn her true feelings about her Dominican culture and about trying to fit into a new culture.

Difficulty: *Average*

Objective: *Essay*

"The Lady and the Spider" by Robert Fulghum

Vocabulary Warm-up Exercises, p. 192

A. 1. terms
2. flings
3. disaster
4. clutches
5. torn
6. fiber
7. poisonous
8. envy

B. Sample Answers
1. F; Favorable comments are positive and approving.
2. F; Wherever means anyplace will do, not one specific place.
3. T; That is exactly what luggage is used for.
4. F; On the contrary, survivors *are* the lucky ones; they lived through what others couldn't.
5. F; Suburban neighborhoods are close to cities.
6. F; Tornadoes are a kind of weather; they begin outdoors.
7. T; Animals are the creatures that live in a zoo.
8. T; Cars are very heavy. It would take someone very strong to do that.

Reading Warm-up A, p. 193

Sample Answers
1. at the spider; *Clutches* means "to grab at."
2. The person who *flings* the spider is trying to get it as far away as possible.
3. (of real danger); *Terms* means "words, or ways of saying something."
4. (not harmful); Some snakes are *poisonous*.
5. (a spider bite); An earthquake that damages a city is a *disaster*.
6. Most spiders have eight legs and eight eyes.; To *envy* means "to be jealous of."
7. walk into a spider web; *Torn* means "ripped."
8. a complicated web; A *fiber* is a long, thin thread.

Reading Warm-up B, p. 194

Sample Answers
1. our family can live through almost anything; Survivors are people who can live through anything.
2. (The place doesn't matter); I don't care where we go, so let's just head off *wherever*.
3. hiking, fishing, and backpacking; A *suburban* area is in between the city and the country.
4. the airline misplaced every piece of our; *Luggage* refers to bags or suitcases used to hold belongings.
5. (hungry bears); *Inhabited* means "lived in."
6. They probably would have been depressed about the missing food.
7. (Rain came pouring down, branches and leaves went flying through the air). *Powerful* means "very strong."
8. The father probably turned around because he knew that a *tornado* can be very dangerous.

Writing About the Big Question, p. 195

A. 1. opinions
2. investigate
3. study
4. test; prove

B. Sample Answers
1. Sometimes it is easy to distinguish between **fact** and **fiction**. A science fiction book about the future is clearly fiction. But in a historical novel, it is harder to tell what is **true** and what is **fiction**.
2. Words such as "I think," "I feel," are signals that you are reading about an **opinion,** not **fact**.

C. Sample Answer

that certain spiders are poisonous.

In order to know what is true about spiders, you would have to study and research the topic. There are many rumors about spiders, and people repeat them without regard to the facts. That is why it is important to have evidence before you say something as though it were a fact.

"The Lady and the Spider" by Robert Fulghum

Reading: Understand the Difference Between Fact and Opinion; Use Resources to Check Facts, p. 196

A. 1. F; 2. O; 3. F; 4. O; 5. F

B. Sample Answers

1. dictionary, encyclopedia, or reliable Web site; A spider has eight legs.
2. encyclopedia or reliable Web site; Spiders eat all kinds of insects and other living animals.
3. dictionary, encyclopedia, or reliable Web site; The word is spelled *arachnid*.
4. encyclopedia or reliable Web site; In temperate climates, two species of spiders are dangerous to human beings (the black widow and the brown recluse).

Literary Analysis: Tone, p. 197

Sample Answers

Informal word: "cinch"

Sentence fragment: "Nice lady"

Short sentence: "This is my neighbor."

Exaggeration: "The neighbor lady thinks the spider is about the size of a lobster."

Surprising idea: "If we had this little six-nozzled aperture right at the base of our spine."

Humorous idea: A woman is terrified of a spider.

Joke word: "AAAAAAAAGGGGGGGGGGHHHHHHHHH"

Contraction: "She's"

Vocabulary Builder, p. 198

A. 1. D; 2. A; 3. C 4. A; **5.** C; **6.** B

B. 1. barometer
2. thermometer
3. parking meter

Enrichment: Songs, p. 199

A. Students should name the song they have chosen, quote several lines from it, and attribute to it a reasonable, meaningful message.

B. Students should describe a design that relates to the message they have attributed to the song.

"The Lady and the Spider" by Robert Fulghum
"Names/Nombres" by Julia Alvarez

Intergrated Language Skills: Grammar, p. 200

Interrogative and Indefinite Pronouns

A. 1. Who [inter] can remember some [indef] of the names Julia Alvarez gave herself?

2. From whose [inter] point of view do the spider and the lady see each other [indef]?

3. None [indef] of Julia's classmates seemed able to pronounce her name correctly.

4. Which [inter] essay do you prefer: the one [indef] by Alvarez or the one [indef] by Fulghum?

5. What [inter] do you think of some [indef] of the lady's and spider's reactions to each other [indef]?

6. What [inter] sort of name is Judy Alcatraz?

B. Students' paragraphs should be four sentences long and include one interrogative pronoun and two indefinite pronouns. Sample response:

Some [indef] of the reactions the spider and lady have to each other [indef] are quite funny. Who [inter] can resist the humor of these mismatched impressions? None [indef] of them is realistic, of course. Which [inter] one [indef] is more frightened of the other [indef], I wonder?

"The Lady and the Spider" by Robert Fulghum

Open-Book Test, p. 203

Short Answer

1. Someone chased by bees would more likely be frenzied since attacking bees would cause a person to act in a wild, uncontrolled way.
   Difficulty: *Average* **Objective:** *Vocabulary*

2. To the spider, the human is a big living creature caught in her web. Anything in the web can be a meal, a piece of meat. However, the woman is also made-up and dressed for work, so she appears to be "painted" to the spider.
   Difficulty: *Challenging* **Objective:** *Interpretation*

3. The lady fears the spider may be in her clothes. Putting on the new outfit will assure that there is no spider living in her clothing.
   Difficulty: *Challenging* **Objective:** *Vocabulary*

4. The statement is a fact because it can be proved to be true. You could check this fact in an encyclopedia.
   Difficulty: *Average* **Objective:** *Reading*

5. This statement is an opinion because there is no way to prove what would happen if human beings made webs.
   Difficulty: *Easy* **Objective:** *Reading*

6. The casual wording and use of the contraction adds to the informal, friendly tone of the essay.
   Difficulty: *Average* **Objective:** *Literary Analysis*

7. Fulghum is saying it is important for living things to keep on going and not give up.

   Difficulty: *Easy*   **Objective:** *Interpretation*

8. The woman will now expect a web to be outside her door so she will be more cautious.

   Difficulty: *Average*   **Objective:** *Interpretation*

9. Sample answers: huge piece of raw-but-painted meat; it's too big to wrap up and eat later; Wrapping packages would be a cinch! The author might have chosen a humorous tone to appeal to more people.

   Difficulty: *Average*   **Objective:** *Literary Analysis*

10. Fulghum uses many short sentences and sentence fragments that mimic someone speaking. The use of these sentences helps set a friendly and informal tone.

    Difficulty: *Challenging*   **Objective:** *Literary Analysis*

Essay

11. Students should note that Fulghum seems to favor the spider. He describes the lady's actions as exaggerated and not logical. Her fear of spiders sends her into a needless terror. She sees the spider as being the size of a lobster with poisonous fangs. When the spider sees a human caught in her web, she logically realizes it is too big to eat and wonders what it will do. Fulghum seems to admire spiders in general. He views them as amazing creatures, and he believes they teach us never to give up.

    Difficulty: *Easy*   **Objective:** *Essay*

12. Students' essays should include some of these observations: A serious essay would not use informal language, exaggeration, and sentence fragments. It might be more scientific, and it might contain longer, more complex sentences and more difficult words. Students are likely to say that they prefer the humorous, informal essay because it is fun and easy to read.

    Difficulty: *Average*   **Objective:** *Essay*

13. Students' essays may include some of these observations: Fulghum supports the idea that spiders are amazing by listing facts about spiders. They have been around for about 350 million years in great quantities and can make webs, a skill that people lack. He uses the song "Eensy, Weensy Spider" to support the idea that spiders can teach us about survival. Some students might find the argument supported by fact more effective. Others might prefer the whimsy of the argument based on the song.

    Difficulty: *Challenging*   **Objective:** *Essay*

14. Students should note that the lady decides what is true through her fear. She is so afraid of spiders that she views the spider as being the size of a lobster with rubber lips and poisonous fangs. Fulghum, on the other hand, uses facts and logic to support his view. He finds spiders to be amazing creatures because they have survived in great numbers for so long. Students will probably agree with this assessment. However, some

students may feel that he gives too much credit to the creatures when he suggests that the song "Eensy, Weensy Spider" indicates that spiders never give up.

Difficulty: *Average*   **Objective:** *Essay*

Oral Response

15. Oral responses should be clear, well organized, and well supported by appropriate examples from the selection.

    Difficulty: *Average*   **Objective:** *Oral Interpretation*

Selection Test A, p. 206

Critical Reading

1. **ANS:** D	**DIF:** Easy	**OBJ:** Interpretation
2. **ANS:** C	**DIF:** Easy	**OBJ:** Comprehension
3. **ANS:** A	**DIF:** Easy	**OBJ:** Literary Analysis
4. **ANS:** A	**DIF:** Easy	**OBJ:** Reading
5. **ANS:** C	**DIF:** Easy	**OBJ:** Interpretation
6. **ANS:** A	**DIF:** Easy	**OBJ:** Reading
7. **ANS:** B	**DIF:** Easy	**OBJ:** Interpretation
8. **ANS:** D	**DIF:** Easy	**OBJ:** Comprehension
9. **ANS:** C	**DIF:** Easy	**OBJ:** Literary Analysis
10. **ANS:** B	**DIF:** Easy	**OBJ:** Literary Analysis

Vocabulary and Grammar

11. **ANS:** C	**DIF:** Easy	**OBJ:** Vocabulary
12. **ANS:** A	**DIF:** Easy	**OBJ:** Grammar

Essay

13. Students may mention Fulghum's use of exaggeration, the scene in which the woman is described from the point of view of the spider, the description of the spider as if it were human, the consideration of what humans might do if they had the capabilities of spiders, and the repetition of the woman's scream.

    Difficulty: *Easy*

    Objective: *Essay*

14. Students should recognize that a serious essay would not use informal language, exaggeration, and sentence fragments. It might be more scientific, and it might contain longer, more complex sentences and more difficult words. Students are likely to say that they prefer the humorous, informal essay because it is funny and easy to read while still making a serious point.

    Difficulty: *Easy*

    Objective: *Essay*

15. Students should note that the lady is terrified by the spider. Her view is based on her fear. She sees the spider as being the size of a lobster with rubber lips and poisonous fangs. Fulghum's view is based on science and his interest in spiders. He thinks spiders are amazing creatures because they have survived in great

numbers for so long. Students will probably find his to be the truer view.

Difficulty: *Easy*

Objective: *Essay*

Selection Test B, p. 209

Critical Reading

1. ANS: A	DIF: Challenging	OBJ: Literary Analysis
2. ANS: C	DIF: Average	OBJ: Interpretation
3. ANS: C	DIF: Average	OBJ: Comprehension
4. ANS: C	DIF: Average	OBJ: Comprehension
5. ANS: D	DIF: Average	OBJ: Reading
6. ANS: A	DIF: Challenging	OBJ: Reading
7. ANS: C	DIF: Average	OBJ: Literary Analysis
8. ANS: A	DIF: Average	OBJ: Reading
9. ANS: D	DIF: Average	OBJ: Interpretation
10. ANS: B	DIF: Challenging	OBJ: Interpretation
11. ANS: B	DIF: Average	OBJ: Reading
12. ANS: A	DIF: Average	OBJ: Comprehension
13. ANS: C	DIF: Average	OBJ: Literary Analysis
14. ANS: B	DIF: Average	OBJ: Literary Analysis

Vocabulary and Grammar

15. ANS: C	DIF: Average	OBJ: Vocabulary
16. ANS: A	DIF: Challenging	OBJ: Grammar
17. ANS: C	DIF: Average	OBJ: Grammar

Essay

18. Students should recognize that the tone of "The Lady and the Spider" is informal, friendly, and humorous. As contributing factors, they should point to contractions, slang, exaggeration, and sentence fragments. They should show how an essay on the same topic might have a different tone—most likely a formal one—and present valid reasons for preferring one tone or the other.

Difficulty: *Average*

Objective: *Essay*

19. Students might mention an instance of exaggeration, the repetition of the woman's scream, and/or the woman seen from the spider's point of view. They should recognize that the humor is appropriate to the essay's casual, informal style.

Difficulty: *Average*

Objective: *Essay*

20. Students should note that the lady decides what is true through her fear. She is so afraid of spiders that she views the spider as being the size of a lobster with rubber lips and poisonous fangs. Fulghum, on the other hand, uses facts and logic to support his view. He finds

spiders to be amazing creatures because they have survived in great numbers for so long. Students will probably agree with this assessment. However, some students may feel that he gives too much credit to the creatures when he suggests that the song "Eensy, Weensy Spider" indicates that spiders never give up.

Difficulty: *Average*

Objective: *Essay*

"The Sound of Summer Running"
by Ray Bradbury
"Eleven" by Sandra Cisneros

Vocabulary Warm-up Exercises, p. 213

A. 1. downtown
2. flex
3. possible
4. tremendous
5. problem
6. clumsily
7. alleys
8. hushed

B. Sample Answers

1. Carly always <u>believes</u> Lauren because she knows Lauren *tells the truth*.
2. The ride looked a little scary so I *didn't feel* <u>absolutely</u> safe going on it.
3. I reached *down* to grab the pencil that had rolled <u>underneath</u> my seat.
4. The <u>arches</u> of Jason's *feet* hurt after a long run.
5. Having a *neat* desk is a <u>valuable</u> way to stay organized.
6. The *bottom* of Jose's sneakers had rubber <u>soles</u>.
7. Douglas *thought* that breaking his arm was <u>painful</u>.

Reading Warm-up A, p. 214

Sample Answers

1. (in the mornings), (truly alone); When no one is awake to make a sound, my house has a *hushed* feeling.
2. (Still sleepy, in the dark); This morning, I *clumsily* tripped up the stairs.
3. <u>Main shopping street, storefronts</u>; I like to go shopping when I go *downtown*.
4. (Empty, shortcut); An *alley* is a small street between buildings.
5. <u>At this hour of the morning</u>, <u>Alex had all the windows to herself</u>.
6. <u>until she couldn't go any faster</u>; I would run as fast as *possible* in a race.
7. Alex *flexed* her muscles for the fast run home; I might *flex* my muscles when playing soccer.

8. <u>Power of movement</u>; I completed a *tremendous* amount of homework this week.

Reading Warm-up B, p. 215

Sample Answers

1. Rubber *soles* last longer than leather *soles* and are lightweight.
2. *Underneath* the tops of sneakers are materials like polyurethane and plastic.
3. (improve performance); Sneakers are *valuable* to me because they help me run faster.
4. <u>can't be seen</u>; The air is *invisible*.
5. Engineers design supports for *arches* to provide balance and prevent foot injuries.
6. The wrong kind of shoes won't support your foot properly.
7. (whether or not that's true); I *believe* kids should respect their parents.
8. It might not be <u>absolutely</u> true that sneakers are the most comfortable shoes; I *absolutely* believe that basketball is the best sport in the world.

Writing About the Big Question, p. 216

A. 1. confirm
2. fiction
3. determine

B. Sample Answers

1. Authors will sometimes include an object that appears throughout a story or book, and that object stands for something. For example, whenever the character wears a red dress, it means she is happy.
2. Sometimes, if the book is well written, it is clear what the symbol stands for. Other times, it is difficult to decipher the symbol, and I have to wait for class discussions to figure it out.

C. Sample Answer

the object becomes associated with those feelings.

One symbol that is widely accepted is the American flag. Most Americans see it as a symbol of freedom and liberty and take pride in it. It is meaningful to people abroad, too, who see it as a symbol of our country.

"The Sound of Summer Running"
by Ray Bradbury
"Eleven" by Sandra Cisneros

Literary Analysis: Symbol, p. 217

1. the end of summer
2. Possible answers: powerlessness, sadness
3. Underlined phrase: <u>with this new pair of shoes, he could do anything, anything at all</u>. Possible answers: freedom, power, hope
4. a sweater

5. Possible underlined phrases: <u>all the years inside of me . . . are all pushing at the back of my eyes when I put one arm through one sleeve</u>; <u>the sweater that smells like cottage cheese</u>; <u>as if the sweater hurts me and it does</u>; <u>all itchy and full of germs that aren't even mine</u>. Possible responses: The sweater symbolizes Rachel's feelings of powerlessness, being misunderstood, being uncomfortable, weakness, embarrassment, insignificance, and smallness.

Vocabulary Builder, p. 218

Sample Answers

A. 2. She <u>seized</u> the dog's leash as he lunged toward the squirrel.
3. The tennis match was <u>suspended</u> due to rainy weather.
4. After a sudden <u>revelation</u>, Charles was able to complete the math problem.
5. Words such as *happiness* and *pride* name concepts that are <u>invisible</u>.
6. Because my coat was <u>raggedy</u>, it was worn and thin.

B. 1. Julia <u>seized</u> the railing as her skates rolled out from under her.
2. The track meet was <u>suspended</u> when heavy rain began to fall.
3. With a sudden <u>revelation</u> of DNA evidence, the detective solved the mystery.
4. The taxi driver turned into an <u>alley</u> to avoid the traffic jam.
5. The flag was faded and <u>raggedy</u> because it had flown during a bad strom.
6. Against the darkened night sky, the black birds were almost <u>invisible</u>.

"The Sound of Summer Running" by Ray Bradbury
"Eleven" by Sandra Cisneros

Open-Book Test, p. 220

Short Answer

1. Douglas is awestruck. He feels his feet "seized" and "suspended." He imagines the speed and power he will feel running in the shoes.
   Difficulty: *Average*   **Objective:** *Interpretation*
2. Three emotions students might write are excitement, joy, and wonder. Mr. Sanderson feels this way because he remembers what it's like to be a boy wearing tennis shoes.
   Difficulty: *Average*   **Objective:** *Interpretation*
3. Mr. Sanderson puts on the shoes and listens to Douglas's rush of words. He suddenly understands how wonderful the tennis shoes are.
   Difficulty: *Average*   **Objective:** *Vocabulary*

4. Rachel is embarrassed that Mrs. Price does not know that she would never wear such an ugly sweater. She is also frustrated that she can't find the right words to convince the teacher that the sweater isn't hers.
   Difficulty: *Average* **Objective:** *Interpretation*

5. An alley is a narrow street between or behind buildings. It would be a good place to get rid of the sweater because it is out of sight.
   Difficulty: *Easy* **Objective:** *Vocabulary*

6. The party won't matter because her day has already been ruined by the incident with the red sweater.
   Difficulty: *Easy* **Objective:** *Interpretation*

7. The symbols help express the characters' feelings. The tennis shoes symbolize Douglas's joy at summer freedom. The itchy, ugly sweater symbolizes Rachel's embarrassment and frustration.
   Difficulty: *Average* **Objective:** *Literary Analysis*

8. They are both items that you can put on and take off—shoes and a sweater. They both also represent strong feelings.
   Difficulty: *Easy* **Objective:** *Literary Analysis*

9. They are different in that the tennis shoes represent positive feelings, while the red sweater represents negative feelings.
   Difficulty: *Average* **Objective:** *Literary Analysis*

10. The problem in each story involves the symbol. Douglas's problem is finding a way to buy new sneakers, his symbol of summer freedom. Rachel's problem is finding a way to rid herself of the red sweater, a symbol of her lack of maturity.
    Difficulty: *Challenging* **Objective:** *Literary Analysis*

Essay

11. Students should make the following observations. Douglas puts on Litefoot tennis shoes. At that moment, he feels light, free, and powerful. Rachel puts on the red sweater. She feels horrified and embarrassed. The situations are different because Douglas has positive feelings and Rachel has negative feelings. They are similar because the objects have power over each character, causing strong feelings.
    Difficulty: *Easy* **Objective:** *Essay*

12. Students' essays should suggest that Douglas would make a good salesperson because he has a great deal of energy, does not give up easily, and is able to convince people to do things. Douglas uses all these qualities to convince Mr. Sanderson to try on the tennis shoes and to allow him to work in order to pay for a pair. Some students might suggest that Douglas would not like this job since it lacks imagination and freedom. Others might say that he would like the job since he is so qualified for it.
    Difficulty: *Average* **Objective:** *Essay*

13. Students should suggest that Rachel would not be as aggressive as Douglas in going after the sneakers. Not having Douglas's way with words, she would never

attempt to convince Mr. Sanderson to let her work off the price of the shoes. Instead, she might just timidly ask her parents to get her the shoes for a birthday present. She might succeed since her birthday is celebrated in the story. Students should also note that Douglas would not be as passive in taking the sweater as Rachel is. He would speak up to Mrs. Price and convince her that the sweater is not his, and he would be confident about the situation.
Difficulty: *Challenging* **Objective:** *Essay*

14. Students should note that Mrs. Price takes the word of Felice Garcia, who says the sweater belongs to Rachel. The teacher probably believes Felice because the girl speaks right up. Rachel, on the other hand, protests "in a little voice" that the sweater isn't hers, and she hesitates while speaking. This might make Mrs. Price think that she is lying. The teacher probably comes to the wrong conclusion because she doesn't know Rachel very well and is overly anxious to settle the ownership of the sweater.
Difficulty: *Average* **Objective:** *Essay*

Oral Response

15. Oral responses should be clear, well organized, and well supported with appropriate examples from the selections.
    Difficulty: *Average* **Objective:** *Oral Interpretation*

Selection Test A, p. 223

Critical Reading

1. ANS: A	DIF: Easy	OBJ: Comprehension
2. ANS: C	DIF: Easy	OBJ: Comprehension
3. ANS: C	DIF: Easy	OBJ: Interpretation
4. ANS: D	DIF: Easy	OBJ: Literary Analysis
5. ANS: D	DIF: Easy	OBJ: Interpretation
6. ANS: B	DIF: Easy	OBJ: Comprehension
7. ANS: A	DIF: Easy	OBJ: Interpretation
8. ANS: C	DIF: Easy	OBJ: Literary Analysis
9. ANS: B	DIF: Easy	OBJ: Interpretation
10. ANS: A	DIF: Easy	OBJ: Comprehension
11. ANS: B	DIF: Easy	OBJ: Literary Analysis
12. ANS: A	DIF: Easy	OBJ: Literary Analysis

Vocabulary

13. ANS: B	DIF: Easy	OBJ: Vocabulary
14. ANS: D	DIF: Easy	OBJ: Vocabulary

Essay

15. In "The Sound of Summer Running," Douglas puts on the Litefoot tennis shoes. At that moment, he feels light and free and powerful. In "Eleven," Rachel puts on the red sweater. She feels horrified and embarrassed. The

experiences are different because Douglas has positive feelings and Rachel has negative feelings. They are similar because the worn objects have power over each character.

Difficulty: *Easy*

Objective: *Essay*

16. Some students will find Douglas more real, because they will identify with his love of summer and new tennis shoes. Other students will find Rachel more real, because like many eleven-year-olds she has a difficult time communicating with adults, is easily embarrassed, and dislikes certain classmates.

Difficulty: *Easy*

Objective: *Essay*

17. Students should note that Mrs. Price believes Felice Garcia, who says the sweater is Rachel's. The teacher probably believes Felice because the girl speaks right up. Rachel, on the other hand, protests "in a little voice" that the sweater isn't hers, and she hesitates while speaking. This might make Mrs. Price think that she is lying. The teacher doesn't know Rachel very well and simply wants to solve the problem.

Difficulty: *Easy*

Objective: *Essay*

Selection Test B, p. 226

Critical Reading

1. ANS: C	DIF: Average	OBJ: Comprehension
2. ANS: A	DIF: Challenging	OBJ: Interpretation
3. ANS: A	DIF: Average	OBJ: Literary Analysis
4. ANS: C	DIF: Average	OBJ: Literary Analysis
5. ANS: D	DIF: Average	OBJ: Literary Analysis
6. ANS: D	DIF: Average	OBJ: Interpretation
7. ANS: C	DIF: Average	OBJ: Comprehension
8. ANS: A	DIF: Average	OBJ: Comprehension
9. ANS: C	DIF: Average	OBJ: Comprehension
10. ANS: C	DIF: Challenging	OBJ: Literary Analysis
11. ANS: B	DIF: Average	OBJ: Literary Analysis
12. ANS: C	DIF: Challenging	OBJ: Comprehension
13. ANS: A	DIF: Average	OBJ: Literary Analysis
14. ANS: D	DIF: Average	OBJ: Interpretation
15. ANS: C	DIF: Challenging	OBJ: Interpretation

Vocabulary

16. ANS: D	DIF: Average	OBJ: Vocabulary
17. ANS: C	DIF: Average	OBJ: Vocabulary

Essay

18. Students should identify the new tennis shoes as the central symbol in "The Sound of Summer Running" and the red sweater as the central symbol in "Eleven."

Students might say that the tennis shoes stand for summer, freedom, power, nature, youth, or Douglas's love of summer. They might say the red sweater stands for the feelings of loneliness, embarrassment, immaturity, or being misunderstood. The two symbols are alike because they are items that can be worn, and they are items about which the main characters have strong feelings. The symbols are different because the tennis shoes represent very positive feelings, while the sweater represents very negative feelings.

Difficulty: *Average*

Objective: *Essay*

19. Students who find Douglas more believable might identify with his attraction to the new tennis shoes and with his love of summer freedom. These students might find it difficult to believe that Rachel, at age eleven, is capable of having complicated ideas about birthdays and also be unable to find the words to defend herself in class. Students might find it hard to understand why Rachel agreed to put on an offensive sweater. Students who find Rachel more believable might say that misunderstandings between student and teacher and embarrassing situations are common for eleven-year-olds. These students might think Douglas's thoughts and words about the tennis shoes are overly sophisticated for a young boy.

Difficulty: *Average*

Objective: *Essay*

20. Students should note that Mrs. Price takes the word of Felice Garcia, who says the sweater belongs to Rachel. The teacher probably believes Felice because the girl speaks right up. Rachel, on the other hand, protests "in a little voice" that the sweater isn't hers, and she hesitates while speaking. This might make Mrs. Price think that she is lying. The teacher probably comes to the wrong conclusion because she doesn't know Rachel very well and is overly anxious to settle the ownership of the sweater.

Difficulty: *Average*

Objective: *Essay*

Writing Workshop Unit 1

Autobiographical Narrative: Pronoun = Antecedent Agreement p. 230

A. 1. her; 2. their; 3. his; 4. they

B. 1. The girls wanted to stop at *their* favorite ice cream shop.

2. Everyone wanted to create *her* own special sundae.

3. Several insisted that *they* be allowed to substitute flavors.

4. Customers in line showed *their* dismay by rolling *their* eyes.

Vocabulary Workshop—1, p. 231

Sample Answers

1. I will *descend* from the top of the mountain. (1)
2. The ramp *descends* toward the lake. (3)
3. The enemy troops will *descend* upon us! (7)
4. The good silver will *descend* to her great-grand-daughter. (5)
5. "The notes *descend* at the end of the song," said the piano teacher. (8)

Vocabulary Workshop—2, p. 232

Sample Answers

1. Aunt Tilly will *lose balance* is she has to walk that far.
2. Missy's plate *dropped* to the ground, shattering into tiny pieces.
3. I watched the diver *plunge* to the bottom of the river.
4. The leaves *fall* gently from the trees in the autumn.
5. The flowers in the garden *increase* every day.
6. It would be so much fun to *ascend* in a hot-air balloon!

Unit 1 Answers

Benchmark Test 2, p. 234

MULTIPLE CHOICE

1. ANS: B
2. ANS: A
3. ANS: A
4. ANS: C
5. ANS: C
6. ANS: D
7. ANS: C
8. ANS: A
9. ANS: C
10. ANS: B
11. ANS: D
12. ANS: D
13. ANS: B
14. ANS: D
15. ANS: A
16. ANS: B
17. ANS: A
18. ANS: D
19. ANS: B
20. ANS: C
21. ANS: C
22. ANS: B
23. ANS: A
24. ANS: B
25. ANS: A
26. ANS: B
27. ANS: D
28. ANS: D
29. ANS: C
30. ANS: D
31. ANS: C
32. ANS: D

ESSAY

33. Students' scenes should follow script form, particularly in using dialogue tags. They should contain dialogue that expresses both facts and opinions.
34. Students should achieve a tone appropriate to the events they recount—humorous, for example, or serious. They should use vivid descriptions to make the event come to life.
35. Students should begin with an interest-grabbing sentence or paragraph. They should present a clear chronological sequence of events that revolves around a central problem or conflict. Students should use vivid details to capture the incident and help readers see and understand the people, places, and events.

Vocabulary in Context 1, p. 240

MULTIPLE CHOICE

1. ANS: B
2. ANS: C
3. ANS: A
4. ANS: C
5. ANS: B
6. ANS: D
7. ANS: D
8. ANS: C
9. ANS: A
10. ANS: D
11. ANS: A
12. ANS: B
13. ANS: B
14. ANS: A
15. ANS: C
16. ANS: A
17. ANS: D
18. ANS: A
19. ANS: B
20. ANS: D